Georg Lukács

Harper & Row, Publishers
New York, Evanston, San Francisco, London

Tactics and Ethics

Political Essays, 1919–1929

This collection first published
in Georg Lukács, Werke, vol. 2,
by Hermann Luchterhand Verlag, 1968
Copyright © Hermann Luchterhand Verlag, 1968
This translation copyright © 1972 by NLB
Introduction copyright © 1972 by Rodney Livingstone

Printed in Great Britain by Harper & Row, Publishers

Translated from the German by Michael McColgan
Edited, with an Introduction, by Rodney Livingstone

Introduction

BY RODNEY LIVINGSTONE

For Georg Lukács the decade 1919–1929 represents a period of sustained political activity, at first in the Hungarian Soviet Republic of 1919 and subsequently in exile in Vienna. His direct experience of events in the turbulent period of history following the end of the First World War and the Russian Revolution furnished him with abundant material for a series of essays on political subjects. Of these only two, the monograph *Lenin* and the collection entitled *History and Class Consciousness* have hitherto appeared in book-form in English.[1] The present volume sets out to make good the lacuna. It contains all the remaining essays (apart from two minor reviews) from volume 2 of the German edition of Lukács's works.[2] The contents range from the analysis of particular events or trends to the discussion of more general problems of a political nature and the revaluation of earlier figures such as Lassalle or Moses Hess. They doubtless vary in importance, but taken together they can be said to provide a full account of the development of Lukács's thought from the moment of his decision to join the Hungarian Communist Party in December 1918 to the moment when he resolved to give up political activity in the face of the violent criticism provoked by the Blum Theses. Moreover, it should now become possible to site *Lenin* and *History and Class Consciousness* in the context of his overall development. A number of the themes developed more fully in the latter work can be found here in embryo and since they often bear on matters of immediate moment they may help to elucidate that important but daunting text.

There is a logic in Lukács's decision to become a Marxist, but there can be no question of a smooth evolution from his earlier position. Even though a number of critics have rightly pointed to the connections between the different phases of his works, the persistence in his maturity of motifs

1. *Lenin*, NLB, 1970; *History and Class Consciousness*, Merlin, London, 1971.
2. *Werke*, vol. 2, Luchterhand, Neuwied, 1968. It is worth recording that this volume does not aspire to completeness. For the omissions see the bibliography in V. Zitta, *Georg Lukács: Marxism/Alienation, Dialectics, Revolution*, The Hague, 1964, pp. 266–9 and I. Mészáros, *Lukács' Concept of Dialectic*, with Biography, Bibliography and Documents, Merlin, 1972.

dating from his earliest, pre-Marxist writings, Lukács himself has always emphasized the changes in his views and has never hesitated to reject lines of thought and even entire books which he regarded as erroneous or superseded. The problem has been compounded by the vexed issue of his various political recantations. But it is important to realize that even if we leave these aside we are still confronted with an *oeuvre* characterized by discontinuity, rapid changes of position and conflicts resolved only with difficulty. This is particularly true of his intellectual development during the First World War culminating in his commitment to Marxism.

At the outbreak of war Lukács was living in Germany, as a lecturer in aesthetics at Heidelberg. His career up to that point had been brilliant but not untypical of his generation of the Austro-Hungarian intelligentsia.[3] He was born in 1885 into a wealthy Jewish family in Budapest. His father was a director of the leading bank in Hungary and had been ennobled by the Hapsburgs. Lukács himself used the honorific 'von' in his publications apparently until 1918. His development was precocious: his first writings appeared in print in 1902, he was a co-founder of the Thalia theatre in 1905 and contributed both to the radical journal *Nyugat* ('The West') and to Oscar Jászi's *Huszadik Század* ('The Twentieth Century'), the organ of the Sociological Society. In 1906 he obtained his doctorate at Budapest University and in 1908 he was awarded a prize for his two-volume *Development of the Modern Drama* (which appeared in 1911 in Hungarian). In the same year the German version of *The Soul and the Forms* was published, a collection of literary essays on Stefan George, Novalis, Theodor Storm, Paul Ernst and on the essay form itself. This work established his reputation as a critic and had a significant influence, e.g. on Thomas Mann's *Death in Venice*. In 1909/10 Lukács went to Berlin and attended the lectures of the philosopher, sociologist and literary critic Georg Simmel. After extensive travels he finally settled in Heidelberg in 1912, where he made the acquaintance of Max Weber and members of the George circle (though there is some doubt whether he actually met George himself), and attended the lectures of the prominent neo-Kantian philosophers Rickert and Windelband. He also became friendly with their most important pupil, Emil Lask, whose ideas exercised an important influence on his own.

3. Accounts of Lukács's life and intellectual development can be found in George Lichtheim, *Lukács*, Fontana, London, 1970; Lucien Goldmann, 'Introduction aux premiers écrits de Georg Lukács', in *Les Temps Modernes*, no. 195, August 1962. See also the 1967 Preface to vol. 2 of the *Werke* in *History and Class Consciousness*, op. cit.

Lukács seems to have had no difficulty in assimilating the culture of Wilhelminian Germany. By contrast, say, with Kafka, in whom the conflicting claims of German, Jewish and Czech cultural identities combined to exacerbate his own sense of estrangement, Lukács does not seem to have experienced divisive pressures of that kind. The increasing dominance of Hungary within the decaying Hapsburg empire and also the greater homogeneity of the small, almost entirely Jewish, bourgeois intelligentsia may have resulted in a greater cultural confidence. It has been pointed out, moreover, that unlike the Russian revolutionaries who for all their Westernizing retained contact with popular, Narodnik movements, the Hungarian left-wing intellectuals were much more deracinated, urban and Jewish in a predominantly rural, peasant country.[4] Their assimilation to western ideas was thereby made easier and more absolute. At any rate the growth of Lukács's views at this time accurately reflects the movement of thought in Germany and the extreme complexity we find in his position mirrors the crisis towards which German civilization was being propelled.

German intellectual life at this time was characterized by the powerful thrust of the empirical sciences and the positivist philosophy which provided them with a rationale. Whereas in England positivism could be readily synthesized with existing traditions of empiricist and utilitarian thought, in Germany it came into direct collision with idealist traditions which endured, although decadent and under attack (e.g. by Nietzsche). In addition to, and reinforcing, technology and science, there was also the coarse materialism of the age of imperialism, whose cynicism, ruthlessness and chauvinism are documented in the novels of Heinrich Mann and the cartoons of Georg Grosz. Both academic philosophers and creative writers were concerned therefore to produce a counterweight to what they saw as the dehumanizing forces of the modern world, the 'approach of nihilism' proclaimed by Nietzsche. What Lukács found in Germany was a variety of ripostes to materialism which ranged from the wilder excesses of irrationalism and mysticism to the haughty individualism of the George circle.

The position of neo-Kantianism in the spectrum of thought is particularly revealing for, paradoxically, Kant's dualism could be used both to strengthen and to undermine the supremacy of the physical sciences. On the one hand, the Marburg philosophers (Natorp, Cohen, Rudolph

4. For a description of Hungarian intellectual life see R. L. Tökés, *Béla Kun and the Hungarian Soviet Republic*, New York and London, 1967, pp. 1–49.

Stammler) upheld Kant's anti-metaphysical bias, and attempted to limit philosophy to logic and the theory of knowledge, insisting that its function was to provide a rationale for the special sciences. On the other hand, the Heidelberg philosophers, Rickert and Windelband, were much more hostile to positivism and used the Kantian distinction between pure and practical reason to establish the autonomy of the humane sciences. They concentrated above all on history, but it is clear that if they could show the validity of history as an alternative to the natural sciences, the proof would apply to the humane and social sciences in general. In this they were supported by the writings of Dilthey whose major project was to provide an adequate epistemology of the historical sciences, a 'critique of historical reason' to supplement Kant.

Lukács felt drawn to the Heidelberg philosophers and equally to Dilthey's vitalism. Of his position at this time he has this to say in *My Road to Marx* (1933):

The neo-Kantian doctrine of the 'immanence of consciousness' corresponded very well to my then class position and world view. I did not subject it to any sort of critical investigation and accepted it unquestioningly as the starting-point of any kind of epistemological inquiry. I did indeed have reservations concerning extreme subjective idealism (the Marburg school of neo-Kantianism as well as Mach's philosophy), since I did not see how the question of reality could simply be treated as an immanent category of consciousness. But this did not lead to materialist conclusions, but rather towards those philosophical schools which tried to solve the problem in an irrationalist-relativist fashion, occasionally tending towards mysticism (Rickert, Simmel, Dilthey).

It speaks volumes for Lukács's early idealism and the state of German philosophy that he rejected the Marburger for their excessive subjectivity! At the same time it offers a pointer to Lukács's own development which we may regard as an attempt to overcome positivism by progressing from a neo-Kantian subjective idealism to a Hegelian objective idealism via the mediation of Dilthey's *Lebensphilosophie*. It should be noted that these neo-Kantian and parallel attempts to defend the autonomy of the spirit avoided having recourse to explicitly metaphysical or religious positions. Inevitably, therefore, the place of religion was often taken by art. Lukács shared in this fashionable aestheticism for a time. In his case this was anything but a frivolous matter; on the contrary, it involved him in a search for authenticity amidst the sterility of modern life. His thought shows a gradual progression in the direction of increased objectivity, passing through the stages of a belief in atemporal essences or 'forms', via Dilthey's intuited verities to arrive at an 'objective' historical dialectic. The revival of Hegelianism is crucial here: while positivism, vitalism and idealism undermined each other, Hegel emerged as the one thinker whose philosophy could claim to be objective and rational as opposed to the ultimate irrationality of idealism, and also human in contrast to the reifications of positivist science.

The entire complex of themes can be seen at work in *The Theory of the Novel* which Lukács wrote at the beginning of the war and which represents a terminal point of his early development.

The outbreak of war in 1914 came as a shock to Lukács. The cultural elite into which he had assimilated showed that its contempt for contemporary German life was perfectly compatible with a chauvinist posture. The ideology of 'non-political' thinkers and poets turned out to be conservative and nationalist in practice. Lukács could not share these sympathies. For one thing his dislike of bourgeois capitalism was too entrenched for him to perform such a volte-face. At the same time there could be no question of his moving towards a more left-wing position. Indeed, the acclamation of the war by the social-democratic parties was a prime cause of his disillusionment. He describes his attitude at the time as 'one of vehement, global and, especially at the beginning, scarcely articulate rejection of the war and especially of the enthusiasm for the war'.[5]

Lukács had no easy transition to Marxism. In *My Road to Marx* he explains that he had read Marx while still at school and was impressed by his contributions to economics and sociology. Nevertheless, Marx had played only a minor role in his development because sociology and economics were themselves regarded as no more than a preliminary stage in his chief interest: aesthetic analysis. Hence his renewed interest in Marx during the war followed his discovery of Hegel with the consequence that economics and materialism were less prominent than the dialectical method and the philosophy of history. As for his contacts with contemporary Marxism, these were confined to the thinkers of the Second International and Rosa Luxemburg's earlier (i.e. pre-Spartacus) works. He knew little of Lenin until after 1917. He absorbed a variety of left-socialist syndicalism, however, through Ervin Szabó, who was himself strongly influenced by Sorel. Lukács is somewhat vague about his own

5. *The Theory of the Novel*, Merlin, London, 1971 (the 1962 Preface included in this volume is especially illuminating).

attitude to Sorel but it is clear that at this time they shared a number of ideas: the dislike of liberal bourgeois democracy, of positivist science, the critique of bureaucracies or of parties likely to become self-perpetuating repressive structures. Even more important perhaps is the emphasis on action, on militancy, on the need to liberate the creative forces of the proletariat. Whereas for Dilthey progress had come of its own accord, and even for Hegel the category of 'becoming' often seems to be the autonomous attribute of spirit, Sorel's voluntarism must have reinforced the philosophy of action Lukács had found in Fichte. Furthermore, the fact that Lukács came to Marxism via idealism and syndicalism rather than through the Second International which he regarded as the home of positivist determinism in philosophy and opportunism in practice explains the crucial role of 'consciousness' in his idea of the revolutionary process.

But the synthesis still lay in the future. Lukács's position was highly contradictory and remained so throughout the war. He wrote in the 1967 Preface to *History and Class Consciousness*: 'I, at least, find that my ideas hovered between the acquisition of Marxism and political activism on the one hand, and the constant intensification of my purely idealistic ethical preoccupations on the other'. But it is noteworthy that he did not evaluate the latter in a wholly negative way: 'For all its romantic anti-capitalist overtones, the ethical idealism I took from Hegel made a number of real contributions to the picture of the world that emerged after this crisis.'

During the war Lukács spent a short time in Budapest (1915/16) where, having been found unfit for military service, he worked for the postal censorship. After returning to Heidelberg in 1916 and again in 1917 he settled in Budapest. Together with Szabó, Karl Mannheim and Arnold Hauser he took part in a 'Free School of the Humanities' which fed the general stream of radical intelligentsia but remained aloof from party politics. During this time and even at the end of the war, Lukács seems to have been thought of as a Tolstoyan ethical humanist. After the collapse of the Austro-Hungarian Empire and the setting-up of the bourgeois democratic government under Count Michael Károlyi, the Hungarian Communist Party was founded by Béla Kun and a number of others who had returned from Russian prisoner-of-war camps. This was in November 1918. Lukács seems to have hesitated for almost a month before he joined and although he was obviously the outstanding mind in the Party he was not made a member of the central committee.

Tactics and Ethics, of which the first three essays were written between Lukács's entry into the Hungarian Communist Party and the rise of the

Hungarian Soviet Republic in March 1919, gives some idea of the inner conflict he underwent. Although his treatment is impersonal it can be understood as an extension of the crisis of the problematic individual of *The Theory of the Novel*. He is replaced here by the revolutionary, a tragic figure compelled to sacrifice his individual morality for a greater collective ethic. The tension Lukács feels is well conveyed by the concluding quotation from Hebbel's grim tragedy *Judith* where the startling juxtaposition of the heroine's action of sacrificing her virtue and killing the tyrant Holofernes, and the revolutionary forced to commit a terrorist action, sets the tone for Lukács's own stance in the Hungarian revolution. In tune with this the essay on 'Intellectual Leadership' launches a scathing attack on bourgeois intellectuals who arrogate to themselves a privileged position in a revolution and opposes to their consciousness the consciousness of the proletariat as a class. This is the first statement in which Lukács advances his distinction between actual and possible class consciousness and it points forward to the discussions in *History and Class Consciousness* and the concept of imputed (*zugerechnet*) consciousness in that work. Consonant with this is the idealist tone of the essay as a whole with its insistence that only Marxism maintains that the course of history is led by the spirit, a spirit however which, far from being the prerogative of an intelligentsia, is located in the proletariat.

Once he had made his commitment, Lukács worked energetically to promote the cause of the revolution.[6] His contribution was far from insignificant both during the Soviet Republic and in the three months preceding it (January–March 1919). With the arrest of Béla Kun and the leading Bolsheviks on 20 February, Lukács was made a member of the central committee together with Szamuely, Joseph Révai, Ernö Bettelheim and Elek Bolgár. For a month (February–March 1919) they made the day-to-day decisions, edited *Vörös Újság* ('The Red Gazette'), wrote propaganda leaflets and organized mass meetings. Without Kun's knowledge they began extensive preparation for an armed uprising in May. It was to begin with a general strike followed by an armed uprising, the execution of bourgeois hostages and a three-day rule of the Budapest *Lumpenproletariat*. The Party would then restore order and form a proletarian republic. The divergence between these proposals and Kun's Bolshevik strategy and tactics points to tensions within the Party which

6. Tökés, op. cit., is more informative about Lukács's part in the Republic than anyone else. Victor Zitta, op. cit., has assembled much material, but he reports it with so much hostility and malice as to render it almost entirely unusable.

were heightened when the plans of this second central committee were overtaken by events. The Entente's renewed demands on Hungarian territorial integrity (the Vyx Note) led to the resignation of the Károlyi government and the Soviet Republic came into being as the result of a merger between the Social Democrats and the Bolsheviks, negotiated with Kun from prison. The alliance triggered off wild enthusiasm for a bloodless revolution, but also provoked searching questions from Lenin about the actual terms, matters on which Kun's reply was a little vague. Doubts were felt also by the 'Old Communists' of the second central committee. Lukács, however, who had protested eloquently against the arrest of Kun in '"Law and Order" and Violence', now wrote the final essay of *Tactics and Ethics*, 'Party and Class', which, with its argument that the alliance represented the emergence of an entirely novel kind of party, provided the Soviet Republic with its ideological rationale. At the same time the article represented a potential threat to the Kun government by asserting that this new party was destined to wither away. That is to say, although Lukács comes increasingly to affirm the necessity for a Leninist vanguard party, his mistrust of party bureaucracies is still lively. Clearly he was worried by certain trends in the Soviet Republic and hoped that the dissolution of the party form would entail the elimination of organized class terror (either as a weapon of the secret police or as capital punishment). In April/May 1919 he protested against the taking of bourgeois hostages. Although he does not recoil from violence he is evidently poles apart from terrorists like Szamuely. In fact throughout the Soviet Republic he seems to have been strongly attracted by 'a certain ascetic type of revolutionary (intellectually I had myself been close to this type at one stage) which had already been born in the French Revolution, amongst the Jacobins, Robespierre's followers'. And he contrasts revolutionaries of this type (among whom he numbers Eugen Leviné and his fellow Hungarian Otto Korvin) with 'non-ascetic' revolutionaries like Engels and Lenin.[7] His unswerving sense of dedication is strongly suggested by the reminiscences of Lajos Kassák who recalls 'his small figure, clutching a revolver, never seeking cover in the foxholes. He had to be recalled from his duties as a political commissar of the army because he entirely lacked any sense of danger at all.'[8] Moreover, his asceticism

7. Interview with András Kovács, *Cambridge Review*, January 1972, p. 91. See also the interview in *New Left Review*, no. 60, March/April 1970, pp. 42–3.

8. Tamás Unguari, 'The Lost Childhood: the genesis of Georg Lukács's conception of literature', in *Cambridge Review*, January 1972, p. 96.

was not simply a matter of temperament, as the essay on 'The Role of Morality in Communist Production' clearly demonstrates. In this essay he assigns to morality a special role: it must be the active component that will protect the revolution from the bureaucratic consequences of a revolution founded on a 'legal order'.

Lukács's principal activities during the Soviet Republic were cultural. He was appointed Deputy Commissar of Education under the socialist Zsigmond Kunfi (whom he replaced after the latter's resignation in June, following an abortive counter-revolution). Despite his subordinate position it is clear that he was the leading spirit in cultural affairs. The Soviet Republic was faced by formidable problems, chief among which were the foreign threats to its territory, the French-supported counter-revolutionary movement in Szeged, the breakdown of the economy, of labour-discipline, the collapse of the monetary system and the vexed question of whether to distribute the great estates to the land-hungry peasantry. Beside such matters as these, cultural affairs were of less moment. But Lukács was not deterred from pushing ahead with far-reaching reforms which may well have been too radical for the short time the Republic had at its disposal. His aim was 'the revolutionizing of the souls through re-education and the establishment of a genuine proprietorship over culture'. According to Jászi he tried to 'create a new spirit of brotherhood, mass faith and a new morality'. The measures he took included the nationalization of private schools (largely in the hands of the Roman Catholic Church), the introduction of eight-grade general schools, the extension of secondary schooling and higher education, the introduction of workers' colleges, the revision of university syllabuses, abolition of traditional text-books (before new ones could be made available). Series of lectures were held on sexual enlightenment, the archaic nature of the family code and monogamy, the irrelevance of religion. The bourgeois treatment of women in the 'social system of possessive males' also came under attack. Some of these measures were undoubtedly precipitate. One instance was the attempt to compel actors to leave Budapest and bring culture to the provinces. The actors regarded this as a blow to their professional prestige and went on strike. In the same way many writers and artists undoubtedly felt threatened by the manner in which the cultural revolution was promoted, as can be seen from a speech by Kunfi obviously aimed at Lukács:

I maintain that the development of science, literature and the arts is inconceivable without an atmosphere of freedom. During the ten weeks of proletarian

dictatorship we have seen ... too many frightened men who should be contri-
buting to literature and the arts ... but do not dare, knowing not what the
menacing words of dictatorship really mean. ...[9]

Nevertheless, it would be misleading to suggest that all these experiments
simply ended in tyranny and the end of free thought. The 'Speech at the
Young Workers' Congress' delivered in June 1919 conveys the spirit of
Lukács's ideas far more faithfully: 'The chief goal of your lives must be
culture; see to it that the new culture has both meaning and purpose.'

With the collapse of the Kun government and the onslaught of the
White Terror, Lukács at first went underground with Korvin and then
escaped to Vienna in October 1919 where he was arrested. The Austrians
were at first inclined to accede to the request of the Hungarian government
to extradite him, and this would have meant his certain death. However,
after a petition signed by Paul Ernst, Thomas and Heinrich Mann and
others, the Austrian authorities relented and he was released at the end of
the year. He then remained in Vienna taking a leading part in the activities
of the émigré Hungarian Communist Party and editing the magazine
Kommunismus in which a number of the essays in the present volume first
appeared:

Our magazine strove to propagate a messianic sectarianism by working out the
most radical methods of every issue, and by proclaiming a total break with
every institution and mode of life stemming from the bourgeois world.[10]

His intransigence is very evident in 'The Question of Parliamentarianism'
which intervenes in the contemporary debate on whether to participate in
parliamentary activities, a debate which was causing splits in the main
European parties. Lukács's formulations are cautious and hedged round
with qualifications, but the preference for workers' councils is unmis-
takable: 'where a workers' council (on however modest a scale) is possible,
parliamentarianism is redundant.' This earned him a rebuke from Lenin
himself:

G.L.'s article is very Left-wing and very poor. Its Marxism is purely verbal; its
distinction between 'defensive' and 'offensive' tactics is artificial; it gives no
concrete analysis of precise and definite historical situations; it takes no account
of what is most essential (the need to take over and to learn to take over, all

9. Quoted in Tökés, op. cit., p. 179.
10. *History and Class Consciousness*, ibid., pp. xiii–xiv.

fields of work and all institutions in which the bourgeoisie exerts its influence over the masses, etc.).[11]

However, between the appearance of the article in March 1920 and Lenin's criticism, Lukács read *'Left-Wing' Communism – An Infantile Disorder* which was published in June. The two together forced him to modify his extreme sectarianism and gradually to adopt a more Leninist and less dogmatic line. Despite this he continued to advocate sectarian solutions at the international level. Thus in Germany he justified the March Action of 1921 in the essays on spontaneity and organization; i.e. he defends the notion that communist parties should take the offensive and act as detonators so as to prepare the workers and increase their class consciousness, rather than pursuing the more cautious line of collaboration where possible with the mass social-democratic parties.

On looking back over his essays of this period Lukács never fails to criticize them severely for their errors of judgement. But to the modern reader these are less important than the fact that he is elaborating an analytical method which comes to fruition in *History and Class Consciousness* and *Lenin*. In *Tactics and Ethics* he had written that 'orthodox Marxism ... is not the "belief" in this or that thesis, the exegesis of a "sacred" book. On the contrary, orthodoxy refers exclusively to *method*.' Each of these essays reasserts the relevance of the Hegelian dialectic in debates that have hardened out into mechanical dogmas: small sect or mass party, spontaneity or party bureaucracy, opportunism or putschism. And on the more theoretical level: are the laws of history scientific, determined by inexorable laws of economics. If so what is the role of consciousness, morality or 'the leap of freedom'? These problems became more acute as the revolutionary wave receded and the problems confronting revolutionaries increased in proportion. Lukács consistently uses the dialectic to forge new, mediating positions: thus opportunism is identified with putschism, its apparent antipole, and opposed to true Marxism: 'the class consciousness of the proletariat as it expresses itself in practical-critical activity.'

These attacks on vulgar Marxism, scientific determinism, economic fatalism, form the hard core of Lukács's theoretical contribution. They seek to show that the entire heritage both of the Second International and of many of its alleged opponents (putschists, adventurists, syndicalists) was hopelessly entangled in bourgeois, reified forms of thought.

11. Lenin, *Collected Works*, vol. 31, London and Moscow, 1960–70, p. 165.

They culminate in the celebrated critical comments on Engels in *History and Class Consciousness*. The publication of this work in 1923 resulted in Lukács's condemnation in 1924 by Zinoviev at the Fifth Congress of the Third International in terms which have linked his name with other 'left' heretics of the twenties, Korsch in particular. Zinoviev's criticism was followed by much more savage treatment by Lukács's rivals in the Hungarian Party (such as László Rudas) and also by the Russian theorist Deborin. Lukács himself came to feel that much of what he had written there was mistaken and that in particular his failure to anchor his discussion of alienation and commodity fetishism in a Marxist analysis of labour proved that economic factors were still neglected in favour of 'abstract and idealist conceptions'.

After 1924 Lukács sees a change in his thought. On the one hand, 'the Third International correctly defined the position of the capitalist world as one of "relative stability"' and Lukács agreed with Stalin about the need to defend socialism in one country. On the other hand, the rise of National Socialism led to his reconsidering the merits of cooperation between the various left-wing movements, and here he diverged from what was to become the official doctrine. His position received its decisive formulation in the Blum Theses in 1928. With the shift in his political views there came also a greater clarification in theory. The reviews he wrote in these years provided him with opportunities to concretize his position on a number of theoretical issues. He himself attached the greatest importance to the essay on Bukharin: 'The most positive feature of this review is the way my views on economics became concretized.' It may well be thought, however, that the reviews of Hess and Lassalle are more substantial. In 'Lassalle' Lukács is concerned to attack what he considers to be a resurgence of the spirit of Lassalle in contemporary social democracy. Even more significant is the philosophical critique which shows that Lassalleanism is rooted in Fichte's concept of a world of absolute sinfulness and that this conception is less revolutionary than Hegel. Here Lukács comes to terms decisively with a tendency that had haunted his own youthful thought. In the review of Hess, Lukács argues that the succession from Hegel to Marx is not mediated by Feuerbach or the Left Hegelians. He thus diverges sharply from a number of thinkers with whom he is often associated, notably the Frankfurt School and Marcuse.

The change in Lukács's political line leading into the Blum Theses did not come about suddenly. It flowed naturally from his participation in

Hungarian émigré politics throughout the twenties. The collapse of the Soviet Republic was followed by a bitter post mortem on its causes, and the émigré movement rapidly split into factions with divergent views on how to continue the struggle in Hungary. As opposed to the official leadership of the Hungarian Party under Béla Kun, Lukács became an adherent of the opposition faction led by Jenö Landler, a veteran unionist who had organized a strike of railway workers at the end of the war and whose experience in union politics at both the local and national level Lukács greatly admired. Under the repressive Horthy regime the hope of a new revolutionary upsurge gradually faded away. But whereas Kun still adhered to maximalist hopes for the emergence of open communist action and a proletarian dictatorship, Landler and Lukács developed a subtle blend of legal and illegal tactics with a view to establishing a bourgeois democracy first. Kun regarded this as opportunism, right-wing deviation, liquidationism. While Kun retained the leadership and the support of the Comintern throughout most of this period, the Landler policy was gradually put into practice, notably in the foundation of the Hungarian Social Democratic Party (MSZMP) in 1925. The programme of this party was worked out by Landler, Révai and Lukács. Its chief slogan, 'the Republic', implied the attempt to establish a legal opposition in Hungary while maintaining close contact with the illegal Communist Party in Vienna. Many of its members were arrested and in any case the party was very small. Nevertheless, Lukács regarded it as an important tactical move and as evidence that his own leftism had been overcome. He contrasts his early sectarianism with that of Kun which he thought was Stalinist in nature and disastrous for the future of Hungarian socialism in practice. There is a consistent line in his essays on this subject from 'Organization and Revolutionary Initiative' and the 'Politics of Illusion – Yet Again' right up to the Blum Theses.

These theses, conceived as a draft programme for the Hungarian Communist Party and known by Lukács's party name, Blum, were written in 1928 and were rejected after much discussion within the Party. Argument turned on whether in some countries the dictatorship of the proletariat should be achieved via a democratic transition. In view of Hungary's backwardness, its largely peasant population and the nature of the regime, Lukács argued in favour of this view. This was opposed not only by Kun but also by the Comintern which at its Sixth Congress had just reversed the United Front politics of the Third Congress. In an Open Letter to the Hungarian Party the Executive Committee argued that 'the

Blum view of the Hungarian Revolution was the chief rightist threat in the Party'. It went on to say:

In the opinion of the political secretariat of the Executive Committee of the Communist International the theses of Comrade Blum (course set for a bourgeois-democratic revolution instead of a proletarian revolution, for the democratic dictatorship of workers and peasants instead of the dictatorship of the proletariat) represent a liquidationist trend in the Hungarian Communist Party. In reality Comrade Blum has taken up a position identical to that of the social democrats: he proposes that the party should conduct its struggle against Fascism on the basis of bourgeois democracy, that its key slogan in this struggle should be the demand for bourgeois reforms; he suggests that the Hungarian Communist Party should be regarded as a party of democratic reforms and that its policy should consist in the abstract propagation of the dictatorship of the proletariat – assuming that the Social Democratic Party does turn out to be an opposition party at all. Comrade Blum discerns the chief task of the Party not in the struggle against democratic illusions, but in the struggle against the 'Nihilism' confronting bourgeois democracy. When he proposes that the Communist Party should proclaim to the workers that bourgeois democracy is the 'best battle-ground', he really puts himself in the position of social democracy. He thus denies that bourgeois democracy tends to develop into Fascism; he thereby leaves the entire third period out of account. These theses have nothing in common with Bolshevism.

This attack, combined with the threat of expulsion, forced Lukács to choose between recantation and the opportunity to work against Fascism within the Communist movement or isolation, the fate of Karl Korsch and others. He chose to retract his views and a self-criticism appeared in *Új Március* in 1929. Unlike his criticism of *History and Class Consciousness*, Lukács held this one to have been dictated by tactical considerations: 'My literary activity after 1930 proves that I have not departed from the essential principles of the *Blum Theses*.' That is to say, a continuity can be traced in the idea of 'democratic dictatorship', in his work in *Der junge Hegel*, his literary activities in the thirties and his support of the Popular Front. In political terms the defeat was total. Landler died in 1928 and this spelt the victory of the Kun faction. With the triumph of Stalinism Lukács retired from politics and henceforth took up that ambivalent position which has been so hotly debated: to some he seemed to be the very incarnation of Stalinism, to others he was the source of an alternative view of Marxism. However that may be, Lukács professed to have left politics behind him without regrets (apart from a brief episode in 1956 when he again became a Minister for Culture in the Nagy government). His later intellectual career belongs largely to philosophy and literary criticism. Its themes and problematics, though to some extent a development of his work in the twenties, are creative about literature and intellectual or cultural history rather than politics.

Tactics and Ethics

TO THE YOUNG GENERATION OF THE COMMUNIST PARTY

Tactics and Ethics[1]

For all parties and classes the position and significance of tactics in the field of political action differ greatly in accordance with the structure and historico-philosophical role peculiar to those parties and classes.

If we define tactics as a means by which politically active groups achieve their declared aims, as a link connecting ultimate objective with reality, fundamental differences arise, depending on whether the ultimate objective is categorized as a moment within the given social reality or as one that transcends it. The principal difference between the immanent and the transcendent ultimate objective is that the former accepts the existing legal order as a given principle which necessarily and normatively determines the scope of any action, whereas in the case of a socio-transcendent objective that legal order is seen as pure reality, as real power, to be taken into account for, at most, reasons of expediency. The 'at most' needs special emphasis, for an objective like that of the French Legitimist Restoration, namely the acknowledgment, in any sense whatever, of the legal order of the Revolution, was already tantamount to a compromise. Even this example, however, shows that the various transcendent objectives, conceived purely in terms of a sociology which is totally abstract and devoid of all values, are to be regarded as being on the same level.

For if the social order which is defined as the ultimate objective already existed in the past, if it were merely a question of reinstating a previous stage of development, then ignorance of the existing legal order represents only an apparent, and not a real, violation of the limits of the given legal orders: one real legal order confronts another real legal order, the continuity of development is not rigidly denied, and the most far-reaching aim amounts merely to cancelling an intermediate stage. Every essentially

1. Both this essay and the two following it ('"Intellectual Workers" and the Problem of Intellectual Leadership' and 'What is Orthodox Marxism?') were written before the dictatorship of the proletariat. The change in the function of ethics consequent upon developments under the dictatorship has given these studies a documentary, historical value. This should be borne in mind while reading all three – it does not apply, however, to the last essay, 'Party and Class' (G.L., 1919). ('Tactics and Ethics', 'What is Orthodox Marxism?', and 'Party and Class' were written in Hungarian and published as *Taktika és ethika*, Budapest, 1919. This English translation is from the German – ed.)

revolutionary objective, on the other hand, denies the moral *raison d'être* and the historico-philosophical appositeness of both present and past legal orders; how far – if at all – they are to be taken into account is therefore an exclusively tactical question.

Because, however, tactics free themselves in this way from the normal limits imposed by the legal order, some new practical criterion has to be discovered which will determine the tactical attitude. Since the concept of expediency is ambiguous, a corresponding distinction must be established between an immediate, concrete aim and an ultimate objective still remote from the ground of reality. For those classes and parties whose ultimate objective has in fact already been achieved, tactics will necessarily be determined by the attainability of the immediate and concrete aims; for them, the gulf which divides the immediate and the ultimate goal, the conflicts arising from this duality, simply do not exist. Tactics here assume the form of legal *Realpolitik*, and it is no mere chance that in those (exceptional) cases where a conflict of this kind does emerge – as, for instance, in connection with war – these classes and parties practise the shallowest and most catastrophic form of *Realpolitik*. They have no choice, for the existence of their ultimate goal admits of no other course of action.

This contrast helps greatly to elucidate the tactics of the revolutionary classes and parties: their tactics are not determined by short-term immediately attainable advantages; indeed, they must sometimes reject such advantages as endangering what is truly important, the ultimate objective. But since the ultimate objective has been categorized, not as Utopia, but as *reality which has to be achieved*, positing it above and beyond the immediate advantage does not mean abstracting from reality or attempting to impose certain ideals on reality, but rather it entails the knowledge and transformation into action of those forces already at work *within* social reality – those forces, that is, which are directed towards the realization of the ultimate objective. Without this knowledge the tactics of every revolutionary class or party will vacillate aimlessly between a *Realpolitik* devoid of ideals and an ideology without real content. It was the lack of this knowledge which characterized the revolutionary struggle of the bourgeois class. An ideology of the ultimate goal existed even here, it is true, but it could not be organically integrated into the planning of concrete action; rather, it developed in a largely pragmatic way, in the creation of institutions which quickly became ends in themselves, thereby obscuring the ultimate objective itself and degrading it to the level of pure, already ineffectual ideology. The unique sociological significance of socialism is precisely that it provides a solution to this problem. For if the ultimate objective of socialism is utopian in the sense that it transcends the economic, legal and social limits of contemporary society and can only be realized through the destruction of that society, it is anything but utopian in the sense that its attainment would entail the absorption of ideas hovering outside or above society. The Marxist theory of class struggle, which in this respect is wholly derived from Hegel's conceptual system, changes the transcendent objective into an immanent one; the class struggle of the proletariat is at once the objective itself and its realization. This process is not a means the significance and value of which can be judged by the standards of a goal which transcends it; it is rather a new elucidation of the utopian society, step by step, leap by leap, corresponding to the logic of history. This implies immersion in contemporary social reality. The 'means' are not alien to the goal (as was the case with the realization of bourgeois ideology); instead, they bring the goal closer to self-realization. It follows that there will be conceptually indeterminable transitional stages between the tactical means and the ultimate objective; it is never possible to know in advance which tactical step will succeed in achieving the ultimate objective itself.

This brings us to the decisive criterion of socialist tactics: the philosophy of history. The *fact* of the class struggle is nothing other than a sociological description and an elevation of events into laws which are effective in social reality; the *meaning* of the class struggle of the proletariat, however, goes beyond this fact. Essentially, of course, the meaning cannot be separated from the *fact*, but it is directed towards the emergence of a social order which differs from that of every previous society in that it no longer knows either oppressors or oppressed. In order that the epoch of economic dependence, which is an affront to human dignity, should come to an end, the blind power of economic forces must, as Marx says, be broken and replaced by a higher power which corresponds more exactly to the dignity of man.[2]

Therefore, to weigh up and understand correctly the contemporary economic and social conjuncture, the true relations of power, is never more than to meet the *prerequisites* for correct socialist action, correct tactics. It does not in itself constitute a *criterion* of correctness. The *only* valid yardstick is whether the *manner* of the action in a given case serves to realize this goal, which is the essence of the socialist movement. Hence,

2. Marx, *Capital*, vol. III, Moscow, n.d., pp. 799–800 (Editor's note).

since this ultimate objective is not served by qualitatively different means; since, rather, the means signify in themselves the progress towards that objective, all means by which this historico-philosophical process is raised to the conscious and real level are to be considered valid, whereas all means which mystify such consciousness – as for example acceptance of the legal order, of the continuity of 'historical' development, let alone the *momentary* material interests of the proletariat – are to be rejected. If ever there was a historical movement to which *Realpolitik* presents a baneful and ominous threat, it is that of socialism.

That means concretely that every gesture of solidarity with the existing order is fraught with such danger. Deriving though they may well do from true inner conviction, our insistent protests that such and such a gesture of solidarity indicates only a momentary, immediate community of interests, nothing more than a provisional alliance for the attainment of a concrete goal, nevertheless do not obviate the danger that the feeling of solidarity will take root in *that* form of consciousness which necessarily obscures the world-historical consciousness, the awakening of humanity to self-consciousness. The class struggle of the proletariat is not merely a class struggle (if it were, it would indeed be governed simply by *Realpolitik*), but a means whereby humanity liberates itself, a means to the true beginning of *human* history. Every compromise made obscures precisely *this aspect* of the struggle and is therefore – despite all its possible, short-term (but extremely problematical) advantages – fatal to the achievement of this true ultimate objective. As long as the present social order persists, the ruling classes remain in a position to compensate, openly or covertly, for whatever economic or political advantages have been won in this fashion. Such 'compensatory' measures effectively worsen the conditions for the continuation of the struggle, since obviously the compromise will weaken the mood of resistance. Tactical deviations within socialism are therefore of more fundamental significance than is the case with other historical movements. The sense of world history determines the tactical criteria, and it is before history that he who does not deviate for reasons of expediency from the narrow, steep path of correct action prescribed by the philosophy of history which alone leads to the goal, undertakes responsibility for *all* his deeds.

It seems to follow from the above that we have also discovered the answer to the ethical problem; that adherence to the correct tactics is in itself ethical. But it is at this point that the dangerous aspects of the Hegelian legacy in Marxism become apparent. Hegel's system is devoid of ethics; in his work ethics are supplanted by the system of material, spiritual and social goods in which his social philosophy culminates. Essentially Marxism has taken over this form of ethics (as we see, for example, in Kautsky's book),[3] merely positing other 'values' than the Hegelian ones, and without raising the question as to whether or not the quest for socially correct 'values', socially correct goals – irrespective of the inner motives of the action – is thereby in itself ethical, although it is clear that the question of ethics can only proceed from these socially correct goals. People who deny the ethical ramifications which arise at this point also deny their ethical possibility, and come into conflict with the most primitive, universal psychological facts: conscience and the sense of responsibility. What all such people are concerned with is not primarily *what* a person did or wanted (that is governed by the norms of social and political action), but whether what he did or wanted and *why* he did it or wanted it was object'vely correct or false. This question of the whys and wherefores, however, can only arise in individual cases, it has no meaning except in relation to the individual, in sharp contrast to the tactical question of objective correctness, the unambiguous resolution of which is only to be found in the collective action of groups of human beings. Therefore we may state the question which confronts us in these terms: 'How do conscience and the sense of responsibility of the individual relate to the problem of tactically correct collective action?'

It is most important at this juncture to establish a mutual dependence, precisely because the two types of action being related are essentially independent of each other. On the one hand, the question whether any given tactical decision is right or wrong is independent of the question whether or not the decision was determined by moral motives on the part of those who act in accordance with it. On the other hand, an action that springs from the purest ethical source can, from a tactical point of view, be completely mistaken. This independence of each other, however, is more apparent than real. For – as we shall see later – once the purely ethically motivated action of the individual brings him into the field of politics, even its objective (historico-philosophical) correctness or

3. Lukács refers here to Karl Kautsky's book *Ethics and the Materialist Conception of History*, Stuttgart, 1906. Kautsky sets out to describe the 'content of the new ethical ideal' which he attempted to deduce 'exclusively from a knowledge of the given material foundations'. The resulting change in values is contained in the formula: 'In scientific socialism the ethical ideal of class struggle is transformed into an economic one' (loc. cit., pp. 69ff.) (Editor's note).

incorrectness can no longer be a matter of ethical indifference. Moreover, by virtue of the historico-philosophical orientation of socialist tactics, a collective action must arise in that one individual will (once the many individual wills have been aggregated) and the governing historico-philosophical consciousness must express itself in him – particularly since the necessary rejection of the immediate advantage in the interest of the ultimate objective would otherwise be impossible. The problem can now be posed in the following terms: what ethical considerations inspire in the individual the decision that the necessary historico-philosophical consciousness he possesses can be transformed into correct political action, i.e. component of a collective will, and can also determine that action?

To re-emphasize the point: ethics relate to the individual and the necessary consequence of this relationship is that the individual's conscience and sense of responsibility are confronted with the postulate that he must act as if on his action or inaction depended the changing of the world's destiny, the approach of which is inevitably helped or hindered by the tactics he is about to adopt. (For in the realm of ethics there is no neutrality and no impartiality; even he who is *unwilling* to act must be able to account to this conscience for his inactivity.) Everyone who at the present time opts for communism is therefore obliged to bear the same *individual* responsibility for each and every human being who dies for him in the struggle, as if he himself had killed them all. But all those who ally themselves to the other side, the defence of capitalism, must bear the same individual responsibility for the destruction entailed in the new imperialist revanchist wars which are surely imminent, and for the future oppression of the nationalities and classes. From the ethical point of view, no one can escape responsibility with the excuse that he is only an individual, on whom the fate of the world does not depend. Not only can this not be known objectively for certain, because it is always possible that it will depend precisely on the individual, but this kind of thinking is also made impossible by the very essence of ethics, by conscience and the sense of responsibility. He whose decision does not arise from such considerations – no matter how highly developed a creature he may otherwise be – exists in ethical terms at a primitive, unconscious, instinctual level.

This purely formal and ethical definition of individual action, however, does not clarify sufficiently the relationship between tactics and ethics. When the individual who makes an ethical decision within himself then follows or rejects a particular tactical course, he moves onto a special level of action, that of politics, and the distinctiveness of his action entails – from the standpoint of pure ethics – the consequence that he must know under what circumstances and how he acts.

The concept of 'knowledge' thereby introduced into the argument requires further clarification. On the one hand, 'knowledge' is by no means to be taken as total understanding of the actual political situation and all its possible consequences; nor, on the other hand, can it be regarded as the result of purely subjective deliberations, where, that is, the individual concerned acts 'to the best of his ability and in good faith'. If the former were the case, every human action would be impossible from the outset; if the latter, the way would be clear for extreme levity and frivolity and every moral standard would become illusory. Since, though, the individual's seriousness and sense of reponsibility constitute a moral standard for every deed, implying that the individual concerned could know the consequences of his deeds, the question arises whether or not, in the light of this knowledge, he could answer for these consequences to his conscience. This objective possibility admittedly varies according to the individual and from case to case, but essentially, both for the individual and from case to case, it is always determinable. Even now, for every socialist, the actual historico-philosophical pressure of the social ideal of socialism determines both the content of the objective possibilities for realizing that ideal and also the very fact that the criterion of possibility should itself be possible. For every socialist, then, morally correct action is related fundamentally to the correct perception of the given historico-philosophical situation, which in turn is only feasible through the efforts of every individual to make this self-consciousness conscious for himself. The first unavoidable prerequisite for this is the formation of class consciousness. In order for correct action to become an authentic, correct regulator, class consciousness must raise itself above the level of the merely given; it must remember its world-historical mission and its sense of responsibility. For the class interest the attainment of which makes up the content of class-conscious action coincides neither with the sum of the personal interests of the individuals belonging to the class nor with the immediate short-term interests of the class as a collective entity. The class interests which will bring socialism about and the class-consciousness in which they find expression signify a world-historical mission – and hence, too, the objective possibility mentioned above implies the question: has the historical moment already arrived which leads – or rather leaps – from the stage of steady approach to that of true realization?

Every individual must, however, be aware that, by the very nature of the matter, we can talk only in terms of a possibility. We cannot conceive of a human science which could say for society, with the accuracy and certainty that characterizes the astronomer's prediction of the appearance of a comet: today the time has come for the realization of the principles of socialism. Likewise, there exists no science which could say: today the time is not yet ripe, we must wait, it will come tomorrow or in another two years. Science, knowledge, can indicate only possibilities – and it is only in the realm of the possible that moral, responsible action, truly human action, is itself possible. For the individual who seizes this possibility, however, there is, if he is a socialist, no choice and no hesitation.

This is not by any means to suggest that action which arises in this fashion must necessarily be morally faultless and unexceptionable. It is not the task of ethics to invent prescriptions for correct action, nor to iron out or deny the insuperable, tragic conflicts of human destiny. On the contrary: ethical self-awareness makes it quite clear that there are situations – tragic situations – in which it is impossible to act without burdening oneself with guilt. But at the same time it teaches us that, even faced with the choice of two ways of incurring guilt, we should still find that there is a standard attaching to correct and incorrect action. This standard we call sacrifice. And just as the individual who chooses between two forms of guilt finally makes the correct choice when he sacrifices his inferior self on the altar of the higher idea, so it also takes strength to assess this sacrifice in terms of the collective action. In the latter case, however, the idea represents an imperative of the world-historical situation, a historico-philosophical mission. In one of his novels, Ropschin (Boris Savinkov),[4] the leader of the terrorist group during the Russian Revolution from 1904 to 1906, put the problem of individual terror in the following terms:

4. Boris Savinkov (1879–1925). Of particular importance to Lukács were the *Memoirs of a Terrorist* (English translation, New York, 1931) and *What never happened. A Novel of the Revolution* (English translation, London, 1919). The latter work treats of the unworldliness of the Russian revolutionaries. In a letter to Paul Ernst of 4 May 1915, Lukács wrote: 'Considering Ropschin's books as documents rather than works of art, I did not at all see them as pathological symptoms, but instead as a new manifestation of the old conflict between a primary ethic (obligation towards institutions) and a secondary ethic (obligations towards the soul). The question of primacy always takes on a peculiar dialectical complexity when the soul is not sufficient unto itself, but is involved in mankind – as in the case of political man, of the revolutionary. Here, if the soul is to be saved, the soul must be sacrificed: starting from a mystical ethic one is forced to become a brutal *Realpolitiker* and to violate the absolute commandment "Thou shalt not kill" – which entails no obligations to institutions' (Editor's note).

murder is not allowed, it is an absolute and unpardonable sin; it 'may' not, but yet it 'must' be committed. Elsewhere in the same book he sees, not the justification (that is impossible) but the ultimate moral basis of the terrorist's act as the sacrifice for his brethren, not only of his life, but also of his purity, his morals, his very soul. In other words, only he who acknowledges unflinchingly and without any reservations that murder is under no circumstances to be sanctioned can commit the murderous deed that is truly – and tragically – moral. To express this sense of the most profound human tragedy in the incomparably beautiful words of Hebbel's Judith: 'Even if God had placed sin between me and the deed enjoined upon me – who am I to be able to escape it?'[5]

5. Judith's actual words are: 'If You (God) place a sin between me and my deed, who am I to quarrel about it with You and to escape from You!' Friedrich Hebbel, *Judith*, Act III, in *Werke*, vol. 1, Munich, 1963 (Editor's note).

'Intellectual Workers' and the Problem of Intellectual Leadership[1]

One of the commonest charges levelled against the socialist conception of history and society by bourgeois intellectual circles – all too often even by the well-meaning – is that socialism makes no allowance for 'intellectual' (*geistig*) forces, that it underestimates the role of these forces in social development, that it looks at and assesses society one-sidedly, even exclusively from the standpoint of material being and physical work. Even when they acknowledge the truth of socialism in all its particulars, such critics insist on the *intellectual* force of the 'intellectual workers' as complementary to progress. They take it for granted, of course, that the 'intellectual workers' will also retain the leading role to which they feel themselves legitimately entitled, not for their own ends, but (as these well-meaning people imagine) in the interests of the society as a whole.

Before discussing the central problem of intellectual leadership, we must first consider those who are concerned to raise it. Are we dealing with a group of individuals or a class? If a class, what is the basis of its composition and what is its position in the process of production? (For it is this which, in the final analysis, determines the differences between the classes.) Straightaway at this point, the largest group is eliminated from the class of so-called intellectual workers: those who, like manual workers, are able to participate in production only by means of their labour power (white-collar workers, engineers, etc.). This group differs sharply from those whose intellectual work is only an accessory to their bourgeois status (major share-holders, factory owners). The class distinction between these two groups is so clear to the objective observer that it is impossible to bring them together under one heading, as the class of 'intellectual workers'. That the economic discrepancy has for a very long time and in many areas not found any corresponding ideological expression is to be attributed above all to the fact that for all members of these oppressed groups the possibility of personal advancement into the oppressing class cannot be denied from the outset and with the same certainty *as is the case with manual workers*. On the one hand, this blurs the boundary lines of such transitions; on the other, it conceals from the individuals con-

1. See footnote 1, p. 3 above.

cerned their true class affiliation. Not that class affiliation alone is the determining factor; before the disappearance of the guilds there existed a similar relationship between master and journeyman which also veiled the sharp contrasts. The special factor is merely the possibility of participating in the privilege of education, which sustains the possibility of advancement into the ruling class for the children of the 'intellectual worker', even if he himself has not managed to make this advance. Those 'intellectual workers' who participate in production therefore belong (*with an unclear class consciousness, at best*) to the same class as the manual workers.

A considerable number of intellectual workers are not directly involved in production, however. What determines to which class they belong? Superficial observation might suggest that herein lies the key to the '*supra-class*' ideology of the petty-bourgeois intellectuals. Since they are not directly interested in the struggle between capital and labour, it is claimed, they are able to become incomparable critics and leaders of social development. But this theory breaks down when we remember, first, that these 'intellectual workers', even if apparently uninterested in the survival or decay of the social order, are profoundly and to the very roots of their existence involved in the *fate of the ideological superstructure* of the social order (civil servants, judges, lawyers, etc.); and secondly, that the way is open for every such individual to work himself up from his semi-proletarian environment into the ruling capitalist classes by serving their material, ideological and power interests or meeting their luxury requirements (writers, lawyers, doctors, etc.).

Not only, therefore, does it denote superficial observation to speak of the 'intellectual workers' as a *homogeneously structured class*, since even within their ranks a clear division into oppressors and oppressed, exploiters and exploited, can be established; more than that, there is no good reason why the group of exploited hack-clerks or legal practitioners should be competent to assume the intellectual leadership of those who belong to the same class, *particularly as the only real characteristic of their position is their clouded class-consciousness.*

Turning aside from these mystificatory slogans, then, what do we mean by the 'intellectual' leadership of society? The task of the old conservative ideology was easy (on account of the then inadequate understanding of the scope of social mechanisms). It needed only to refer to great men who by their 'genius' had given a creative lead to the development of mankind. Nowadays – at least in sociologically half-educated circles – such claims can no longer be taken seriously. What is involved in the question of 'intellectual leadership'? Everybody knows and acknowledges that forces independent of human consciousness and its ability to set goals and make evaluations keep the development of human society going, even if consciousness is unable to recognize the true essence of that society, the class stuggle and the changes in productive relations. The ideological standpoints at present under discussion grasp, albeit in veiled form, the automatic nature (i.e. the complete independence from consciousness) of social development, but accuse Marxism of claiming that this automatic process is totally exclusive. They therefore feel themselves specially cut out to contribute something which will provide both an aim and a direction for development to what is in itself an aimless movement. It is at this point that the *epistemological* question of the leadership of society arises, which in our view *only* Marxism has shown itself able to answer. No other social theories have managed even to pose the question *unambiguously*. The question itself is twofold, even if both parts point in only one direction. First, we have to ask: what must be the nature of the forces moving society and the laws which govern them so that consciousness can grasp them and human will and human objectives can intervene in them significantly? And secondly: what must be the direction and the composition of human consciousness so that it can intervene significantly and authoritatively in social development?

Posed thus clearly, the epistemological question contains certain important assumptions which neither can be nor need to be proved, yet constitute the basis of the existence and the cognizability of society – like the fundamental principles of geometry for the theory of space. The first such thesis is: that the development of society is determined exclusively by forces present within that society (in the Marxist view, by the class struggle and the transformation of the relations of production). The second: that the direction of this development can be clearly determined, even if it is not yet fully understood. The third: that this direction has to be related in a certain, albeit still not fully understood fashion, to human objectives; such a relationship can be perceived and made conscious, and the process of making it conscious exerts a positive influence on the development itself. And finally, the fourth thesis; that the relationship in question is possible because, although the motive forces of society are independent of every *individual* human consciousness, or its will and its objectives, their existence is inconceivable except in the form of *human* consciousness, human will and human objectives. Obviously the laws which have to become effective in this relationship are reflected for the most part in an obscure or distorted manner in the consciousness of individual human beings.

Such a method of posing the question – the Marxist method – provides immediately the only possible, unambiguous and meaningful answer. 'Intellectual leadership' can only be one thing: the process of making social development conscious, the clear understanding of what is essential as opposed to obscure and distorted slogans; the 'knowledge', in other words, that the 'laws' governing social development, their complete independence of human consciousness, their similarity with the play of the blind forces of nature, are a mere appearance which can survive only until those blind forces have been awakened to consciousness[2] by this knowledge. Hence, the primary *truly epoch-making significance of Marx's social theory is that the development of social consciousness has been effected in this way within, and only within, the confines of society.* Marxist social theory put an end to the unbridgeable dualistic separation of social reality and human objectives which had made the previous theories of the great Utopians (Fourier, Owen) so hopelessly unattainable. Every Utopian scheme, however penetrating a critique of the given social situation it may have offered, however desirable it may have appeared as an ideal to be attained, has failed to determine the mode and the means necessary for its realization and has therefore come to nothing. Utopia has always remained a pious wish, the acceptance or rejection of which necessarily

2. The concept of consciousness was first noted and elucidated in classical German philosophy. 'Consciousness' refers to that particular stage of knowledge where the subject and the object of knowledge are substantively homogeneous, i.e. where knowledge takes place *from within* and not *from without*. (The simplest example is in man's moral knowledge of himself, e.g. his sense of responsibility, his conscience as contrasted with the knowledge of the natural sciences, where the known object remains eternally alien to the knowing subject for all his knowledge of it.) *The chief significance of this type of knowledge is that the mere fact of knowledge produces an essential modification in the object known: thanks to the act of consciousness, of knowledge, the tendency inherent in it hitherto now becomes more assured and vigorous than it was or could have been before.* A further implication of this mode of knowledge, however, is that the distinction between subject and object disappears, and with it, therefore, *the distinction between theory and practice.* Without sacrificing any of its purity, impartiality or truth, theory becomes action, practice. To the extent to which knowledge, as the consciousness of the known object, imparts greater vigour and assurance to the natural development of that object than would have been possible without it, it has already and in the most immediate fashion involved itself in immediate practical action, in the transformation of life through action (G.L.'s note).

remained a voluntary decision on the part of each individual human being. Marx, on the other hand – and it is in this that he distinguishes himself most clearly from the great Utopians who preceded him – took over, as it stood, the greatest legacy of Hegelian philosophy: the concept of development as meaning that the mind develops homogeneously from complete lack of consciousness to a clear, ever-growing self-consciousness. Only the superficiality and philosophical philistinism of his successors have obscured this crucial concept. Unable to comprehend Hegel's conception of history, they have turned historical development into a wholly automatic process, not only independent of, but even qualitatively different from consciousness. Clearly it is then impossible for them to establish a meaningful relationship between development on the one hand and consciousness and conscious action on the other. But Marx did more than simply take over the Hegelian theory of development: he also modified it essentially through his critique – not, as the vulgar Marxists assume, by the mere substitution of 'materialism' for 'idealism' (empty phrases), *but on the contrary, by essentially enriching and deepening the Hegelian concept.* The essential feature of Hegel's prodigious world system was its view of nature and history as one great homogeneous process, the essence of which is the development of its ever-clearer consciousness of itself (the Spirit). According to Hegel's philosophy, the Spirit in nature is still wholly unconscious. Man, on the other hand, in his so-called spiritual life, becomes ever more conscious, until finally, through institutional systems, through art and religion, he rediscovers himself in philosophy. Marx was altogether too sober and profound a thinker to apply this method to the investigation of nature. Moreover – and decisively – he did not separate out such abstract and interconnected phenomena as law, art, religion and so on, in order to discover in them stages of development, but he searched for and found, *in the process of the homogeneous development of society*, that consciousness which constantly searches for and finally finds itself.

Uncomprehending non-Marxists have often wondered why Marxism, above all other theories, should possess such world-revolutionizing force. The answer, which all those who understand Marx properly take for granted, is already contained in the foregoing. Its force derives from the fact that *Marx recognized the class struggle as the moving force in the development of society and the laws governing that struggle as the laws of social development generally*. He thereby raised the real moving force of world history (which until then had moved blindly and unconsciously), the class struggle, into consciousness. The class-consciousness of the proletariat, developed on the basis of Marxist theory, shows for the first time in the history of mankind that the real moving factors of history do not operate unconsciously (or in accordance with imaginary motives, which amounts to the same thing) like component parts of a machine: only after they have attained consciousness do they become the true moving forces. It was in the class-consciousness created by Marxism that the spirit, indeed, the very meaning of social development, emerged from its previously unconscious state. By the same token the laws of social development ceased to be blind, catastrophic and fatal powers: they awoke to self-awareness, to consciousness. If, as the historians of philosophy rightly claim, the decisive achievement of classical German philosophy was the perception of this consciousness of the Spirit, then, equally, Engels was correct to point out that the proletariat is the sole legitimate heir to that philosophy – and, as we might add – *its true executor.*

But proletarian class-consciousness is in itself only a step towards this consciousness, for, as a mere given quantity, it simply establishes the relationship of the immediate interests of the proletariat to the laws governing social development. The ultimate goals of development remain abstract ideals, situated at a new – utopian – distance. In order for society to *become truly self-conscious,* a further step is necessary: *the class-consciousness of the proletariat must itself become conscious.* This means understanding above and beyond direct class-consciousness, above and beyond the immediate conflicts of class interests – that world-historical process which leads through these class interests and class struggles to the final goal: *the classless society and the liberation from every form of economic dependence.*

Class-consciousness alone (the exclusive acknowledgement of immediate economic interests as it finds expression in so-called social-democratic *Realpolitik*) cannot provide this understanding, but merely a yardstick for the correctness of *immediate tactics.* Historical situations arise, however – *the moments of world crisis* – in which even the tactics demanded by immediate interests are pursued blindly (the position of the Social Democratic parties during the war), in which even class-consciousness, confronted with the ultimate necessity, adopts the stance of complete unconsciousness, in which even actions dictated by class-consciousness operate like blind forces of nature. The need in such moments is, as I have already stated, for the class-consciousness of the proletariat to become conscious: *conscious of the world-historical mission of the proletarian class-struggle.* It was this consciousness which drove Marx to create the new philosophy that was to revolutionize the world and build it up again. It is this consciousness which makes Lenin the leader of the proletarian revolution. This consciousness – in Hegelian terms, the development towards self-consciousness of society, the self-discovery of the Spirit seeking itself in the course of history – the consciousness which recognizes its world-historical mission; this consciousness alone is cut out to become the intellectual leader of society.

Hence we Marxists not only believe that the development of society is directed by the so-often disparaged Spirit, but we also know that it was only in Marx's work that this spirit became consciousness and assumed the mission of leadership. But this mission cannot be the privilege of any 'intellectual class' or the product of any form of 'supra-class' thinking. The salvation of society is a mission which only the proletariat, by virtue of its world-historical role, can achieve. And *only through the class-consciousness of the proletarians* is it possible to achieve the knowledge and understanding of this path of humanity that is essential to 'intellectual leadership'.

What is Orthodox Marxism?[1]

The philosophers have only interpreted the world in various ways; the point is to change it (Marx, Eleventh Thesis on Feuerbach).

This extraordinarily simple question stands at the centre of a debate which has raged for decades in both bourgeois and socialist writings. On the one side, vehement attacks have been made on those doctrinaire Marxists who, like the medieval Schoolmen, did not proceed from the facts, but strove to approach the truth by constant justification of their bible. On the other side, the Marxists have fallen out even among themselves, unable to agree on precisely those theses the acceptance of which is the *sine qua non* of being an orthodox Marxist. The development of science has overtaken many of Marx's original theses – these critics of Marx, however, demand whether criticism has a right even then to draw the line at any particular thesis. Of course not; we who claim to be orthodox Marxists are no less insistent than they, but in our view the question as to whether someone is or is not a Marxist is not determined by his conviction of the truth of individual theses, but by something quite different: *the method*. Let us assume – though this is not to admit – that the development of science had proved all Marx's assertions to be false. We could accept this scientific criticism without demur and still remain Marxists – as long as we adhered to the Marxist method. In order to understand Marxism properly, therefore, we must elucidate the essence of this method. In so doing we shall come to see that every attempt to deviate from the path of orthodoxy, by 'improving' or 'developing' the Marxist method, has in fact rendered Marxism more superficial.

Marx's method is the revolutionary dialectic. Before proceeding to elucidate the concept of the dialectic, let us deal with the immediate question: how can a theory, a theoretical method, be revolutionary? The foregoing study provided an answer to this question. The theory can be revolutionary *only insofar as it transcends the difference between theory and practice.* As the mere fact of correct thought produces an essential change in the object at which that thought is directed, so putting the correct thought consistently into practice will result in the transformation of reality.

1. This is the first version of the essay which later appeared, greatly extended, as Section I of *History and Class Consciousness*, London, 1971, pp. 1–26. See also footnote 1, p. 3 above (Editor's note).

Marx took over the dialectical method from classical German philosophy, and in particular from Hegel. The essential feature of this method, which has revolutionized science, is that concepts cease being rigid schemata, which, once defined, never again change their meaning, nor are they isolated thought-structures, to be understood only in the abstract, but rather *living realities*, which cause a process of uninterrupted transition, of sudden change. Understood in this way, these concepts create a process in which individual concepts necessarily change *into the opposite of their original formulation*, into their own negation, there, just as in the rejection of the negation, to be reconciled in a higher unity, and so on to infinity. Thus Marx, to quote the famous example, establishes that the development towards capitalism and the organized regimentation of production has proceeded so far by virtue of the necessity of its development, that capitalism itself, which arose through the exploitation of the immediate producers, must be destroyed; that, in other words, the expropriators must be expropriated.[2] In this respect, therefore, capitalism represents the denial of personal property based on one's own work. And with the inevitability of a natural process it brings about its own negation: the negation of the negation, a new higher unity.

The vulgarizers of Marxism, led by Bernstein, have donned a 'scientific' mask and attempted to eradicate the dialectic from Marxist thought, claiming that it is an obsolete legacy of Hegelian philosophy, unfit to occupy a place in modern science, which constructs its theories only on the 'facts' of 'reality'. They even accuse Marx himself of having violated the facts and realities to accommodate his method, and demand in its place an 'impartial' scientific method. But they fail to understand that to eradicate the method 'dialectically' is to rob Marxism of its revolutionary rigour and strength. *For no amount of mere empirical research, i.e. mere accumulation of facts, could ever make the inevitability of revolution, the necessity for revolutionary action above and beyond the transient characteristic of any given movement, either intelligible or acceptable.*

Only the dialectic is adequate to this task. Only with the help of the dialectic can we understand in what way every concept *must* change into its opposite, in what way every system of production and every social order *must create, by and in itself,* the elements of its own disintegration and destruction. Without the dialectic we should stand perplexed in a labyrinth of unordered and unorderable facts, appealing in vain to the facts to guide our actions. For facts can never direct meaningful action. They can

2. See *Capital*, vol. I, London, n.d., pp. 760–3.

always be valued and considered in hundreds of ways; and those who look *only* to the facts for guidance will flounder helplessly back and forth between conflicting possibilities. They will become eclectics and opportunists, like Bernstein and with him the German, indeed, almost the whole of the European Social Democratic movement.

But even Bernstein's opponents, the self-styled guardians of orthodox Marxism, Kautsky and the vulgar Marxists, have continued to trivialize the dialectical method and with it the revolutionary impetus of socialism. It is not enough simply to assert that the destruction of capitalism is inevitable and that it will be liquidated, not by gradual development, but by revolution; the assertion must follow *from the essence of the method*. Only then does revolution become more than an empty slogan (as with Kautsky); *only then does it give meaning and direction to all thoughts and actions, only then does it become a necessary and living unity of theory and practice*. Kautsky and his followers have abandoned, albeit not openly, the dialectical method. Whereas Bernstein declared openly that for him the ultimate objective meant nothing, the movement, however, everything, Kautsky and company have attributed to the ultimate objective the role of some supernatural deity, preserving it in a sublime state remote from every aspect of immediate reality. *In their actions, therefore, they have remained every bit as opportunistic as the Bernsteinites*. Their notion of the ultimate objective remains constant: a fine-sounding phrase with which to round off effectively appropriate speeches, articles and books, and occasionally, too, for use in the drafting of an impressive, but ineffective, pamphlet. But their ultimate objective is *totally unsuited to guiding their actions in a revolutionary direction*. For it is of the essence of the dialectical, revolutionary method *that there is no essential difference between movement and ultimate objective*. In the language of the Hegelian dialectic, the thesis, which in this context has been taken over almost unaltered by Marx and Engels, runs as follows: the constant increase of quantitative differences suddenly changes at a certain point into a qualitative difference. It is not our task at this juncture either to demonstrate the truth of this thesis or to indicate its application in the works of Marx and Engels. Here we need only point out that, for Marx, revolution means neither 'a gradual and peaceful development', as the opportunists would have it, nor a succession of putsches, as the false interpreters claim, but a sudden change from the normal and always organic development of the working-class movement to the overthrow of the capitalist order: a sudden change from increasing quantity to quality. Every moment of the normal working-class movement, every wage increase, eveiy reduction in working hours, etc., is therefore a revolutionary act: together they make up that process which at a certain point suddenly changes into something qualitatively new. This in turn makes capitalist production impossible. *But these individual moments can only be transformed into revolutionary action within the unity of the dialectical method.* For those who see only the individual moments, the working-class movement is reduced to a reformist wage-bargaining movement. At the moment of sudden change, of revolution, they will stand anxious and helpless, fearful for the 'successes achieved', even though these successes, seen in isolation, serve at best to secure the petty-bourgeois affluence, the embourgeoisement, of the workers. Yet such individuals are no more helpless when confronted with the reality of revolution than those who are incapable of recognizing the revolutionary essence of individual moments and integrating them into their consciousness in a revolutionary way. For, from the revolutionary standpoint, the possibility of revolution and the 'ripeness' of the circumstances are nothing other than the instant where this sudden dialectical change occurs. True, this moment is a possibility latent within every instant of time, but it cannot be predetermined with the same certainty with which the astronomer is able to calculate the appearance of a comet. *Because of its dialectical nature this instant of time cannot vault from possibility to reality until the workers' movement is conscious that for them theory and practice, like movement and ultimate objective, constitute a single unity.* When every single moment of the movement is considered consciously from the standpoint of the totality, when every single moment is brought to effect consciously as a revolutionary deed – then and only then will the movement overcome its helplessness in the face of the reality of revolution. No longer will the reality of revolution crash down on the working-class movement like an unforeseen catastrophe, as it does on the vulgar Marxists and most of the leaders of the European labour movement; instead, it will come as the fulfilment of its hopes, for which it was both inwardly and outwardly prepared, as it was for the possibility of that sudden dialectical change in every single moment of action.

Hence the following fundamental principle of the dialectical method, the theory of the Hegelian concrete concept, becomes clear. Briefly, it means that the whole takes precedence over the parts, *that the parts must be construed from the whole and not the whole from the parts.* In his struggle against bourgeois economics, Marx attaches crucial importance to this question. Bourgeois economics, he points out, considers the individual elements of the economic process in isolation and constructs its system of the economy on the basis of the 'reciprocal effect' of these elements. Thus, while it can explain how production proceeds under given circumstances, it is unable to explain how these circumstances themselves arise, in other words how the historical process which creates them in the first place itself comes into being.[3] For this reason both bourgeois economics and bourgeois sociology remain incapable of advancing even conceptually beyond the framework of the conditions determining production in bourgeois society. They regard these conditions as eternal laws, as a necessary by-product of human existence, whereas they are in fact exclusively historical in character, brought into being within the context of the capitalist order and destined to disappear along with that order (e.g. capitalist private property, the bourgeois family, the constitutional state).

The same theoretical mistake is made even by the syndicalists, who consequently lose themselves in the labyrinth of reactionary pettybourgeois agitation. From the abstraction of economic concepts interpreted in isolation they deduce the abstract nature of the whole social order, seeing it in other words as something estranged from real life. They infer the complete alienation of the bourgeois system of production from these facts (which, of course, are crucial for the working-class movement also) but they fail to go beyond mere negation, and abstract rejection. Inevitably, therefore, they see no way leading into the future, to the new society of the proletariat. They criticize sharply individual institutions of bourgeois society (e.g. parliamentarianism), perceived in isolation and abstractly, but are unable to offer any alternative to them but the abstractly revolutionary élan of a proletariat without concrete goals. The working-class movement and the general strike become in their eyes ends in themselves, part and parcel of the mythology, and thereby excluded from history conceived of as a great and necessary process – in exactly the same way as the bourgeois system of production, which they so vehemently criticize, is excluded if conceived of in bourgeois terms.[4]

3. Marx, *The Poverty of Philosophy*, Moscow, n.d., p. 117. In this book Marx provides a rigorous critique of those 'misinterpreters' of the dialectical method who, like Proudhon, arrive at dialectical antitheses by counting up the good and bad sides of a concept or an institution taken in isolation. They then seek the higher synthesis, the negation of the negation, in the avoidance of errors, the bad sides. This critique is also relevant to many contemporary vulgar Marxists (G.L.'s note). (See *The Poverty of Philosophy*, pp. 124–6 – ed.)

4. We would draw the attention of readers interested in philosophical problems to the

The genius of Marx's method reveals itself precisely in the avoidance of these two abstract extremes. *Marx always sees the whole from the standpoint of an even more comprehensive totality, that of a great socio-historical process.* No other thinker has ever considered society less abstractly and more determinedly from the standpoint of action and real life. At the same time, he never saw the contrast between the concrete and the abstract as an excuse for stopping at mere feelings, merely instinctive action. For Marx, as a true pupil of Hegel, the concrete is not the antithesis of what is grasped intellectually, but on the contrary: it is something *that only the mind can grasp.* The concrete is concrete, he says, because it is the combination of many determinants, that is to say, the unity of the diverse. The thinking mind perceives this combination as a process, as a result and not as a beginning, although it is the real starting-point.[5] The true starting-point, therefore, is the complete whole, the concrete totality, and all parts, whether a moment of the movement or a phenomenon of social or economic life, can and must be understood only by proceeding from this whole, from the correct insight into the whole. The chief task of thought – which, left to itself, is always ready to consider individual phenomena and moments in isolation – is in every case to revert to this starting-point, to raise itself to this unity of the whole, whence alone it is possible to avoid considering the individual phenomena and moments abstractly. *It is this unconditional hegemony of the totality, of the unity of the whole over the abstract isolation of the parts, which constitutes the essence of Marx's social theory, the dialectical method. To adhere to this method (and not just to regurgitate individual phrases) is to be an orthodox Marxist.* Marx himself was the first to recognize that economic concepts are historically and not eternally determined; the first, therefore, to see not only the phenomena of social life from the standpoint of the complete transformation of production, but even the revolutionizing of production itself from the standpoint of world history. Like the classical German philosophers, particularly Hegel, Marx perceived world history as a homogeneous process, as an uninterrupted, revolutionary process of

fact that syndicalism is related to authentic Marxism as Hegel, correctly interpreted, is related to the philosopher of syndicalism, namely Bergson. This question, however, is not one we can discuss here (G.L.'s note).

5. See *Beiträge zur Kritik der Nationalökonomie* ('Contributions to a Critique of Political Economy'), German edition, p. XXXVI. The Hungarian translation regrettably omits this introduction, so indispensable to an understanding of Marx's method (G.L.'s note).

liberation. But unlike them – and it is precisely in this respect that he far surpasses them – Marx recognized tħe true motive forces of this process, the class struggle and the transformation of the relations of production, and was able to integrate them into the concrete totality of the world-historical process, into the process of liberation. And it is this which enables us to understand that – and how – Marx could comprehend the capitalist system of production and social order as both necessary and, at the same time, doomed to destruction. Only the dialectical method of Marx makes it possible to view social phenomena in this way: to recognize first, that they are necessary, and, secondly, that they are at the same time also transient and destined to perish. Both points of view are crucial: the former as a guard against the abstract Utopianism to which all petty-bourgeois social reformers incline; the latter as a corrective to the over-estimation of the power and indispensability of the given institutional orders which characterizes the vulgar Marxists, who *allow their actions to be dictated by the 'facts', instead of making their actions work on and transform reality itself.*

Revolutionary action is not possible except on the basis of the unity forged between these two standpoints – which means, in turn, on the basis of the dialectic. Even in this respect, the vulgar Marxists have managed to trivialize the theory of reality which Marxism took over from classical philosophy. In so doing they have forfeited all revolutionary rigour and élan. *Marx's theory of reality is not the same as the everyday notion of reality which already and actually exists, replete with chance and contingency.* Reality for him is something that necessarily exists, a necessarily given stage in the homogeneous and total process of history. And although it forms the basis of being in general, it can be thrown into relief in its true reality, in its complete unity, by the mind. The vulgar Marxists, on the other hand, have allowed themselves to be misled by Marx's criticisms of petty-bourgeois revolutionaries, where he constantly defended reality against empty and merely abstract intellectual constructions. *Consequently the vulgar Marxists have confused the Marxist concept of reality with the concept of being in general.* Intellectual chaos of this kind had and still has fatal consequences in practice. For instance, the vulgar Marxists regarded the World War, the mere existence of the World War seen in isolation from the world-historical process, as true reality, instead of seeing in it the unity of the decaying process of imperialistic capitalism and accordingly focusing the actions of the proletariat as a decisive factor on the world revolution necessarily emerging from it. Hence they became opportunists where the war was concerned, both in their tactical approach and in their conformist actions. They failed to perceive what lay behind and beyond the war: the world revolution, the true Marxist reality of the war, the only action which could have served as a meaningful criterion of tactics. Opportunism, the politics of trimming, was the only possible outcome of this trivializing of the concept of reality, and if there were no other proof that those old enemies, Kautsky and Bernstein, stand on a par with each other in this respect, the brotherly cooperation into which they were swept headlong by the war is evidence enough. Lenin and Trotsky, as truly orthodox, dialectical Marxists, paid little attention to the so-called 'facts'. They were blind to the 'fact' that the Germans had won and had secured for themselves the military opportunity to march into Petrograd at any time, to occupy the Ukraine, and so on. Lenin and Trotsky understood the true reality, the necessary materialization of the world revolution; it was to this reality, not to the 'facts', that they adjusted their actions. And it was they who were vindicated by reality, not the apostles of *Realpolitik*, who, swaying to and fro like reeds in the wind, judging their actions only by the 'facts', changed their tactics after every victory or every defeat and stood helpless when it came to making real decisions.

What else could they do? *Decisions, real decisions, precede the facts.* To understand reality in the Marxist sense is to be the master and not the slave of the imminent facts. The vulgar Marxist turns helplessly from left to right; helplessly, because facts which succeed one another in isolation necessarily seem to point sometimes in one direction and sometimes in the other, and because dialectical knowledge is needed in order to come to grips with their labyrinthine complexity.

Today, too, the proletariat faces similar decisions. Its leaders, their minds blunted by vulgar-Marxist notions, are still anxiously awaiting guidance from these 'facts'. Has the time for revolution really arrived? Is the system of production ripe for the proletariat to take into its own hands? We can tell them straightaway that they will look in vain for a decision emanating from the 'facts'. A situation where the 'facts' point unambiguously and unmistakably to the revolution will never come about. And all their 'conscientious' testing of all the 'data' will prove just as futile. Some of the data will always be frightening; what chance is there, then, of a revolution ever being initiated by people whose 'conscientiousness' is, so to speak, risk-free? *The message of reality, meanwhile, Marxist reality, the unity of the historical process, is quite clear: the revolution is here.*

And every orthodox Marxist who realizes that the moment has come when capital is no longer anything but an obstacle to production, that the time has come for the expropriation of the exploiters, will respond to the vulgar-Marxist litany of 'facts' which contradict this process with the words of Fichte, one of the greatest of classical German philosophers: 'So much the worse for the facts.'

Party and Class[1]

21 March 1919[2] is a day of historical significance, not only in the life of the Hungarian proletariat, but also in the development of the world revolution. Briefly, an event occurred on that day which also proved crucial in making it possible at all. It was an event that in Russia took eighteen months of hard fraternal struggle on the part of the proletariat to bring about. On that day *the Social Democratic Party accepted without any reservations, as the basis of their activity, the communist, Bolshevik programme.*

The practical significance of this event hardly needs to be discussed at any length. For if one thing is certain, it is that the strength of the proletariat lies in its being united and organized. Those who doubt this and might have expected the victory of the proletariat to come about through a putsch were taught a sharp lesson by the events of 21 March. The very

1. First appeared in Hungarian under the title 'The Theoretical Significance of the Restoration of Proletarian Unity' in a pamphlet, *Documents on Unity*, 1919 (Editor's note).

2. The Soviet government in Hungary came into existence on 21 March 1919, after the previous regime, led by Count Michael Károlyi, had collapsed under the pressure of renewed territorial demands on Hungary by the Allies. (The Vyx ultimatum of the previous day had demanded the secession of Debrecen, the second largest town, and a large chunk of the surrounding territory.) Károlyi said in his resignation that he 'was handing power over to the Hungarian proletariat'. This consisted of the Social Democratic Party, and the Communist Party which had been formed in November 1918 by Béla Kun and other prisoners of war, returning from Russia. The agreement between the two parties stated inter alia that 'in the name of the proletariat the party immediately takes all power into its hands. The dictatorship will be exercised through councils of workers, soldiers and peasants. The plan to convene a national assembly thereby becomes obsolete. . . . To secure the power of the proletariat and offer resistance to allied imperialism, a complete and close military alliance shall be concluded with the Russian Soviet Republic.' In a letter to the Hungarian workers of 27 March 1919 Lenin wrote: 'You have given the world a still finer example than Soviet Russia, in that you have been able to unite all socialists from the outset on the platform of a real proletarian dictatorship' (see Jane Degras, *The Communist International, 1919–43, Documents*, London, 1956). For a detailed, if hostile account of the whole course of the revolution see R. L. Tökés, *Béla Kun and the Hungarian Soviet Republic*, New York and London, 1967 (Editor's note).

fact that the proletarian parties united, the unity of the class expressing itself in party unity, ensured that power passed without violence and bloodshed into the hands of the proletariat. And the events of the last days have proved beyond doubt that the proletariat knows how to wield this power and use it to build the society which corresponds to its goals. At the same time they show that this new-found unity of the Hungarian proletariat makes it capable of even faster and more resolute action than was possible for the divided Russian working class during its revolution.

This unity is based, like all actions of the proletariat, on *theoretical unity*. The whole proletarian movement distinguished itself clearly from those of other classes inasmuch as its roots and its starting-points were always exclusively theoretical. Since the practice of other classes was determined by transitory interest groupings and since those classes lacked comprehensive unity (which theory, and theory *alone*, can provide) they could only totter to and fro in the labyrinth of external events. The actions of the proletariat, on the other hand, have consistently followed a straight path leading to the goal, for they have always been undertaken on previously clarified theoretical premises. Where external events have come into play, they have at most influenced immediate tactics; they have never directed these actions in their totality.

The historical documents relating to those events are illustrated on these pages. If we consider the events themselves from the standpoint of the theory of proletarian action, we will discover that the end of the social revolution is the conclusion of the last great crisis of the proletarian movement, the crisis which is conditioned by the attitude of the proletariat under the domination of imperialistic finance capital. Short-sighted and petty-bourgeois thinkers will see a contradiction here: as if the crisis of society were beginning properly only now, with the systematic, revolutionary action of the proletariat. In truth, however, construction and destruction are just as organically connected and inseparable as life and death, as all opposites, indeed, which petty-bourgeois thought, try as it might, will never succeed in reconciling. Just as now in the destructive deeds of the proletariat with which it crushes the material and spiritual organs of oppression of the bourgeois state, the highest and purest constructive powers are manifesting themselves, so the crisis of the last years and decades has prepared the way for the revolution of the proletariat. To put the most obvious manifestation of this crisis in a nutshell: the real goals and possibilities of the actions of the *proletarian class* had come into dialectical conflict with that particular form of *party organization* which provided the only possible framework for such actions.[3] Many people have pointed out the irreconcilable antagonisms between class and party: in Hungary Ervin Szabó[4] has been particularly critical. In the heat of the battle, however, those critics of the party organization who attack this possibility of proletarian action have failed to appreciate adequately the necessity of this form of the party as a *transitional formation*. They do not realize that the antagonism between the actions of the class and the actions of the party is anything but clear-cut, with one side obviously right and the other equally obviously wrong. Rather, it is a dialectical antagonism, one in which both forms of action, though mutually exclusive and opposed to each other, are yet *equally necessary*.

In other words, not only are both equally right or wrong, as the case may be, but the existence of the one demands the existence of the other, and they can no more exist without each other than they can avoid warring with each other. The essence of this crisis in the class struggle of the proletariat is that, on the one hand, the existing relations of power demanded the organization of a party, but that, on the other, those same power relations made of this party organization an element which hindered the actions of the proletariat. The crisis could not be overcome, therefore, by one side proving itself right *vis-à-vis* the other, but only by the *reconciliation in a higher unity* of both seemingly mutually exclusive standpoints. Both in fact dissolved in a higher unity, thereby ceasing to exist as independent, isolated and mutually antagonistic entities.

This higher unity is the unified proletariat, as a ruling class in society. That pure form of communism which derived its theoretical foundations from the earliest works of Marx and Engels, both of whom cooperated in determining its frame of reference, was the work of a small revolutionary

3. See e.g. the *Works of Marx and Engels*, vol. II, p. 405 (G.L.'s note). Cf. e.g. *The Communist Manifesto*, Marx/Engels, *Selected Works*, vol. I, p. 44, as well as the *Beschlüsse der delegierten Konferenz der internationalen Arbeiterassoziation, abgehalten zu London vom 17 bis 23 September 1871*, in Marx/Engels *Werke*, vol. 17, p. 422 (Editor's note).

4. Ervin Szabó (1877–1918), historian and sociologist. A convinced Marxist, he edited a three-volume edition of Marx, for which he wrote an introduction that remains classical in Hungarian literature. As the leader of the left wing of Hungarian social-democracy, he played a unique role in educating a whole generation of socialist intellectuals, and had a considerable influence on Lukács himself. From 1904 he became prominent in the Hungarian socialist party by rejecting the model of the regimented German party in favour of anarcho-syndicalist methods (Editor's note).

group. The nature of contemporary power relations necessitated unmistakably pure revolutionary tactics, which could not be obscured either by temporary cooperation with other classes (as, for example, in 1848),[5] or by isolated, independent experiments. These tactics were disturbed by the class movement of the proletariat as it grew stronger. The proletariat was becoming too strong to withdraw from political activity, which at that time related so immediately to its many interests. On the other hand, however, the proletariat was not yet strong enough to impose its will and its interests on society. *The external organizational expression of this inner conflict, this dichotomous situation, is the party.*

The modern concept of the party emerged in capitalist society. Apart from the complexity of the conflicts of interests within the ruling class (whose unity can only reveal itself *vis-à-vis* the proletariat), the basis of its existence is the lack of both clear class affiliations and a correspondingly clear consciousness among broad sections of capitalist society (the petty-bourgeoisie, intellectuals, peasants). Whenever such groups exerted influence on or were brought into political actions, it was not and could not be through the kind of pure class organization produced by the creative power of the proletariat. The essence of organization in a party rests, therefore, on the *lack of clear class-consciousness*. In ideological terms, the party appears to represent the interests of the 'whole society' and not just those of the individual classes. That this is pure ideology and nothing else is demonstrated by the fact that parties, insofar as they are actually politically effective, have always served, openly or covertly, the interests of a *class with a clear and highly-developed class-consciousness* (large-scale capital, big landowners). The object of the ideological façade is simply to inveigle social groups without any clear consciousness into acting as the train-bearers of such interests. Where a party seriously believes that it 'stands above and beyond the classes', it condemns itself from the outset to inactivity (e.g. the Radical Party).

Let us now consider what it meant for the proletariat to fit its actions into the organizational framework of the party. It meant first and foremost that the area, the form and the scope of action sank to the level of party struggles, a level which essentially involves compromise, uncertainty and opportunism. It meant, further, that the party of the proletariat was forced, as a necessary consequence of the activities within its own organizational

5. See e.g. Marx's interpretation of the tactics of the French proletariat in February 1848, in *Class Struggles in France 1848–1850*, in *Selected Works*, vol. I, pp. 145ff. (Editor's note).

framework, to accept the forms of capitalist society. Its criticisms in word and deed of those forms were futile as long as it continued to take part in elections, parliamentary life, and so on. To all intents and purposes it accepted capitalist society. The upshot was the deep gulf between words and deeds which has characterized the movements of recent years. This situation was further aggravated when, as a necessary consequence of the organizational form, countless non-proletarian elements were able to attach themselves to all the 'parties of the proletariat'. As long as large masses of the petty-bourgeoisie were joining the party and thereby strengthening the interest of large-scale capital, every non-proletarian element could only weaken the organs of the proletariat.

And yet – the organizational form of the party was a necessary transition in the proletarian movement. Its inner contradictions are not to be regarded so much as the consequences of deviations, but rather as inner, *dialectical* contradictions. It is the historical mission of the proletariat to destroy class society. In the fulfilment of this task lies the only possibility for the proletariat, as the lowest class in the social order, to become, temporarily at least, the ruling class. I say temporarily because, if the proletariat is to become the ruling class, it must necessarily destroy the class organization of society.[6] The transition, then, involves the organization by the proletariat, as ruling class and in accordance with its own ideas of the *whole of society*. This necessity finds expression in the party organization, but in such a way – and it is here that the dialectical conflict is rooted – that the true nature of the proletariat's mission is again obscured. The form in which the proletariat organizes itself represents, after all, the initial active stages in the emergence of the proletarians from the merely oppositional, utterly negative attitude which necessarily debilitated the proletarian movement in its earliest development. It is the first attempt to form the totality of society in its own image. But within the framework of the bourgeois state this positively creative standpoint could only express itself in a distorted form. As long as the proletariat was not in a position where, by seizing power, it could at one and the same time destroy the edifice of bourgeois society and construct its own, its constructive and destructive energies could not be united in joint action. Rather, those energies were bound to remain opposed in an inner, insuperable contradiction. This contradiction is, of course, not to be understood in terms of bourgeois thought: as if, that is, the party organization embodied the forces longing impatiently for action, and the opposing tendency the destructive

6. Cf. Marx, *The Poverty of Philosophy*, op. cit., pp. 196–7.

forces. On the contrary: as in all proletarian action, these two opposites are united in both. Nowhere, however, do they retain their really clear forms; certainly not in the party, for the proletariat could not develop within the framework of the bourgeois state and its destructive work had manifested itself only in inadequate forms, as 'oppositionalism' inside or outside Parliament. Not even in the party organizations and the tendencies which rejected Parliament, however, did this unity of opposites retain a clear form (syndicalism). In this case the unity of constructive and destructive work broke down because the scope of the action involved had been determined by the bourgeois state; here, too, negation meant 'opposition', albeit illegal, and construction meant any kind of organization 'within society'.

The basis of this crisis was the bourgeois state's power of self-preservation, coupled with the belief of the proletariat in this power. As soon as this power began to waver, or, alternatively, as soon as the proletariat made up its mind that its aim was the destruction of the bourgeois state and saw this aim as an imperative – from that point on, the state lay in ruins. *The outstanding achievement of Russian Bolshevism was that it embodied, for the first time since the Paris Commune, this consciousness and world-historical self-awareness of the proletariat.* For that reason the Communist Party was no longer a party in the same sense as the socialist parties opposing it. Quite the contrary: *the essential character of the communist parties lies in the radical break which they make with actions conducted within the framework of a party organization.* In accusing the Communist Party of causing a setback to the socialist movement, a retrogression to the first stages of the movement, its enemies could not have been more mistaken. They allowed themselves to be deceived by the similarity of superficial, external features, and failed to understand the dialectical antagonism between the first and the concluding phases in the class struggle of the militant and ambitious proletariat – an antagonism which manifests itself precisely in a certain external similarity. This similarity reveals itself in as much as both phases, the first and the last, represent *a pure activity of the proletariat, a complete break with all limitations on action imposed by a party organization.* Whereas in the first phase such activity can be assigned a significance which negates the party organization, the same – or rather, a similar – phenomenon in the final phase signifies *that the proletarian movement has outgrown the organizational framework of the party,* that the development of the relations of production has proceeded so far as to allow the proletariat to take all power into its own hands.

The theoretical difference between the social-democratic and the communist parties emerged chiefly, then, in their assessment of the balance of forces between, on the one hand, imperialistic finance capital, and, on the other, the proletariat with its correct or incorrect understanding of the last phase in its struggle for liberation. In this respect there can be no doubt that a union of the two parties was possible only on the basis of the unconditional acceptance of the communist programme, particularly since the profound theoretical difference was becoming more acute and obvious as the conditions for the realization of such a union developed to maturity. The communists had already said 'yes', and for them there was no question of compromise. It was up to the social democrats: if they could convince themselves that conditions *had* actually reached that critical stage of maturity, then – and only then – was union possible. As soon as they realized the true position – and that is what happened on 21 March – they were able, without in any way sacrificing deeply held opinions, to give their full support to the communist platform and put behind them those forms of action (party organization, class collaboration, etc.) which their own erroneous assessment of historical development had imposed upon them.

The question is clearly a theoretical one. But it was not theoretical discussions, not the weapons of 'persuasion', which resolved it. Discussions, indeed, could not possibly provide the answer. Both sides had already written volumes full of arguments on how to judge the situation. But from the outset they carried no conviction, for it was impossible to understand with arguments, any arguments, the deepest source of conviction of all: namely, the united and resolute will of the proletariat to seize power. All other indications adduced as evidence that conditions were ripe or unripe touched only the surface. Nothing but the unity and will of the proletariat can destroy the old society and build the new. *The conditions for the destruction of capitalism reached maturity, that is to say, when this resolute will in the proletariat awoke and became conscious.*

The unity of the proletariat and hence the possibility of a dictatorship of the proletariat were created simply and solely by the proletariat itself. It did not come about because the leaders of two parties had 'come to an agreement' and 'overcome' their outstanding differences. On the contrary, the proletariat started to move as a result of its own unified strength. Aware of its possibilities and guided by the brilliant light of its own self-consciousness, the proletariat created its own unity, its own strength and its own form. The so-called 'leaders' were merely the executors of this will, the source and goal alike of which is unity. They merely gave a theoretical form to this will, which then manifested itself in the actions of the proletariat (in that direct unity of theory and practice).

Every proletarian is an orthodox Marxist by nature of his very class position. The position arrived at by the theoretician only after arduous intellectual work is one which the proletarian, precisely because he belongs to the proletariat, already and always occupies – provided that he remains aware of his true class affiliation and the consequences which this entails. What the theory of communism has constantly proclaimed – that the proletariat must now seize power – remained mere theory until the proletariat itself absorbed it into its own consciousness. And that is exactly what happened on 21 March.

That meant, however, that the raison d'être *of the Social Democratic and even of the Communist Party no longer existed.* Not only because the dictatorship of the proletariat no longer recognizes any parties in the old sense, or even because it ruthlessly crushes the party organizations of the bourgeoisie at the same time as it destroys its class organizations; but above all because the *raison d'être* of all parties has simply disappeared. The Social Democratic Party was built on the hypothesis that the proletariat on its own was not in a position to seize power and impose its will on the totality of society. That is why the Social Democratic Party was a party. When the dictatorship of the proletariat became a reality, that entire world in which the Social Democratic Party operated as a party of the many was destroyed. But if even the social democrats regarded it from this standpoint as a necessary evil that they had to function as a party, how much truer this is for the Communist Party. For the communists had consciously organized themselves within the framework of a party precisely and only in order to be able to destroy all forms of party organization. They aimed to function as a party only until such time as the situation which they already clearly understood was consciously perceived by the whole proletariat. It was no great sacrifice for them to give up their party organization, especially as their whole existence was based on the negation of the old party forms. In rejecting their own organizational form they brought about that new unity which was the reason for their working together in a party in the first place. The new unity was *the organized dictatorship of the unified proletariat.* It is to the everlasting credit of the Hungarian proletariat that it has created this unity entirely from within itself. The proletarian masses in Russia could not create the framework of the new proletarian society – and hence their own unity – by themselves; this had to be achieved by a vanguard movement of the proletariat through fraternal struggles. In Hungary, on the other hand, the proletariat itself laid the foundations of its dictatorship with unswerving determination. None of the leaders of the proletariat, irrespective of his position before the unification, did anything more than put its intentions into effect.

The parties have ceased to exist – now there is a unified proletariat. That is the decisive theoretical significance of this union. No matter that it calls itself a party – the word party now means something quite new and different. No longer is it a heterogeneous grouping made up of different classes, aiming by all kinds of violent or conformist means to realize some of its aims within class society. Today the party is the means by which the unified will of the unified proletariat expresses itself; it is the executive organ of the will that is developing in the new society from new sources of strength. The crisis of socialism, which found expression in the dialectical antagonisms between the party movements, has come to an end. The proletarian movement has definitely entered upon a new phase, the phase of proletarian power. The most prodigious achievement of the Hungarian proletariat has been to lead the world revolution conclusively into this phase. The Russian revolution has demonstrated that the proletariat is capable of seizing power and organizing a new society. The Hungarian revolution has demonstrated that this revolution is possible without fratricidal struggles among the proletariat itself. The world revolution is thereby carried another stage further. And it is to the lasting credit and honour of the Hungarian proletariat that it has been able to draw from within itself the strength and the resources to assume this leading role, to lead, not only its own leaders, but the proletarians of all countries.

Early Writings
1919–1922

Speech at the Young Workers' Congress[1]

Now that the dictatorship of the proletariat has been realized, all proletarian organizations, even the young workers' movement, are having to change their function. Before the revolution, our main concerns were the struggle against militarism and the economic and political issues; the struggle for education and culture was only one of many.

But even before the dictatorship of the proletariat, this struggle was one of the major concerns of the young workers' movement. Prolonged campaigns were waged, many involving hardship and self-denial, in order to force even minimal concessions from those who were unwilling to give anything to the workers, especially young workers, the group most blatantly denied access to science and culture. With the change of function since the revolution, the struggle for culture, self-education and learning must become the central activity for young workers.

It seems at first glance as if, in relation to the movement as a whole, you are thereby setting yourselves a somewhat less ambitious goal than before. But that is a very superficial observation. Capitalist society is essentially one in which economic forces rule society in a completely arbitrary and untrammelled fashion, like blind forces of nature. Everything else – science, beauty, morals – is only a consequence and a product of these uncurbed, autarchic, blind and aimless forces. The victory of the proletariat has radically changed the situation: society has taken the direction of the economic elements into its own hands.

The ultimate aim is to do away with the iniquitous and disastrous autonomy of economic life, to make the economy, production, serve the needs of mankind, humanitarian ideas and culture. In turning aside from the economic struggle and devoting yourselves to cultural tasks, therefore, you are devoting yourselves to that area of social leadership which will constitute the dominant concern of a future society. If learning is now the most important task, the question arises: what and how must you learn? It is clear that the role of the young workers is crucial in this respect. All of us who are fighting for the victory of the proletariat are – without exception – the corrupted victims of capitalism. Our task now is

1. First printed in Hungarian in *Vörös Vjság*, 21 June 1919 (Editor's note).

to enable the spirit and morality of our youth to develop freely, and in this work we need your help.

It is also in your own interest to engage in the cultural struggle, so that we can realize our own culture and determine which of the achievements of past centuries are still valid, which of them we can use and which of them are useless. We therefore implore you to learn. The chief goal of your lives must be culture; see to it that the new culture has both meaning and purpose. For it is your spirit that will determine the entire content of this new culture; everything depends on how you learn and develop. The construction of this new society, the society of socialism, for which we fought and are still fighting, is your task and your responsibility.

Yet even if there is no longer any economic conflict, do not forget the struggle which you waged against militarism. The economic conflict may have been partially resolved; the proletariat is nonetheless still at war. And though you do not need to take part directly in the struggle, you are necessarily involved through your inner participation, through the task entailed in learning. In the interests of our ultimate objective we are continually forced to compromise. We cannot afford to be particular about the means we adopt. We have to do everything in our power to further the class interests of the proletariat. You, on the other hand, are not directly involved in this struggle. Your task is to wage a political struggle free from compromise and to set a moral standard for the wider struggle. For there must be a point in the struggle for the interests of the proletariat, where the flame burns absolutely clearly, where the struggle is uncompromising, completely pure, immaculate. This point is to be found in the spirit of our youth. And believe me, in every struggle and every conflict it is of the utmost importance that such a point should exist, where there are no compromises, where the struggle of the proletariat proceeds in a completely pure and unrelenting form.

No matter what functional changes the young workers' movement has undergone – as long as you remain true, your role now and in the future will be that of the vanguard of the revolution. (*Heavy and sustained applause and cries of 'Bravo'.*)

'Law and Order' and Violence[1]

Our opponents, the government socialists and the bourgeois politicians, claim with equal emphasis and equal stridency that they represent law and order, truth and persuasion by argument. The alternative we offer, as a well-known government socialist eagerly pointed out, is nothing but brute force and a resort to 'bestial instincts'. The events of the last few days have brought home clearly, even to the most prejudiced observers, the mendacity of this comparison. Here in the columns of the *Internationale*, led by Béla Kun, we do nothing but arouse the 'bestial instincts' of the immature, is that not so? And while we, the 'so-called communists' who were thrown out of the Social Democratic Party because of our 'inability and lack of character', proceed with our terrorist methods, our 'police comrades' have used the weightiest of arguments to convince Béla Kun that the system of the People's Government is constitutional, that it is based exclusively on the rule of law and that it shuns all weapons other than those of truth and persuasion. It is high time the People's Government stripped off its mask and showed itself for what it really is: a determined and ruthless defender of the class interests of the bourgeoisie. It is high time it said: yes, we admit it, the primary function of this system is to defend by any means at its disposal that self-same imperialistic capitalism which was conclusively broken in the war and is now driving the whole of Europe into its own state of bankruptcy. The

1. This article first appeared in Hungarian during the Hungarian Soviet Republic, as a supplement to the bi-weekly magazine *Die Internationale*, nos 3–4, 1919. It had been written somewhat earlier, however, immediately after 20 February 1919, when a riot in Budapest had led to the arrest of 68 communists on charges of conspiring against public order and inciting to riot. Among those arrested were Béla Kun and most of the key personnel of the Hungarian Communist Party. Károlyi's government which was responsible for the arrests was a coalition which included a number of social-democratic ministers. The article was printed along with the following explanatory note: 'These lines were written while the immediate impact of the arrests was still fresh. The repressive measures carried out against us by the [Social Democrat] Party leadership and the People's Government put a stop to the publication of the *Internationale*, although the type had already been set, and it also prevented the appearance of this little article. However, we do not believe that the lapse of time has diminished the essential truth of the position taken up there and so we print it as it stands.' (Editor's note.)

government should say it without beating about the bush – then we could at least regard it as an honest and worthwhile opponent. But let it admit this openly rather than try to conceal its counter-revolutionary activities as if it were only intent on serving the workers and the interests of the working class. Let it say this quite frankly, and then we shall see whether the Hungarian proletariat, the class of the workers, is prepared to spill the blood of its brothers to achieve this goal; then we shall see whether in the interests of this goal, and not misled by lying and false slogans, it is prepared to destroy those who sacrifice their lives in the struggle for the working class.

But no one dares to speak out. There are, of course, 'popular laws' to safeguard the 'achievements' of the revolution, but even here no one dares to say in public that these laws were enacted as an attack on those who take the revolutionary nature of the revolution seriously. Word has it that we are now threatened with a counter-revolution. True enough. But how can you defend yourself with a counter-revolution against the true counter-revolutionaries? For appearances' sake a few house-searches were carried out and a few notorious, embarrassingly obvious counter-revolutionaries were arrested, only to be released after a few days, armed with first-class moral testimonials. And it was precisely the most stubborn lackeys of the old order who praised the government most fulsomely for this 'patriotic' action. What it showed beyond a shadow of doubt, such journals claimed, was that there are no counter-revolutionaries among the bourgeois politicians. Without such an investigation, they went on, the endeavours of such people (which are in fact paving the way for an organized counter-revolution) would have been misjudged from the outset. Now, however, the People's Government itself has testified to their good character: consequently, it is they who are the true supporters of the revolution. The matter is now closed, and the gentlemen concerned can continue their activities in peace. Having offered up this 'sacrifice' of an 'impartial' investigation to the Social Democratic Party, they have now decided that it is our turn, the turn of the 'true counter-revolutionaries'.

The attitude of the bourgeois parties is easily understood. They are indeed defending the 'achievements' of the October revolution. It is very much in their own vital interests to say that the revolution is 'over', that it has 'achieved' its aims – and that it is now high time everybody cooperated for the sake of 'order', simply in order to re-establish order. Of course, even their calculations will not work out, for the counter-revolution which they are so blithely allowing to develop is hardly going to make a distinction between moderate and immoderate revolutionaries, even if it could. Once the combination of finance capital and agrarian feudalism, the self-same system which – seemingly – collapsed in the October Revolution, regains its strength, it will sweep away the petty-bourgeois radicals just as much as those bourgeoisified social-democratic leaders who fondly imagine that they can protect a few 'achievements' by leading the revolutionary movement of the proletariat into petty-bourgeois political channels.

I repeat: we can understand such tactics, however pathetic and hope-less, when they come from the 'revolutionary' bourgeoisie. But what are we to make of the 'revolutionary' policies of those who lead the Social Democratic Party? Do these wretched people not know or do they not want to see that no revolution has ever stopped halfway, that 'cooperation' between classes with conflicting interests is dangerous, even as a temporary measure, because it gives the class which controls the power apparatus a chance to recuperate and, as soon as it has recuperated, get its own back on the entire revolution! Marx's classic studies of the 1848 revolutions demonstrated the consequences of the 'parliamentary cretinism' indulged in by the trend-setting petty-bourgeois politicians of the day. It is easy to understand why the petty-bourgeois parties at that time were in such a tearing hurry to set up parliamentary forms: they feared a revolution of the proletariat. And what does the present leadership of the Social Democratic Party fear? All signs point to the same conclusion: that they too fear a revolution of the proletariat.

This is neither the time nor the place to go into the reasons for the development of this situation. It was necessary, however, to make at least some reference to them. For not only does the present factual context provide incontrovertible evidence for our assertions; it is also impossible to understand, except in terms of the situation as we have described it, the fierce and unrestrained hatred felt by the Social Democratic Party leaders towards us 'so-called communists'. It is this hatred which diverts their attention from their true enemy, the incipient counter-revolution; it is this hatred which robs their sense of morality of any discrimination and purity. The cause of this hatred is, simply, that we 'so-called communists' express openly all the things that all socialists ought anyway to be thinking. They do in fact think these things (at home, behind closed doors) and they even say so (in confidential whispers and only to trustworthy friends) – but they lack the courage to acknowledge them publicly as their true convictions.

Paradoxically, the attempt to eliminate communism indicated that the conscience of true socialism had been stirred. And the hatred with which the social-democratic leaders confronted what they themselves recognized in their heart of hearts as right was a desperate defence against the voice of their own conscience.

Great writers who really understand the workings of the human soul have many times described the lengths to which men will go in the attempt to free themselves from the torments of their bad conscience; the way in which they manage to entangle and deceive both themselves and others in a web of lies; their ability to descend to the most terrible depths of sinfulness – and all to silence the warning voice of bad conscience within themselves. The simplest way of doing this is to falsify reality. If a man can persuade himself that the person he hates because he sees in him the embodiment of his own bad conscience does not, after all, represent the principle which is in fact embodied in him; if he can persuade himself that something quite different is at issue, that his own treachery and cowardice are only a legitimate defence against the wickedness of the other, then he has apparently achieved his objective. But only apparently, only briefly. For the truth cannot be extinguished. It is futile to heap abuse on those who proclaim it, futile even to get rid of them: the truth remains in the world, and it will triumph over all self-deception, slander and violence.

It was just this kind of bad conscience which determined the tactics of the Social Democratic Party leadership *vis-à-vis* the communists. Their aim was to convince themselves and others by hook or by crook that our position is not the only possible and the only correct one that is consistent with the whole logic of socialism. They had to represent the question to themselves and to others in such a way as to make it seem that they had been 'forced' by our use of naked violence to defend themselves, and – since (through our fault) it was impossible to come to an understanding with us by means of arguments – had 'perforce' to resort to the weapons of violence. Unfortunately, the communists were not prepared to provide them with sufficient opportunities for the application of violent means of any such 'legitimate self-defence'. Such opportunities had, therefore, to be created, had to be provoked. Whenever we attempted to continue our activity of enlightening the people and making them conscious (the ultimate objective, of course, being a dictatorship of the fully-conscious proletariat and the construction of a new social order on the ruins of the old), they tried with all their might to provoke a violent incident, in order to have a pretext and an opportunity to drown our efforts in blood.

Not a day passes without every spontaneous (whether through immaturity or understandable bitterness) mass demonstration being blamed on the communists. Now and then some of the bourgeois papers retract their initial untrue allegations, but the *Népszava* never does. No opportunity is missed to make this kind of attempt at provocation at communist meetings. (There was an instance last week in Újpest, where only the patience and discipline of those of our comrades who were present helped us to ensure that the People's Government did not emerge victorious from the affair, as it has now done.)

The same thing happened with a demonstration in front of the *Népszava*.[2] All the indications are that the fracas which took place came about through counter-revolutionary provocation. What is absolutely certain is that the Communist Party had nothing to do with what happened there. But no one bothered to find that out. The truth? What did the truth matter to the masters of truth? A chance to eliminate the communist leaders presented itself, and they took it ecstatically with both hands. For their thought processes have become so petty-bourgeois that they even believe that mass movements are 'created' by individuals, 'unscrupulous agitators', and not by the compelling necessities of economic revolutions. Their methods are those of Tzarism, which also believed it could escape its fate if it despatched all those who had perceived and propagated the verdict of world history on the Tzarist regime to Siberia or the scaffold.

They are deluding themselves, just as their predecessors deluded themselves – the Tzars and those around Ludendorff and Tisza.[3] For what human strength is able to achieve in history is nothing other than a process of making conscious the necessity of world history. We have recognized and – by proclaiming the text – attempted to rouse the proletarians to consciousness of this necessity. For we realized that, once this conscious awareness exists, that is, a correct perception of the true interests of the proletariat, there is nothing which can hold back the emergence of a new world order. To be sure, we also realized and proclaimed that

2. *Népszava* ('The People's Voice'), a socialist daily. The riot which resulted in the mass arrest of the communists took place outside its offices; in the course of the disturbances four policemen were shot by anarchist soldiers (Editor's note).

3. Count Kálmán Tisza: Prime Minister of Hungary during World War I, assassinated in 1918 (Editor's note).

this new world order – like every social order – can only come about through violence. We know full well that capitalism, under sentence of death, will fight with all the means at its disposal in order to survive. But we cannot understand why those whose vocation in life ought to be to make the proletariat conscious in a revolutionary sense, oppose precisely this process with violence. We cannot understand why, at the very moment when the ideas which they have constantly proclaimed could be put into effect, they should place themselves at the service of the old order and use the means of the old order in an attempt to prevent the proletariat from becoming conscious. 'Poor misguided people', Béla Kun said to the policemen who attacked him; poor misguided people, we say to the workers who are still unable to recognize their true interests and their honest spokesmen.

But all those who believe they can hold back the course of world history by resorting to social-democratic 'law and order' are deluding themselves. We will continue the propaganda work of our imprisoned leaders. And if we, too, are eliminated, others will take our place. Attempts based on the pretext of provocation to prevent the best of us from carrying on with our educational work will fail. It is futile for them to abandon Béla Kun to the bestial rage of misguided men. No one believes their denials: they were out to have Béla Kun killed by 'police comrades'. If the counter-revolutionaries of Székesfehérvár could escape unscathed in spite of the documentary proof of their counter-revolutionary activities – during the October Revolution they protected the military hangman, General Lukasich, 'with their own lives' – then a 'legal' procedure could have been devised for the Béla Kun affair. But just as they also recoiled from 'legal' methods then, so in this case they were terrified by the mere thought that Béla Kun might have to be set free again after a certain time. It seemed simpler to eliminate him, just as Scheidemann and his supporters eliminated Liebknecht and Rosa Luxemburg. Afterwards, however, when even their carefully-laid plan somehow misfired, they attempted to pass the whole business off as an insignificant incident, of the kind today's leaders often had to contend with under the old system. And *Népszava* is not even annoyed with the police, whose indignation it considers to be understandable and excusable, but rather with *Est* whose – admittedly malicious – report uncovered what was actually intended and what went wrong. This much is true, however: Béla Kun was maltreated by the same policemen who had previously arrested the present-day leaders. On the first occasion, however, they were not considered 'comrades'. Their brutality had not yet been sanctioned by the moral backing of the Social Democratic Party, and the police chiefs did not dare to throw their victims publicly into the still 'uncomradely' jaws of their bestial underlings. No matter, all their efforts are in vain: the truth will out, and the persecution of those who proclaim it will only accelerate its realization.

We shall not follow the Social Democratic Party leadership on this path of 'law and order', persuasion and truth. We will remain on our own path, which we know to be the only correct one: in defiance of all 'legal' violence, we will continue to rouse the proletariat to consciousness, to make it fully aware of its world-historical mission. And when the proletariat has achieved self-awareness, it will pass its verdict on those who wanted fratricidal war, whose hands are stained with the blood of our comrades, and who impeded the process of the world's salvation. We await that verdict with complete confidence and unshakable faith. And we know that we shall be able to answer for our deeds. We wait confidently. And we are not alone in knowing what the verdict will be: our opponents, the murderers and executioners of the honest leaders of the proletariat – they know, too.

The Role of Morality in Communist Production[1]

The ultimate objective of communism is the construction of a society in which freedom of morality will take the place of legal compulsion in the regulation of all behaviour. Such a society necessarily presupposes, as every Marxist knows, the end of class divisions. For, whether or not we think it possible for human nature in general to permit a society based on a moral code (and in my view, the question cannot be put in these terms) – the power of morality cannot become effective, even given a decisively affirmative answer, as long as there are still classes in society. Only one mode of regulation is possible in society: the existence of two, one of which contradicts the other or even merely deviates from it, could only lead to a state of complete anarchy. If, however, a society is divided into several classes, or if – to put it another way – the interests of the human groups who make up society are not the same, it is inevitable that the regulation of human behaviour will conflict with the interests of the indubitably decisive group, if not, indeed, of the majority of human beings. But human beings cannot be induced to act voluntarily against their own interests, they can only be compelled to do so – whether this compulsion be of a physical or of a spiritual kind. As long as there are different classes, therefore, it is inevitable that the function of regulating social behaviour will be fulfilled by law, and not by morality.

But such a function of law does not end with the imposition of a mode of behaviour on the oppressed classes in the interests of their oppressors. The class interests of the ruling classes must be enforced even *vis-à-vis* the ruling class itself. This second source of the necessity of law, the conflict of individual and class interests, is of course not exclusively a consequence of the division of society into classes. It is true, however, that this conflict has never been as acute as under capitalism. Moreover, the very conditions of existence of capitalist society – the anarchy in production, the constant revolutionizing of production, production based on motives of profit, and so on – make it impossible from the outset to unite individual and class interests harmoniously within one class. However self-evidently individual and class interests have coincided whenever the capitalists con-

1. First appeared in Hungarian in *Szocialís Termelés*, 1/11, 1919 (Editor's note).

fronted other classes (either the oppressed or other oppressors, e.g. agrarian feudal classes or capitalists of a different country) – whenever, that is, the class is obliged to adopt a position to ensure the general possibility and direction of the oppression – it has nonetheless always proved impossible to unite individual and class interests once the realization of that oppression has become concrete, once the question has been posed: who is to become the oppressor, and whom, how many and to what extent is he to exploit? Class solidarity in the capitalist classes is only possible when they look outwards, not when they are concerned only with themselves. This is why, within these classes, morality could never have replaced the power of law.

The class situation of the proletariat, in both capitalist society and that which will emerge from the defeat of capitalism, is exactly the opposite. Properly conceived, the interest of the individual proletarian cannot be realized in its abstract potentiality, but only in reality itself through the victory of his class interests. The very solidarity propagated as an un-attainable social ideal by the greatest bourgeois thinkers is in fact a living presence in the class interests of the proletariat. The world-historical mission of the proletariat manifests itself precisely in the fact that the fulfilment of its own class interests will entail the social salvation of mankind.

This salvation, however, will not simply emerge as the outcome of a merely automatic process determined by natural laws. The victory of the idea over the egoistic will of individual human beings is of course clearly implicit in the class-dominating nature of the dictatorship of the proletariat; it is possible that the immediate aim of the proletariat is likewise a class hegemony. Nevertheless, the consistent implementation of this class hegemony will destroy class differences and bring into being the classless society. For if the class hegemony of the proletariat is to become truly effective, it can only liquidate class differences economically and socially by – in the final analysis – forcing all human beings into that democracy of the proletariat which is only an inner form of the manifesta-tion of the dictatorship of the proletariat within the framework of the class. The consistent implementation of the dictatorship of the proletariat can only end with the democracy of the proletariat absorbing the dictator-ship and making it superfluous. After classes have ceased to exist, dictatorship can no longer be exercised against anybody.

The state, the chief cause of the exercise of legal compulsion, the cause whose removal Engels had in mind when he said that 'the state withers away',[2] thereby ceases to exist. The question is, however: what is the pattern of this development within the proletarian class? This is where the question of the socially effective function of morality becomes problematic. It certainly played an important part in the ideologies of the old society, but never made any substantial contribution to the development of social reality itself. Nor could it, because the social pre-conditions for the development of class morality and its validity within a class – namely the same orientation of individual and class interests – are present only in the proletariat. It is only for the proletariat that solidarity, the subordination of personal interests to those of the collective, coincides with the interests, correctly conceived, of the individual. That social possibility now exists, inasmuch as all individuals belonging to the proletariat can subordinate themselves to the interests of their class without detriment to their personal interests. Such freedom of choice was not possible in the bourgeoisie, where order could only be enforced by law. For the bourgeoisie, morality could only mean – assuming that it exercised any real control over behaviour at all – a principle that went beyond class divisions and the existence of a class: in other words, individual morality. This kind of morality unfortunately implies a level of human culture which can become a general factor, effective for the total society, only in a much later epoch.

The gulf between behaviour based on merely selfish interests and pure morality is bridged by class morality, which will lead humanity into a new spiritual epoch, into, as Engels says, the 'realm of freedom'.[3] But I repeat: this development will not be a consequence of the automatic necessity of blind social forces – it must be a consequence of the free decision of the working class. For, after the victory of the proletariat, compulsion will be necessary within the working class only insofar as individuals are unable or unwilling to act in accordance with their own interests. If compulsion, the organization of physical and spiritual violence, prevailed in capitalist society even within the ruling class, it did so of necessity, because the individuals who comprised a class had been led by the exorbitant demands of their individual interests (greed for profit) to the dissolution of capitalist society. In contrast, the individual interests of every single proletarian, will, provided he assesses them correctly, strengthen society. What matters is the correct understanding of these interests, the attainment of that moral strength which enables one

2. F. Engels, *Anti-Dühring*, London, 1969, p. 333 (Editor's note).
3. ibid., p. 336 (Editor's note).

to subordinate inclinations, emotions and momentary whims to one's real interests.

The point at which individual and class interests converge is in fact characterized by increased production, a rise in productivity and a corresponding strengthening of labour discipline. Without these things the proletariat cannot survive, without them the class hegemony of the proletariat disappears – without them (even if we disregard the disastrous consequences entailed in such a dislocation of the class for all proletarians), no single person can develop fully, not even as an individual. For it is clear that those aspects of the power of the proletariat which are most oppressive and whose immediate consequences every proletarian feels most keenly – namely, shortage of goods and high prices – are a direct result of slackening labour discipline and declining productivity. To effect a remedy for this state of affairs and thereby raise the level of the individuals concerned, the causes of such phenomena must be removed.

There are two possible remedies. Either the individuals who constitute the proletariat realize that they can help themselves only by voluntarily setting about the strengthening of labour discipline and thereby raising productivity; or, where they as individuals are incapable of doing so, they create institutions which are in a position to carry out this necessary function. In the latter case they create for themselves a legal order by means of which the proletariat compels its individual members, the proletarians, to act in accordance with their class interests. The proletariat then exercises dictatorship even against itself. Where the interests of the class are not correctly perceived and voluntarily adhered to, such measures are necessary if the proletariat is to survive. They also, however – and we must not disguise the problem from ourselves – involve great dangers for the future. If, on the one hand, the proletariat creates its own labour discipline; if the labour system of the proletarian state is built on a moral basis; then the external compulsion of the law will automatically cease with the abolition of the class structure of society. In other words, the state will wither away. This liquidation of the class structure will of itself create the beginning of true human history – as Marx prophesied and hoped. If, on the other hand, the proletariat adopts a different course, it will be obliged to create for itself a legal order which cannot be abolished automatically through historical progress. In that case a tendency could evolve which would endanger both the physiognomy and the achievability of the ultimate objective. For if the proletariat is compelled to create a legal order in this way, that legal order must itself be overthrown – and who can tell what convulsions and sufferings will be caused by the transition from the realm of necessity to the realm of freedom via such a circuitous path?

The question of labour discipline, therefore, does not relate simply to the economic existence of the proletariat; it is also a moral question. Which in turn makes it clear how correct Marx and Engels were when they asserted that the epoch of freedom begins with the seizure of power by the proletariat. Progress is already no longer governed by the laws of socially blind forces, but by the voluntary decision of the proletariat. The direction which social development takes depends on the self-consciousness, the spiritual and moral character, the judgment and altruism of the proletariat.

Thus the question of production becomes a moral question. It depends on the proletariat whether or not 'the pre-history of man', the power of the economy over men, of institutions and compulsion over morality, will now come to an end. It depends on the proletariat whether or not the real history of mankind is beginning: that is, the power of morality over institutions and economy. True, social development created the possibility in the first place, but now the proletariat has actually in its hands not only its own destiny, but the destiny of mankind. The criterion for the readiness of the proletariat to take the control and leadership of society into its own hands is thereby given. Until now the proletariat has been led by the laws of social development; henceforth, the task of leadership is its own. Its decision will determine the development of society. Every individual in the proletariat must now be conscious of this responsibility. He must feel that it is he himself, his everyday work performance, which will determine when the truly happy and free epoch begins for mankind. It is inconceivable that the proletariat, which, under far more difficult conditions, has so far remained true to its world-historical mission, should now abandon this mission at the very moment when it is at last in a position to fulfil it through deeds.

The Question of Parliamentarianism[1]

I

It is generally claimed nowadays that the question of parliamentarianism does not involve principles, but is a merely tactical problem. In a limited sense this is no doubt correct, yet as a general statement it is far from clear. Apart from the fact that, in practice, those who put forward the idea are almost to a man supporters of parliamentarianism – which means that to do so almost invariably involves adopting an affirmative position – the assertion that tactics and not principles are of the essence of any particular question tells us precious little; particularly since – in the absence of a real epistemology of socialism – it in no way clarifies the relationship between a tactical question and the basic principles.

1. This article, which appeared in *Kommunismus*, 1/6, 1920, was Lukács's contribution to the debate on parliamentarianism, an issue which profoundly affected all the members of the Third International. Since Lukács frequently refers to the events in the German Communist Party, the following background information may be useful. The German Communist Party (KPD) had come into existence in December 1918/ January 1919, when the Spartacus League broke away from the left-wing Independent Socialists (USPD) because of the latter's decision to take part in the elections for the first post-war Reichstag. After the murder of Rosa Luxemburg and Karl Liebknecht (January 1919), the leadership passed to Paul Levi, who at the Second Congress of the KPD at Heidelberg (October 1919) forced through his own 'Theses on Parliamentarianism', advocating participation in elections. This split the party and those hostile to Levi broke away and founded the Communist Workers' Party (KAPD). Faced with the challenge from this party as well as the growing strength of the right-wing reaction in the country as a whole (as seen in the Kapp Putsch of March 1920) the Fourth Congress of the KPD (in Berlin in April 1920) resolved to participate in the elections in June. Here the KPD gained 2% of all votes cast and sent Levi and Clara Zetkin to the Reichstag. In December of that year the party joined forces with the left wing of the USPD, adopting the name of United Communist Party of Germany (VKPD). From then on the rejuvenated KPD was firmly committed to parliamentary action. Lukács's article appeared three months before Lenin's own essay on the subject, *'Left-wing' communism – an infantile disorder*. Lenin considered that Lukács's view was a symptom of the left-wing malady, and the Kun faction repeatedly attacked him for the positions he adopted here. See pp. *xvi–xvii* above for Lenin's remarks on the subject (Editor's note).

We cannot at this point go into the problem in any detail – yet one thing must be emphasized. Tactics are the practical application of theoretically established principles. Consequently they form the link connecting the objective and the immediately given reality. They are therefore determined from two sides; on the one hand, by the irrevocable principles and objectives of communism; on the other, by the constantly changing historical reality. There have been repeated references to the flexibility of communist tactics (or, at least, what such tactics ought to be). If we are to understand correctly what this means, we must not forget that *the non-rigidity of communist tactics is the direct consequence of the rigidity of communist principles*. It is precisely because the immutable principles of communism are adequate to the task of transforming the ever-changing reality in a vital and fruitful way that they are able to maintain this flexibility. All forms of *Realpolitik*, all forms of unprincipled action become rigid and schematic the more rigidly, schematically and stubbornly the emphasis is put on their 'principle-free' character (e.g. German imperialist politics). For the constant element amid change, the constitutive amid profusion – these cannot be supplanted by *Realpolitik* in any shape or form. Only a theory which is able to influence facts fruitfully and, in turn, to profit from the facts, is truly adequate. Where it does not exist, it will be replaced by habit, convention and routine, none of which are able to adapt themselves to the demands of the moment.

Precisely because they are rooted in theory, in principles, communist tactics have nothing in common with those of bourgeois or petty-bourgeois social-democratic *Realpolitik*. Hence, when a question facing the Communist Party is defined as a tactical question, we have to ask ourselves several things. First, on what principles is the tactical question concerned contingent? Secondly, in which historical situation are such tactics applicable in accordance with this contingency? Thirdly, what is to be the character, likewise in accordance with this contingency, of the tactics? And fourthly, how is the connection of the individual tactical question with the other individual tactical questions to be conceived – again bearing in mind their connection with the questions of principle?

2

In order to determine accurately the significance of parliamentarianism as a tactical question for communism we must always proceed, on the one hand, from the principle of the class struggle, and, on the other, from the concrete analysis of the present, actual stage in the balance of material and ideological forces between the opposing classes. This gives rise to the two decisive questions. First: *when* does parliamentarianism come under consideration at all as a weapon, as a tactical instrument of the proletariat? Secondly: *how* is this weapon to be used in the interests of the proletarian class struggle?

The class struggle of the proletariat is by its very nature a denial of bourgeois society. That, however, by no means implies the kind of political indifference towards the state which Marx correctly ridiculed, but on the contrary a form of struggle in which the proletariat does not allow itself in any way to be bound by the forms and means which bourgeois society has developed for its own purposes; a form of struggle in which the initiative lies wholly with the proletariat. However, it must not be forgotten that the proletarian class struggle can only seldom develop in this totally pure form. This is primarily because the proletariat, although by virtue of its *historico-philosophical mission* engaged in constant struggle against the very existence of bourgeois society, very often finds itself in *given historical situations* on the defensive *vis-à-vis* the bourgeoisie. The idea of the proletarian class struggle is a tremendous offensive against capitalism; history makes this offensive appear as if it were imposed on the proletariat. Hence, the tactical position which the proletariat occupies at any one time can most simply be described in terms of its offensive or defensive nature. The self-evident conclusion is that in defensive situations tactical means must be employed which fundamentally contradict the idea of the proletarian class struggle. The employment of such means, though necessary, is therefore constantly fraught with the danger that they might jeopardize the purpose for which they are used, the class struggle of the proletariat.

Parliament, the bourgeoisie's very own instrument, can therefore only ever be a *defensive weapon for the proletariat*. The question of 'when' to make use of it thus resolves itself: it will necessarily be a phase of the class struggle in which the proletariat, whether because of the external balance of forces or in consequence of its own ideological immaturity, is unable to employ its own particular offensive means in its fight against the bourgeoisie. For every Communist Party, then, taking up parliamentary activity implies *the realization and the admission that revolution is unthinkable in the foreseeable future*. In that case, if it is forced on to the defensive, by all means let the proletariat use the forum of parliament for agitational and propagandistic purposes; let it exploit the possibilities afforded members of parliament by bourgeois 'freedom' as a substitute for forms of expression otherwise denied it; let it make use of the parliamentary struggles with the bourgeoisie in order to gather its own forces, in preparation for the really basic struggle against the bourgeoisie. Clearly, such a phase may well last for a considerable length of time, but that in itself does nothing to alter the fact that, for a Communist Party, parliamentary activity *can never be anything more than a preparation for the real struggle*, can never be the actual struggle itself.

3

Even more difficult to determine than the point in time at which parliamentary tactics can be employed is the manner in which a communist faction should conduct itself in parliament. (Incidentally, the two questions are closely connected.) The examples cited are almost always those of Karl Liebknecht[2] and the Bolshevist faction in the Duma. But both show how difficult it is for communists to strike the correct mode of parliamentary conduct and what extraordinary abilities such conduct demands of communist deputies. The difficulty can be briefly summarized as follows: the communist deputy must fight parliament within parliament itself – and, moreover, using tactics which are not for a single moment based on the methods of the bourgeoisie, on parliamentarianism. This does not mean simply 'protesting' against parliamentarianism or 'attacking' it in 'debates' (all such gestures remain parliamentary and legal, and add up to nothing more than revolutionary phrase-mongering), but rather attacking parliamentarianism and bourgeois hegemony *through action* in parliament itself.

The sole purpose of such action must be to prepare ideologically the transition of the proletariat from the defensive to the offensive; to force the bourgeoisie together with its social-democratic accomplices to expose their class dictatorship in a way which could jeopardize its very continuance. If communist tactics are to unmask the bourgeoisie in parliament, therefore, they must go beyond verbal criticism (which amounts

2. Most recently by Karl Radek in *Die Entwicklung der Weltrevolution und die Taktik der kommunistischen Parteien im Kampfe um die Diktatur des Proletariats* ('The growth of the world revolution and the tactics of the communist parties in the struggle for the dictatorship of the proletariat'), Berlin, 1920, p. 29 (G.L.'s note).

in many cases to mere revolutionary sloganizing, easily tolerated by the bourgeoisie) to the stage where the bourgeoisie is provoked to act more openly and to reveal its true nature by actions which at the given moment are to its own disadvantage. Since parliamentarianism is a defensive tactic for the proletariat, it is imperative to organize the defensive in such a way that the proletariat nonetheless retains the tactical initiative, in such a way that the onslaughts of the bourgeoisie rebound on their authors with disastrous consequences.[3]

It is to be hoped that this brief and somewhat crude exposition illustrates sufficiently clearly the great difficulties entailed in such tactics. The chief difficulty, to which parliamentary parties almost without exception succumb, lies in managing to transcend parliamentarianism in a real sense within parliament itself. For even the most vehement criticism of a measure taken by the ruling class remains so much hot air, so much revolutionary sloganizing, as long as it fails to reach out beyond the confines of parliament; as long as it does not result at the same time in sparking off the class struggle itself, bringing out more clearly the class antagonisms and hence accelerating the emergence of the ideology of the proletariat. Such shortcomings are the ultimate basis of opportunism, the greatest pitfall for parliamentary tactics: any parliamentary activity which does not essentially and effectively transcend parliament, or does not at least move in the direction of shattering the parliamentary framework, is opportunistic. Even the most severe criticism levelled *within* that framework changes absolutely nothing. On the contrary: the very fact that severe criticism of bourgeois society appears *possible* within the confines of parliament serves, just as the bourgeoisie would wish it, to confuse the class-consciousness of the proletariat. Indeed the myth of bourgeois parliamentary democracy depends precisely on the ability of parliament to appear not as an organ of class oppression, but as the organ of the 'entire people'. All forms of verbal radicalism which use the opportunities afforded by parliament to reinforce the illusions of the unenlightened sections of the proletariat about this myth are opportunistic and contemptible.

---

3. These tactics are surely what Engels has in mind in his frequently (and for the most part intentionally) misunderstood preface to *Class Struggles in France*, when he says that the parties of order are destroyed by the state of 'legality' they have themselves created. There can be no doubt that Engels is describing a defensive situation (G.L.'s note). (See Engels, preface to *Class Struggles in France*, in *Selected Works*, vol. I, pp. 135–6 – ed.)

Parliament must therefore be sabotaged *as parliament*, and parliamentary activity propelled beyond mere parliamentarianism. However, in addressing themselves to this task, the parliamentary representatives of the communists will encounter a further tactical difficulty, which could well jeopardize their work even when the danger of opportunism seems to have been overcome. In spite of all the efforts of the communist faction in parliament, the danger nevertheless exists that the initiative and hence tactical superiority will remain with the bourgeoisie. If one of the sides in the struggle succeeds in imposing on the other such conditions of struggle as will be to its own advantage, the question of tactical superiority is thereby settled. It has already been emphasized that any struggle which abides by parliamentary conventions represents a tactical victory for the bourgeosie.

So, in very many cases the proletariat has to choose between the devil and the deep blue sea: either it evades the decisive struggle (by sticking to parliamentary forms and thereby running the risk of opportunism), or it carries out a policy of moving beyond parliamentarianism and appealing directly to the masses – but at a time when such action can only benefit the bourgeoisie. The present situation of the Italian proletariat provides the clearest example of this insoluble dilemma.[4] The elections – which the communists openly contested as a large-scale 'agitational' campaign under their own banner – brought the party a large number of mandates. What now? Either participation in the 'positive work' of parliament, which is what Turati and company want, resulting in victory for opportunism and the decline of the revolutionary movement. Or outright sabotage of parliament, resulting sooner or later in a direct collision with the bourgeoisie – and that when it does not lie within the power of the proletariat to choose the moment of the collision. This last point should not be misunderstood: we do not, of course, proceed on the ludicrous assumption that the 'moment' for revolution can be 'selected'. On the contrary, we believe that revolutionary outbreaks are spontaneous mass actions in which the role of the party is to make the people conscious of their objective and to point the way forward for the struggle. But it is precisely this spontaneity which is endangered if the collision is triggered

4. With the exception of the small 'abstentionist' faction of Bordiga, the Italian Socialists (PSI) took part in the elections of November 1919 and gained 150 seats to become the largest parliamentary party. Filippo Turati was the leader of the right wing of the party. The Second Congress of the Third International called for his expulsion (together with the other right-wing leaders) in the summer of 1920 (Editor's note).

off in parliament. Parliamentary action either turns into empty demonstrations (resulting eventually in the exhaustion and lethargy of the masses) or leads to successful provocative measures on the part of the bourgeoisie. The Italian parliamentary party – fearful of the latter possibility – vacillates blindly between meaningless demonstrations and the covert opportunism of revolutionary phrase-mongering. (It is not, of course, only in relation to the methods chosen that tactical mistakes have been made; there have also been what we might call tactical mistakes of substance, e.g. the petty-bourgeois demonstration for the republic.)

4

This example brings home quite clearly how dangerous an 'electoral victory' can be for the proletariat. For the greatest danger at present facing the Italian party is the distinct possibility that its anti-parliamentary activity in parliament will destroy parliament – even though the Italian proletariat does not yet have the ideological and organizational maturity necessary for the decisive struggle. The contradiction between electoral victory and unpreparedness throws into sharp relief the weakness of those arguments in favour of parliamentarianism which see in it a kind of 'military parade' of the proletariat. After all, if the 'votes' won represented the number of real communists, these reservations would be redundant, and the necessary ideological maturity would already exist.

What this also shows clearly, however, is that electoral agitation has serious drawbacks, even as a mere propaganda device. The propaganda of the Communist Party must serve to clarify the class-consciousness of the proletarian masses and awaken them to the necessity of the class struggle. Accordingly it must be directed towards accelerating as far as possible the process of differentiation within the proletariat. Only in this way is it possible to achieve the position where, on the one hand, the conscious and resolute nucleus of the revolutionary proletariat (the Communist Party) will develop both quantitatively and qualitatively; and on the other hand, the party, through the object-lesson it provides in revolutionary action, will galvanize the support of the half-conscious sectors and lead them to revolutionary consciousness of their situation. Electoral agitation is an extremely dubious means of bringing this about. Casting a vote in an election is not only not real action, but – what is far worse – it is sham action, the illusion of action. Its effect, therefore, far from raising consciousness, is actually to cloud consciousness. A seemingly huge army arises, only to capitulate utterly the moment it becomes necessary to stand firm (German Social Democracy in August 1914).

Such a state of affairs is a necessary consequence of the typically bourgeois nature of the parliamentary parties. Like all organizations of bourgeois society, the bourgeois parliamentary parties have as their ultimate, albeit seldom conscious object, the obfuscation of class-consciousness. As a dwindling minority of the population the bourgeoisie is able to maintain its hegemony only by recruiting into its retinue all those sectors which are materially and ideologically uncertain and unclear. The bourgeois parliamentary party is consequently an amalgam of the most diverse class interests (from the capitalist point of view, of course, the apparent compromise is always greater than the real one). And yet, whenever the proletariat takes part in elections, it almost invariably has this kind of party structure imposed on it. The mechanism of all such elections, in which the objective is necessarily as great a 'victory' as possible, has a life of its own which always influences the slogans in the direction calculated to attract the 'fellow-travellers'. And even where this has not happened – or at least not consciously so – the whole election technique involves the seduction of 'fellow-travellers'. This in turn involves the fatal danger of the separation of attitude and action, thus fostering bourgeois tendencies and opportunism. The educational work of the communist parties, its impact on the unclear and unsure sectors of the proletariat, can become really fruitful only when it stiffens their revolutionary conviction through the object-lesson it provides in revolutionary action. The effect of all election campaigns is exactly the opposite – as it must be, bearing in mind their essentially bourgeois nature – and only very occasionally can it really be overcome. Even the Italian party succumbed to this danger. The right wing regarded affiliation to the Third International and the demand for a republic of soviets as a mere election slogan. The process of differentiation, the *real* winning over of the masses to communist *action* can therefore *begin* only later (and in all probability in less favourable circumstances). Precisely because they are not directly related to action, election slogans exhibit a remarkable propensity for blurring differences and uniting the most divergent tendencies. At this particular stage of the class struggle, where what matters most is the real, active unity of the proletariat, not the sham unity of the old parties, such attributes are more than suspect.

5

Among the almost insuperable difficulties confronting communist activity in parliament is the inordinate degree of independence, even licence, customarily enjoyed by the parliamentary group in party affairs. It goes without saying that this is an advantage for the bourgeois parties.[5] But what is useful for the bourgeoisie is almost always of dubious use to the proletariat. That is also true in this case: there is no prospect of avoiding the dangers of parliamentary tactics outlined above unless *parliamentary activity is completely and absolutely subject to the extra-parliamentary leadership of the Central Bureau.* This seems to be theoretically self-evident, but experience has taught us that the relationship between party and parliamentary faction is almost always inverted, with the party being pulled along in the wake of the parliamentary faction. That, for instance, was Karl Liebknecht's experience during the war, when he appealed – without any success, of course – to the Reichstag faction to respect the binding nature of the party programme.[6]

Even more problematic than the relationship between *parliamentary faction and party* is that which exists *between* the former and the workers' council. The difficulty involved in posing the correct theoretical question again casts a harsh light on the problematical nature of parliamentarianism in the class struggle of the proletariat. As *organizations of the entire proletariat* (both conscious and unconscious) the workers' councils *by their mere existence point the way forward beyond bourgeois society.* They are by their very nature revolutionary and organizational expressions of the growing significance, the ability to act and the power of the proletariat. As such, they are the true index of the progress of the revolution. For everything that is achieved and attained in the workers' councils is wrested from the defiant grasp of the bourgeoisie, and is therefore valuable not simply as a result, but chiefly as a means of education for class-conscious action. Attempts (like those of the USPD) to 'anchor the workers' councils in the constitution', to assign them a legally established field of activity, therefore indicate a new peak in 'parliamentary cretinism'. *Legality is the death of the workers' council.* As an offensive organization of the revolutionary proletariat the workers' council can exist only insofar

5. This is connected with the advantages accruing to the bourgeoisie from the so-called separation of the powers of government (G.L.'s note).

6. Karl Liebknecht, *Klassenkampf gegen den Krieg* ('Class Struggle against the War'), Berlin, 1915, p. 53 (G.L.'s note).

as it threatens the existence of bourgeois society, only insofar as it struggles for and prepares, step by step, the destruction of that society and hence the construction of the proletarian society. Legality in any shape or form – i.e. integration into bourgeois society, with *precisely defined limits* to its competence – would transform its existence into a sham: the workers' council would turn into a cross between a debating society and a poor man's parliamentary committee.

Is it at all possible, then, for workers' council and parliamentary faction to exist side by side as tactical weapons of the proletariat? Since the one is essentially offensive and the other essentially defensive, it would be simple to deduce that they are complementary.[7] Any such attempt to reconcile them, however, overlooks the fact that, within the class struggle, offensive and defensive are dialectical concepts, each of which embraces an entire world of activity (in both cases, individual offensive and defensive measures) and can only be applied to a particular phase of the class struggle, after which the other can be applied. The difference between the two phases can be defined most succinctly and at the same time – for the question under discussion – most clearly in the following way: the proletariat remains on the defensive until the process of disintegration of capitalism has begun. Once this phase of the economic development is under way – regardless of whether or not this transformation has become conscious, or, indeed, whether or not it appears to be 'scientifically' verifiable and demonstrable – the proletariat is *forced on to the offensive*. However, since ideological development does not conveniently coincide with the economic process, since it does not even run absolutely parallel with it, the objective possibility and necessity of the offensive phase of the class struggle seldom finds the proletariat adequately prepared ideologically. As a result of the economic situation, it is true, the spontaneous activity of the masses moves in a revolutionary direction, but it is constantly being diverted into the wrong channels or even completely sabotaged by opportunistic leaders who neither will nor can free themselves of the habits of the defensive phase. Consequently, in the offensive phase of the class struggle it is no longer simply the bourgeoisie and its followers who stand opposed to the proletariat, but *its own former leadership*. Our criticism should therefore no longer be directed primarily against the bourgeoisie (on whom history has long since passed judgment), but rather against the right wing and the centre of the workers' movement, against social democracy, without whose assistance capitalism would not have the

7. Max Adler's proposal of the workers' council as a second Chamber (G.L.'s note).

slightest prospect in any country of overcoming, even temporarily, its present crisis.

Proletarian criticism, however, is not merely verbal; it is *active criticism*, a process of education through revolutionary action, an object lesson. For this purpose the workers' councils are the most effective instrument conceivable. For, far more important than all the individual gains which they can achieve for the proletariat, is their educational function. *The workers' council spells the death of social democracy.* Whereas in parliament it is quite possible to conceal actual opportunism behind revolutionary slogans, the workers' council is compelled to act – otherwise it ceases to exist. Such action, which should be under the conscious leadership of the Communist Party, will bring about the disintegration of opportunism and give rise to the criticism which is necessary today. No wonder the social democrats fight shy of the self-criticism which is now being imposed upon them. The progress made by the soviets in Russia between the first and the second revolution demonstrates clearly where this development is bound to lead to.

Theoretically and tactically, then, we have defined the respective roles of workers' council and parliament: *where a workers' council* (on however modest a scale) *is possible, parliamentarianism is redundant.* It is even dangerous, for it ensures by its very nature that the only form of criticism possible within its confines is criticism of the bourgeoisie, not proletarian self-criticism. Before the proletariat can enter the promised land of liberation, however, it must first go through the purgatory of such self-criticism. Only thus can its own character in the capitalist epoch, as exemplified most precisely by the nature of social democracy, be dissolved, rejected and thereby purged.

The Moral Mission of the Communist Party[1]

I

Like all Lenin's writings this latest pamphlet[2] deserves to be studied most carefully by all communists. He reveals yet again his quite extraordinary ability to grasp what is decisively new about a new phenomenon in the development of the proletariat; his ability to comprehend its very essence and to make it comprehensible in the most concrete way. Whereas his earlier writings were largely of a polemical nature, concerned mainly to examine the fighting organizations of the proletariat (primarily the state), this one deals with the present development of the embryonic new society. Just as the capitalist form of production, with its labour discipline dictated by economic compulsion (hunger), was superior to the naked violence of serfdom, so the free cooperation of free human beings in the new society – even in the field of productivity – will far surpass capitalism. It is precisely in this respect that the social-democratic defeatists of the world revolution are most sceptical. They point to the slackening of labour discipline, the fall in productivity – in short, to the inevitable concomitants of the disintegrating capitalist economic system. And with an impatience and intolerance matched in intensity only by their patience and tolerance towards capitalism they point out that these things did not change *immediately* in Soviet Russia. Lack of raw materials, internal struggles and organizational difficulties count as excuses in their view *only for capitalist states*; their line is that a proletarian social order ought to mean the internal and external transformation of all conditions, an all-round improvement in the situation, from the very first moment that that order is born. Genuine revolutionaries, and above all Lenin, distinguish themselves from such petty-bourgeois utopianism by their lack of illusions. They know what can be expected, not only of an economy ruined in the World War, but also – and above all – of *human beings* who, under capitalism, have been spiritually corrupted and depraved and indoctrinated with

1. First appeared in *Kommunismus*, 1/16–17, 1920 (Editor's note).

2. 'A Great Beginning' in *Selected Works*, London, 1969, pp. 478–97 (*Collected Works*, vol. 29) (Editor's note).

egoism. However, freedom from illusions never leads the true revolutionary to lose heart or to despair; his understanding of the situation as it really is serves rather to strengthen his faith in the world-historical mission of the proletariat. This faith can never be shaken, no matter how long it takes to realize it, no matter how often it is beset by adverse circumstances. It accepts all these disruptions and obstructions, but never allows them to distract him from his goal and the indications of its imminence.

The communist Saturdays, the mobilization to work which the Russian Communist Party has taken upon itself, have been discussed frequently and from many different points of view. Understandably, the main emphasis has always been put on their actual and possible economic consequences. But however important these may be, the communist Saturdays and the possibility and form of their origins are significant in a further sense, one which takes us far beyond their immediate economic consequences. 'The enormous historical significance of the communist Saturdays is that they reveal to us the purposeful and voluntary initiative of the workers in the development of labour productivity, in the transition to the new work discipline, in the creation of socialist conditions in the economy and in life generally.'[3]

The non-Russian communist parties are frequently criticized for imitating the Russian example too slavishly in their actions and their demands. It seems to me that in several (by no means inessential) respects, the exact opposite is the case: the European communist parties either cannot or will not examine the true sources of the Russian movement's strength – and even when some of the lessons strike home they cannot raise the necessary strength to translate them into action.

The communist Saturdays, as the first seeds of the transition from a capitalist to a socialist economic order, as the starting-point for the 'leap from the realm of necessity into the realm of freedom', are *in no sense institutional measures of the Soviet government, but moral actions of the Communist Party*. And it is precisely this vital and decisive aspect of the reality of the Russian Communist Party which has been least appreciated by its sister parties, who, far from copying its example, have hardly ever drawn the correct and necessary conclusions from its achievements.

3. Cf. Lenin, *Selected Works*, London, 1969, p. 488 (Editor's note).

If there is one commonplace which cannot be too strongly emphasized, it is that *the communist party is the organizational expression of the revolutionary will of the proletariat.* It is therefore by no means bound to embrace the whole of the proletariat from the very outset; as the conscious leader of the revolution, as the embodiment of the revolutionary idea, its task is rather to unite the most conscious sections, the vanguard, the really revolutionary and fully class-conscious workers. The revolution itself is brought about necessarily by the natural laws governing the economic forces. The duty and the mission of communist parties everywhere is to supply the revolutionary movement – which to a large extent arises independently of them – with *a direction and a goal* and to lead the elemental outbreaks sparked off by the collapse of the capitalist economic order on to the only viable path of salvation, on to the dictatorship of the proletariat.

The old parties were compromise combinations, heterogeneous collections of individuals, and consequently very quickly became bureaucratized, very quickly gave rise to an aristocracy of party officers and subalterns who were cut off from the masses. The new communist parties, on the other hand, should represent the purest expression of the revolutionary class struggle, the transcending of bourgeois society. However, the transition from the old society to the new implies, *not merely an economic and institutional, but also and at the same time a moral transformation.* Let there be no misunderstanding: nothing is further from our thoughts than the petty-bourgeois utopianism of those who fondly imagine that social change can only be brought about through an inner transformation of human beings. (Not the least indication that this is a petty-bourgeois notion is the fact that its proponents – whether consciously or not – thereby relegate the transformation of society to some dim and distant point in the timeless future.) On the contrary, we insist that the transition from the old to the new society is a necessary consequence of objective economic forces and laws. For all its objective necessity, however, this transition is precisely the transition from bondage and reification to freedom and humanity. For that reason *freedom cannot be regarded simply as a fruit, a result of historical development. There must arise in that development a moment where freedom itself becomes one of the driving forces.* Its significance as a driving force must constantly increase until the time comes when it takes over completely the leadership of a society which has now become human, when 'mankind's pre-history' comes to an end and its true history is able to begin.

The beginning of this phase seems, in our view, to coincide with the rise of revolutionary consciousness, with the founding of the communist parties. For every Communist Party – as long as it does not merely stand in *opposition* to bourgeois society, but actively embodies its *negation* – represents far more than just the antithesis of the old social-democratic parties. It signifies in fact the beginning of their destruction and disappearance. The greatest tragedy of the workers' movement has always been its inability to tear itself completely free from the ideological matrix of capitalism. The old social-democratic parties have *never even seriously tried to do so*: they have remained essentially bourgeois parties, with all the accompanying characteristics: compromise, vote-catching, cheap-jack demagogy, intrigue, social climbing and bureaucracy. Hence coalitions with bourgeois parties are not merely the consequence of objective, political necessity; they spring from the inner structure, the real essence of the social-democratic parties. It is therefore easy to understand why, in the truly revolutionary, albeit not fully conscious elements of the workers' movement, voices should have made themselves heard denouncing, not only the corrupt petty-bourgeois and counter-revolutionary nature of the old parties, *but the whole idea of parties as such*. One of the chief reasons for the emergence and the attraction of syndicalism is doubtless to be found in the *ethical rejection* of the old parties.

The Russian Communist Party never succumbed to these dangers. Instead of the usual dilemma – old style party or syndicalism, bureaucratic organization or destruction of the party – they devised a clear 'tertium datur', a third approach. It is this third approach whose *consequences* we can now discern in every facet of the Russian Revolution. So far, however, we have been too cowardly and too idle to recognize its *basis* and incorporate it as a driving force into our own movements.

3

The basis of this power of the Soviet Communist Party is to be found, first, in its internal organization; secondly, in the way in which it conceives its task and mission; and thirdly (as a consequence of the first two) in the manner of its effect upon its members. In contrast to the old social-democratic parties and most non-Russian communist parties, it is a closed, not an open party. Not only does it not try to recruit anybody and everybody to its ranks (one of the chief causes of corruption and compromise); it does not even accept all those who want to join. Such people are sifted through the ranks of the so-called sympathizers ('Friends of the Communists'), of whom those who meet the *moral* demands made of a Russian communist are admitted to the party itself. The party, however, is by no means concerned with merely increasing its membership, but rather with the quality of those who remain in its ranks. For this reason the party uses every opportunity arising from the tremendous exertions of the Revolution to *purge its ranks.* 'The war mobilization of the communists,' says Lenin, 'helped us in this respect: the cowards and blackguards turned their backs on the party. That sort of reduction in the number of members represents a significant *growth* in the strength and reputation of the party. We should continue the purge by exploiting the initiative of the "communist Saturdays".'[4] This purging of the party is therefore based on 'a constant *stepping-up of demands* in relation to real communist achievements'.[5]

The internal construction of the Russian Communist Party takes us on to the second aspect of our discussion, the mission of the party in the revolution. The Communist Party, as the vanguard of the revolution, should always be at least one step ahead of the development of the masses. Just as the Communist Party was already conscious of the necessity of revolution at a time when the broad masses felt at most a vague dissatisfaction with their situation, so consciousness of the realm of freedom ought already to be a vital factor in the various communist parties and a decisive influence on their actions, particularly if the masses who follow them are not yet in a position to tear themselves free ideologically from the corrupt matrix of capitalism. Such a role for the Communist Party does not of course acquire complete actuality until the setting-up of the government of Soviets. For once the proletariat has established its power *institutionally*, everything depends on whether the *spirit* which informs those soviets is really the spirit of communism, of the new humanity which is now emerging, or just a new disguise for the old society. Only the Communist Party can embody this cleansing, purifying and dynamic principle. Since the transformation in forms of government cannot possibly bring about an inner transformation in human beings at the same time, it is inevitable that all the evil aspects of capitalist society (bureau-

4. Cf. op. cit., p. 495 (Editor's note).
5. ibid.

cracy, corruption, and so on) will find their way into Soviet institutions. There is a grave danger that these institutions will degenerate or ossify even before they have had a chance to develop properly. This where the Communist Party must intervene as critic, model, bulwark, organizer and reformer. It is the only body which is in a position to do so.[6]

Having educated the proletariat for revolution, then, the Communist Party must now educate the whole of humanity in freedom and self-discipline. But it can only fulfil this mission if it practises its educational work among its members from the very beginning. It would, however, be completely un-Marxist and non-dialectical thinking to attempt to separate forcibly the two developmental phases mentioned above. On the contrary, their relationship is one of constant mutual interpenetration, and no one can ever determine exactly where the one begins and the other ends. The human ideal of the realm of freedom must therefore be a conscious principle governing the actions and motivating the lives of all communist parties from the very moment of their inception. Organizational forms, raising consciousness by means of education and propaganda – these are crucial and essential means. But they are far from the only ones. Most important – indeed, in the last analysis, the decisive factor – is *what communists themselves achieve as human beings*.

The Communist Party must be the primary incarnation of the realm of freedom; above all, the spirit of comradeliness, of true solidarity, and of self-sacrifice must govern everything it does. If it cannot achieve this, or if it does not at least exert itself seriously to put such ideals into practice, the Communist Party will no longer be distinguishable from the other parties, except by virtue of its programme. There is even the danger that this unbridgeable gulf which separates it programmatically from the opportunists and the waverers will gradually become obscured, with the result that it could soon be nothing more than the 'extreme left wing' of the 'workers' parties'. That in turn would present a further, more immediate danger (already posed in accentuated form by the rhetorical recognition of the Third International by the parties of the centre): namely, that the qualitative distinction between the communists and the other parties would degenerate into a merely quantitative one and in time even disappear altogether. The less a Communist Party puts its ideals into practice both organizationally and spiritually, the less able it will be, not only to counter effectively this widespread inclination to compromise, but also to *educate*

6. Cf. the article by Comrade Vladimir Sorin, 'The Communist Party and Soviet Institutions', in *Kommunismus*, 1/8–9 (1920), pp. 283ff. (G.L.'s note).

the unconscious but really revolutionary elements (syndicalists, anarchists) to become true communists.

Compromise and disintegration spring from the same source: the inadequate inner transformation of communists themselves. The more the communists (and with and through them the Communist Party) have cleansed themselves of all the dross of capitalist, social-democratic party life, such as bureaucracy, intrigues, social climbing, etc., the more their party solidarity turns into true comradeship and spiritual solidarity – the better able they will be to fulfil their mission. Then and only then will they be in a position to gather revolutionary forces, strengthen the irresolute, rouse the unconscious to consciousness – and push aside and destroy once and for all the scoundrels and the opportunists. The revolutionary period which we now face will be rich in protracted and difficult struggles; it will provide us with countless opportunities for this self-education. Our Russian comrades provide the most instructive example, both in organizational and human terms, that we could wish for. It is high time we *began* to emulate their example in this country, too.

Opportunism and Putschism[1]

No intelligent communist who is honest with himself will be willing or able to conceal the fact that all the communist parties (with the exception of the Russian party) are bound to undergo a severe crisis. This crisis, the seeds of which have been present ever since the founding of the communist parties, has from time to time become acute. In the early stages it manifested itself in the prevalence of putschist tendencies. Blanquism, which Bernstein, Marx himself and – most decisively – the Bolsheviks rejected, in fact haunted the thoughts and actions of many otherwise honest and committed comrades, in the shape of the illusion that the proletarian revolution could be achieved at one blow through the resolute and selfless action of a small well-organized vanguard group. To all appearances the communist parties were on the point of overcoming the confusions inherent in this doctrine, which was bound to come into particular prominence with the disintegration of the state power apparatus in Central Europe immediately after the war had been lost.

This impression is reinforced by the fact that the significance of the other, internal and hence more important reason for the emergence of putschist leanings in the communist parties is likewise showing a tendency to decline. The very nature of the matter makes it inevitable that the first people to be gripped by revolutionary movements will be those sectors of the working class which, although instinctively revolutionary, have not previously been organized and therefore lack experience in the class struggle. On the other hand, it is precisely the elite of organized working-class trade unionists which will exhibit marked opportunistic and conservative tendencies. However, in proportion as these latter sectors are also affected by the collapse of capitalism as its consequences extend to their own immediate economic situation, and in proportion as they are thereby revolutionized, the elemental revolutionary feeling of the proletarian masses becomes imbued with the revolutionary consciousness of the true class struggle, with conscious dialectical Marxism. (The significance of the previously mentioned sectors of the working class for the

1. First published in *Kommunismus*, 1/32, 1920 (Editor's note).

fate of the revolution still holds good, but it undergoes a change of function.)

Instead, other internal dangers now seem to be looming up. With the growth of the parties, especially where the proletarian party of the Third International has not emerged through a struggle and split with the old party but has attained the majority position and the leadership from within the party (as in Italy and possibly soon in Czechoslovakia), and with the gravitation of opportunistic or at least vacillating groups towards the Third International (the Longuet[2] group and the Independent Socialists), the danger grows ever more acute. Every day brings fresh and increasingly clear signs that the entry of such groups will lead to the communist parties themselves being invaded by the spirit of opportunism. It looks, therefore, as if the true Marxist communists are now having to wage a struggle on two fronts, right and left, as if Marxism itself has been forced into a middle position in the communist movement. Against this it must be stressed – and, as far as the present discussion allows, theoretically demonstrated – that *we are dealing in both cases with the same danger to the spirit of communism*; that in the decisive theoretical area of basic principles, both opportunists and putschists occupy the same ground, and consequently only too often achieve very similar results in practice.

The same theoretically crucial weaknesses are common to both groups: on the one hand – to put it purely negatively – they are unable to understand *the revolution as process*: on the other hand – and this is, as it were, a positive fault – *they wrongly assess the value of organization* for the revolutionary movement. We could just as well say that they both overrate the importance of organization, except that this would be misleading to the extent that it could be interpreted as support for anarcho-syndicalist tendencies – something no communist can afford to countenance. If, in contrast to the communists, the opportunists and the putschists wrongly assess the significance of organization, it is not in relation to organization in general, but exclusively *as regards the role and function of organization in the revolutionary movement*. Without organization – indeed, without

2. The efforts of Jean Longuet and his friends to join the French Communist Party at its foundation in December 1920 were frustrated by an unprecedented intervention from Zinoviev in the form of a telegram which stated that 'the draft resolution signed by Longuet and Paul Faure proves that Longuet and his group do not wish to dissociate themselves from the reformist camp. They have been and still remain determined agents of bourgeois influence on the proletariat. . . . The Communist International can have nothing in common with the authors of such resolutions' (Editor's note).

highly centralized and disciplined organization – the Communist Party is inconceivable. For the Communist Party, however – and this is what distinguishes it from opportunist and putschist groups – organization is not the prerequisite of action, but rather a constant interplay of pre-requisite and consequence evolving during action. Indeed, if either of these aspects has to preponderate, then it must be the conception of organization as consequence rather than as prerequisite. Rosa Luxemburg writes: 'The rigid, mechanical and bureaucratic view is not prepared to allow the validity of the struggle except as the product of organization at a certain level of strength. The living dialectic of development, on the con-trary, causes organization to arise as the product of the struggle.'[3] It is hardly necessary to give examples illustrating the kind of thinking and action peculiar to the opportunists; their whole business of totting up ballot papers and party pamphlets, their lying in wait for the 'moment' when sufficient proletarians are sufficiently well organized – this is all general knowledge. The reasoning of the putschists, however, is strikingly similar. No matter that they tot up revolvers, machine guns and so on instead of ballot papers; no matter that the 'good organization' is not enshrined in an election apparatus or a trade union, but in an illegal military organization – it makes precious little difference to their theoretical principles. The putschists, too, regard organization and action as two distinct stages, organization as the preparation and the revolution itself as the mobilization and battle. This mechanical division of the revolution-ary process necessarily leads them to exaggerate grossly the significance of the mere actual seizure of power by the proletariat. They believe it is legitimate to regard the seizure of power as the conclusion, or at least as the culmination, of the revolutionary process, although it is in fact nothing more than a very important, crucial stage (but only one stage, neverthe-less) in the class struggle. They are therefore bound to overlook completely the fact that their resources, and especially those of their 'organization', are not only inadequate for the following, truly decisive struggle, but are absolutely inappropriate to it. The opportunists also see the moment when power is seized in a false light. Even though they generally attempt to eradicate its significance from the consciousness of the proletariat by meaningless waffle about 'gradual development', 'transitional stage' and the like, their incorrect assessment can very often give rise to situations where the actual seizure of power is not only over-rated, but is even dealt with in practice in putschist fashion. The call to set up the Munich Soviet

3. Rosa Luxemburg, *Massenstreik*, new edn, p. 46 (G.L.'s note).

is a characteristic example: even though the genuine communists whole-heartedly opposed the move and declined to take any part in it at all, the first, apparently genuine, Soviet Republic of Bavaria came into being as a result of the putsch staged by the majority socialists, independents and anarchists. And whereas, once it had been established, the communists devoted all their energy to turning this bogus sovereignty of the proletariat, this paper power, into a real dictatorship of the proletariat, the actual instigators of the putsch – those to the right and left of Toller[4] – when they were not pursuing sham achievements were blatantly sabotaging every genuine revolutionary measure in the class struggle.

This is no coincidence. It is no coincidence that the Independent Socialist Party is at the centre of this fraternal mélange of opportunism and putschism. It is also no coincidence that the seizure of power could not come quickly and 'vigorously' enough for so-called left-wing radicals like Laufenberg and Wolffheim,[5] but that, on the other hand, these self-same people are only too eager to 'consolidate' this kind of proletarian 'sovereignty' for the struggle against entente capitalism by concluding an armistice with the bourgeoisie. For if 'organization' is viewed in mechanical terms and over-emphasized, it is inevitable that the *totality* of the revolutionary process will be neglected in favour of the *immediate visible result* and forced into the background.

4. Ernst Toller, the Expressionist dramatist, was one of the leaders of the Bavarian Soviet Republic, which was overcome by force of arms in May 1919 after existing for less than a month. The Bavarian Communist Party, led by Eugen Leviné, at first dismissed the revolution as 'a comedy', but came to its defence when attack by government troops was imminent. After Munich was taken, Leviné and hundreds of others were executed with or without a trial. Toller escaped with five years' imprisonment. His account of the revolution can be found in his biography *Eine Jugend in Deutschland* (English translation, *I was a German*, London, 1934) (Editor's note).

5. W. Laufenberg and K. Wolffheim had come out in favour of a policy of 'National Bolshevism', i.e. cooperation with the right-wing nationalist German parties on an anti-Versailles, anti-west and anti-social-democratic platform. These ideas, communicated to Lenin through Radek, were rejected and Laufenberg and Wolffheim were expelled from the KPD. In an Open Letter the Executive Committee of the Communist International took issue with the matter as follows: 'The German Communist Labour Party split from the German Communist Party because it considered the Communist Party's tactics opportunist; at the same time it accepted as members Laufenberg and Wolffheim . . . advocates of civil peace with the bourgeoisie if the bourgeoisie recognized the governments of the workers' councils, before that bourgeoisie had been destroyed and broken by the proletariat. . . . Thus their policy amounted in fact to the establishment of a sham Soviet republic' (Cf. Jane Degras, *The Communist International, 1919–43, Documents*, vol. 1, London, 1956, pp. 95–6) (Editor's note).

Only the totality of the revolutionary process can provide a guide-line for revolutionary action. In his *Critique of the Gotha Programme*,[6] Marx stressed that 'the law can never be more highly developed than the economic formation of the society and the level of cultural development which that formation conditions'. His remarks are equally relevant to the forms of organization of the proletariat in its class struggle. These too are, on the one hand manifestations, on the other weapons, of the class struggle, and their development, strength, usefulness, improvement, etc. are dependent on the development of that class struggle. As soon as an organizational form reaches the level of independence, this aspect of the totality is lost sight of. And since, when that disappears, the true criterion for action also disappears, there remain as results and criteria only the immediately perceptible results of the struggle. These, however – irrespective of whether they are successfully concluded tariff agreements or armed uprisings – *cannot possibly, viewed in isolation, provide criteria either for the actions of the proletariat or even for the correct utilization of the immediate situation.*

The theoretical roots of this fatal misinterpretation of revolutionary Marxism extend far back into the past. They first manifested themselves clearly in the struggle between Willich, Schapper and Marx, and later – with consequences that are still discernible in all present-day debates – in the Bernsteinian contrast between evolution and revolution. There is no point in combating the theory of gradual evolution with revolutionary slogans, no matter how ardent and heartfelt, unless it is understood that to talk about such a contrast at all – regardless of whether one adopts a positive or a negative attitude to it – means *to abandon the Marxist standpoint altogether*. For Marxism conceives the whole process of capitalist development and, within it, that of the burgeoning of proletarian energies, as a single great coherent process. The vast expanse of time embraced by this development, the long pauses, the lengthy periods of (seeming) inertia, the setbacks, the moments of quiescence – must never be allowed to conceal the revolutionary character of its totality from the proletariat, least of all from its class-conscious avant-garde. Communist tactics must therefore be adapted to this dual character of the revolutionary workers' movement. On the one hand, they must never lose sight of the oneness and the totality of the revolutionary process. On the other hand, however, they must always view this same totality from the standpoint of the 'demands of the day'. They must at all times constitute *revolutionary*

6. In *Selected Works*, vol. II, London, 1950, p. 23 (Editor's note).

Realpolitik, which means that each of the two concepts on which they are based must remain *equally* important. It is only when this understanding of the oneness of the process and the corresponding tactics are forsaken; when the opportunists have managed to distort the meaning of the process; when development is understood as 'peaceful evolution' and *Realpolitik* as abandonment of the revolution – it is only then that putschism acquires (apparent) revolutionary justification. In such cases the armed uprising, the seizure of power 'at any price', can indeed appear as a really revolutionary act. If, on the other hand, *the process itself is conceived of as being by its very nature revolutionary,* and if armed uprisings are seen as necessary stages along the route – in certain situations even absolutely necessary stages – but essentially and certainly in principle no different from the other stages, the entire rationale of putschism is shattered, not only for theoretical and agitational, but for practical purposes, too, and its petty-bourgeois foundations will expose themselves of their own accord to every intelligent worker.

In saying this, we are at the same time clearly defining the tactics to be adopted by communists *vis-à-vis* putschism: every activity, however (seemingly) petty, however directly geared to everyday demands, *must be imbued with revolutionary spirit.* And revolutionary spirit means, in this practical sense of the word, nothing more nor less than acting consciously in the spirit of the revolutionary process, using every available opportunity to intensify the class antagonisms and make the proletariat conscious of this intensification.

This is only possible if every single action of the proletariat is governed by the perspective of the total movement and if this oneness with the entire revolutionary process becomes an active part of proletarian consciousness. If this does not happen, then those workers who are revolutionary-minded but have not yet achieved full class-consciousness must inevitably regard the taking up of arms in the defence of their interests as the only revolutionary course of action. For it is not only in theory that opportunism and putschism are related phenomena.

Putschism can only flourish on soil prepared by opportunism. Consequently, the existence of putschist tendencies in the working class must compel every true communist to undergo *self-criticism,* to examine whether in fact his own tactics do not at some point contain opportunistic elements.

'*The chief fault of all previous materialism,*' says Marx,[7] 'is that the

7. First Thesis on Feuerbach in *The German Ideology,* Moscow, 1968, p. 659 (Editor's note).

object' is not grasped 'as human, sensuous activity, subjectively, as praxis,' as 'objective activity'. Hence the failure of Feuerbachian, contemplative materialism to grasp the significance of 'revolutionary, practical-critical activity'. The vulgar Marxism of the opportunists has lapsed back into this Feuerbachian stage of development – and all the (apparent) activity of the putschists cannot raise them above the same standpoint of mere contemplation. Which is why both tendencies share a thoroughly mechanistic view of historical development, and why in both conceptions of the class struggle the notion of *the revolutionary activity of the masses* simply disappears, and with it the notion of the raising of their revolutionary consciousness, which is at once the fruit and the foundation of their revolutionary activity.

There are further similarities between opportunists and putschists: on the one hand they underestimate the spontaneity of the masses as against actions which are 'prepared' and organized in advance; on the other, where the movement itself is concerned (no matter whether it is a question of wage increases or of armed uprisings), they attempt, not simply to make it conscious and lead it in the communist spirit, but rather to actually 'make' it. Hence their activities – however insistently both camps designate them as *Realpolitik* in contrast to the merely 'theoretical' considerations of the true Marxists – cannot ever be anything but illusory, lacking as they do any perceptible foundation in reality. There is only one real foundation of activity: the class-consciousness of the proletariat as it expresses itself in 'practical-critical activity'. Every action, however straightforward and *realpolitical* its slogans might otherwise be, is doomed to operate in a void unless it takes as its starting-point the spontaneity of the masses, unless its objective is to make conscious those unconscious demands which have given rise to that spontaneity, unless it attempts to lead that spontaneity in the right direction, in the direction of the totality of the revolutionary process. Every worker is an orthodox Marxist – however unconscious of the fact he himself is initially: this is the unspoken premiss of communist activity. He is so by virtue of his class situation, which necessarily places him at the centre of the revolutionary process. But it is only through the object-lesson of the class struggle and the active leadership of the Communist Party in that struggle that the worker can be made conscious of this, his inescapable class situation, and all its consequences. Opportunists and putschists inhibit this process in equal measure, albeit by different means: the former by taking the immediate situation, isolated and removed from the total context, as the starting-point of their tactics; the latter by setting their sights on a goal which is not yet a potentiality, not yet spontaneously (even if unconsciously) envisaged by the mass, and by attempting to achieve it without any direct relationship to the mass.

The mechanical conception which vulgar Marxism has of the class struggle separates, as we can see, the 'preparation' for the revolution from the 'revolution' itself. Consequently it separates the organization from the mass and isolates the individual moments of the struggle from their totality. In abandoning the concept of the totality of the revolutionary process, it becomes incapable of grasping the role of consciousness in revolutionary development and of adjusting revolutionary action to the development of revolutionary class-consciousness. The opportunists imagine that they can gradually inculcate the 'maturity' necessary for revolution in the proletariat by means of – characteristically peaceful – 'propaganda work'. The putschists, on the other hand, ignore the question altogether: they simply foist their own revolutionary 'consciousness' on the masses. Both approaches are equally mechanistic, for both see in the development of proletarian class-consciousness something that could itself only be conceived of independently of the revolutionary struggle. In doing so they relinquish the most important, indeed, in a revolutionary sense the absolutely decisive, weapon in the struggle. As long as the communists adhere to the only genuine Marxist method; as long, that is, as they attune their tactics to this unity of class struggle and class-consciousness; as long as they imbue every one of their actions with revolutionary spirit and thereby lead the proletariat towards 'practical-critical activity', they will not even have to fight especially hard to defeat opportunism and putschism.

If they stray from this path, however, no amount of eloquent polemics can save them from this twofold danger. *For the revolution itself is a great process of maturation of the proletariat.* The proletariat can win only if it constitutes itself as a class in and through the struggle. But it can only then become a class when it develops true class-consciousness within itself. Class-consciousness, however, can arise only through the development of consciousness of class-specific, revolutionary action. All other talk of the 'ideological maturity' of the proletariat remains idle chatter, regardless of whether it recognizes or denies such 'maturity'.

The proletariat as a class exists initially only economically, only objectively; it is the class struggle itself which actually makes this objective, scientific reality of the class subjective, makes it conscious, brings it into real, active, vital life. Because of their mechanical notion of the class struggle, opportunists and putschists alike are bound to have a static view of the concept of the class, seeing it as a once-and-for-all, unalterably given fact, and not as something dynamic which emerges, grows and brings itself to life in the course of the struggle. However, it is only when the constitution of the proletariat as a class is regarded *as the goal and the tendency of the revolution* that we can discover a firm basis for the constantly changing tactics of communist activity. The economic, scientific reality of the class is of course the starting-point for tactical considerations. But the other reality, the living reality of the class effected by the proletariat – this is possible only as the goal of revolutionary action. Every genuine revolutionary act diminishes the tension, the gulf between economic being and active consciousness of the proletariat. Once this consciousness has reached, penetrated and illuminated being, it is immediately possessed of the power to overcome all obstacles and to complete the process of revolution.

In explaining his motion dissociating himself from the Willich-Schapper faction, Marx wrote with incomparable clarity:[8] 'For them revolutions are not the product of the realities of the situation but the result of a *mere effort of will*. What we say to the workers is: "You will have 15, 20, 50 years of civil war and national struggle and this not merely to bring about a change in society but also *to change yourselves*[9] and prepare yourselves for the exercise of political power." Whereas you say on the contrary: "Either we seize power at once, or else we might as well just take to our beds." Just as the word "people" has been given an aura of sanctity by the democrats, so you have made an idol of the word "proletariat". Like the democrats you ignore the idea of revolutionary development and substitute for it the slogan of revolutions.'

8. *The Cologne Communist Trial*, London, 1971, pp. 62–3. August Willich (1820–78) and Karl Schapper (c. 1812–70) were leading members of the Communist League in London after the collapse of the 1848 revolutions on the Continent. In September 1850 the League was divided on the issue of whether there was an objective revolutionary situation. Willich, Schapper and the majority thought there was and pressed for immediate action. Marx, Engels and their supporters, who included a majority on the central committee, disagreed and proposed a split in the League which was carried and in effect spelt the end of the League's effective existence. Willich later emigrated to America and became a general in the Civil War, Schapper was reconciled with Marx and became a member of the General Council of the First International (Editor's note).

9. G.L.'s italics.

The Crisis of Syndicalism in Italy[1]

The latest great battle of the Italian workers is over. The concrete demands have been largely met. The occupied factories have once more been abandoned and handed over to their former 'legal' owners.[2] The net result, however, is an air of peculiar confusion, characterized most clearly by the fact that – *all parties concerned consider themselves the victors*. Thus the *Corriere della Sera* talks of a 'triumph for the moderate elements, in the Italian workers' movement'. 'It was a triumph of courage: it was shown that the sensible elements, once they had summoned up the courage to take a firm stand, could and did win' (21 October). Giolitti's sense of victory manifests itself even more clearly. In a telegram reprinted in the *Neue Freie Presse* of 4 November, he declares: 'Inaccurate and false reports were disseminated abroad, even as regards the control of the factories by the workers. The misunderstandings were brought about by the enormous differences in the meaning of the word "control" between the English and the Italian languages. In America and England "control" virtually means command and statutory authority, whereas in Italy it means "check". I am far from being an advocate of *the Bolshevization of Italian industry*, but I am convinced that I can be of use to our industry in the manner in which I have striven to act so far. For the worker who understands the real conditions will adjust his claims to these actual conditions; in this way the damaging mistrust of the worker towards the factory owner will disappear. On the other hand, this moral improvement

1. First appeared in *Kommunismus*, 1/40, 1920 (Editor's note).
2. After an abortive general strike in April 1920 trouble flared up in Italy in August of that year when the refusal of the factory owners to discuss wage increases with the engineering union led to a campaign of passive resistance and obstructionism, i.e. the workers reported each day and stayed in the factories to forestall a lock-out, but did no work. The dispute soon escalated into a revolutionary action in Turin when the employers proclaimed a lock-out (31 August) and the workers occupied the factories permanently, setting up factory councils and starting up production under their aegis. However, outside Turin mass support was lacking and by October the workers were forced to give up the factories and return to work on the basis of a compromise settlement laid down by the Prime Minister, Giovanni Giolitti (Editor's note).

in the worker will have beneficial effects on production, because it is an incentive to work, which – I repeat – is our only hope of salvation.'

But the chaos is even greater, as is evidenced by the prevalence of a victory mood even amongst large sections of the workers. It is not only *Avanti* which is proclaiming the victory of the workers; in syndicalist circles, too, the agreement reached is being seen as a victory. Even the revolutionary syndicalists are of the opinion that it was only the vacillating conduct of the 'top men' which prevented the movement from achieving total victory. The first, greatest and most revolutionary uprising of the Italian workers has ended in an *intellectual status quo*.

It is at this point that we must begin a principled examination of the crisis in which, in our view, the Italian working-class movement now finds itself. That is, we have to examine the tactics adopted in this particular struggle. The manner in which the struggle was waged provides very important lessons for the working-class movement in general, all the more so since the present, extremely complicated situation in Italy is by no means merely the product of unique conditions and circumstances, but rather the necessary consequence of the purely syndicalist tactics pursued in the course of the struggle. It is a situation, in other words, which will in all likelihood repeat itself – albeit in variously modified forms – in every Western European country (and in America), all those countries which lack the tradition of a revolutionary party but have instead a tradition of revolutionary syndicalism. It is therefore of the utmost importance that we recognize in good time the principle involved in the problematical situation of the Italian proletariat, so that we can draw the correct conclusions as quickly as possible.

The Moscow Congress[3] and the Italian metalworkers' movement shed a remarkable degree of light on each other, and therefore complement each other in a manner which is most instructive. In Moscow the syndicalist ideology was definitively and theoretically defeated, and in the theses which the congress ratified (after deliberations in which representatives of the Italian syndicalists, the International Workers of the World (IWW) and the Shop Steward movement also took part), the ways in which its inherent dangers could be avoided in practice were indicated.

3. This was the second Comintern Congress which opened on 19 July 1920 in Petrograd and then adjourned to Moscow, where the proceedings lasted from 23 July to 7 August. The theses referred to were drafted by Zinoviev and dealt with the role of the Communist Party in the proletarian revolution. Their complete text will be found in Degras, op. cit., vol. 1, pp. 129ff. (Editor's note).

In Italy the world proletariat was given an object-lesson in the dangerous limits of a purely syndicalist action. The Moscow theses would possibly have struck large sectors of the Italian proletariat as dogmatic or as rarified theory. But the only lesson which even these sectors can possibly draw from the taking over of the factories is that adherence to the theses, and that alone, presents the possibility of escaping from the critical situation into which the Italian proletariat has stumbled.

The fifth thesis of the Congress on the role of the Communist Party in the proletarian revolution reads in essence as follows: 'The Communist International rejects most emphatically the view that the proletariat can achieve its revolution without an independent political party. *Each and every class struggle is a political struggle.* The goal of this struggle, which inevitably transforms itself into a civil war, is the capture of political power. However, political power cannot be seized, organized and directed except by means of some kind of political party. It is only when the proletariat as leader possesses an organized and experienced party with strictly defined goals and a clearly worked-out programme of immediate measures, in the fields of both internal and foreign policy, that the conquest of political power will not appear as a chance episode, but will serve rather as the starting-point for a lasting communist construction of society by the proletariat.

The same class struggle demands likewise the centralized coordination and the concerted leadership of the various forms of the proletarian movement (trade unions, consumer cooperatives, factory councils, educational work, elections and so on). Only a political party can fulfil this function of a coordinating and leading centre. To refuse to create and to strengthen such a party, to refuse to subordinate oneself to it, is to forego unity in the leadership of the individual proletarian fighting forces which are pushing forward on the various battlefields. *The class struggle of the proletariat demands a concentrated form of propaganda which illuminates the different stages of the struggle from a united standpoint and directs the attention of the proletariat at every appropriate moment to certain tasks common to the entire class.* That cannot be achieved without a centralized political apparatus, that is, outside the framework of a political party.

Objectively, therefore, the propaganda put out by the revolutionary syndicalists and the supporters of the IWW against the necessity of an independent workers' party served and serves only to support the bourgeoisie and the counter-revolutionary social democrats. In their propaganda against a Communist Party, which they want to replace exclusively by trade unions or some kind of formless general workers' unions, the syndicalists and the industrial workers are at one with avowed opportunists.

The revolutionary syndicalists and industrial workers want to fight against the dictatorship of the bourgeoisie, but they do not know how. They cannot see that the working class without an independent political party is a rump without a head.

Revolutionary syndicalism and industrialism represent a step forward only by comparison with the obsolete, muddled counter-revolutionary ideology of the Second International. However, by comparison with revolutionary Marxism – that is, with communism – syndicalism and industrialism represent a step backwards.

The general strike alone, the tactics of folded arms, will not enable the working class to defeat the bourgeoisie.

The proletariat must resort to armed uprising. Those who understand that will also have to grasp the fact that an organized political party is essential, and that formless workers' unions are inadequate.

The revolutionary syndicalists frequently talk of the great role of a determined revolutionary minority. Well, a really determined minority of the working class, a minority which is communist, which intends to act, which has a programme, which intends to organize the struggle of the masses – that is precisely what the communist party is.

These guide-lines for revolutionary communist activity fit exactly the present situation in Italy. The Italian workers acted in a revolutionary manner. Passive resistance as the answer to the challenge of the industrial bosses was a correctly conceived and a bold step, which, as Comrade Zinoviev makes clear (*Kommunismus*, nos 36/37), was very damaging for the capitalists. The occupation of the factories followed necessarily and logically from this state of affairs. But the syndicalist ideology which inspired these revolutionary workers finally led the movement into a blind alley. It is of course true that the workers occupied the factories; it is also true that they demonstrated with admirable discipline and maturity that without capitalists they are able, not only to produce, but even to increase production. But the question which confronted the Italian proletariat at the decisive moment was: *How can it get out of the occupied factories again?*

Obviously it is not opportunistic, *realpolitical* considerations which prompt this question. The fear, which was even expressed in communist quarters (*Rote Fahne*, no. 409), that the movement would fail owing to its isolation (to the withdrawal, for example, of credit facilities by the banks, and so on) is one which we do not consider wholly valid. First, for practical reasons. The Italian proletariat has demonstrated on several occasions that it can look after itself even in this kind of situation. For instance, the dock workers in Ancona withdrew 70,000 lire from a local bank and used it to pay the wages; similarly, the labour office in Verona issued assignats on the strength of the raw materials present in the occupied factories. There are many other such examples. Secondly and above all, however, for reasons of principle. Even assuming that the movement had embraced the whole of the working class, that the entire economy, the entire economic apparatus had been in the hands of the workers, they would still have been in the same critical situation as the one they actually found themselves in, *because and as long as the power of the capitalist state remained unimpaired*. During the entire movement *not a single step* was taken in the direction of shaking that power; such a step was not even attempted.

The explanation lay and lies primarily in the syndicalist ideology of the workers. The great and fatal flaw in syndicalist thinking is that it localizes the antagonism between labour and exploitation, centring it on the *immediate area of exploitation*, the factory. Hence it confronts the workers only with the capitalists, not with the capitalist state. Thus it is that syndicalism, although it emerged as opposition to the opportunism of the social-democratic parties, has never managed to overcome precisely the essence of their opportunism. It must by now be evident to every Marxist who can think properly that the salient difference between reformism and revolution lies precisely in the understanding and assessment of the capitalist state. Only by falsely judging the state, by neglecting the Marxist theory of the state, was it possible to conceive of the activity of the workers' parties as opposition within the state, as a struggle for, rather than a struggle against, the state. However, in rejecting (correctly) parliamentary-cum-oppositional opportunism, the syndicalists also rejected all forms of meaningful political activity. In doing so, they have in essence put themselves on the same footing as the opportunists after all. Which is why Jouhaux, Merrheim and Co. failed just as ignominiously in the war as the Scheidemanns, Renaudels and Hendersons did.[4] Even

4. Leon Jouhaux (1879–1954), a reformist member of the French and international trade-union movement; Alphonse Merrheim (1881–1925), French trade-union leader and syndicalist; after 1905 he became one of the leaders of the Metal-Workers' Federation and the CGT; Pierre Renaudel (1871–1935) – one of the reformist leaders of the

that section of the syndicalists which has maintained its determination and desire for revolutionary action cannot possibly cope with the present, decisive phase of the class struggle – as long as it clings to the apolitical ideology of syndicalism.

And in Italy today this is still very largely the case. The trade unions, headed by D'Arragona, have of course opportunistic reasons for wanting to continue the struggle exclusively at the trade-union level. It is not just that their weapons are exclusively trade-union weapons – their objective, too, is *trade-union control of the factories*. And it is *only within these limits* that the strong, revolutionary-syndicalist minority is extending the struggle beyond the demands of the opportunists. Thus *Umanita Nova* (12 October) writes: 'Even today the extension of the occupation is the best way, the way which will ensure the continuation of productive work and saddle the enemy with the responsibility for any monstrous and futile carnage. *It is revolution without chaos and with the fewest sacrifices.*'

Even *Umanita Nova*, therefore, is incapable of perceiving correctly the dilemma of the workers' situation. Which is, namely: *either they must abandon the factories*, which represents in any event, no matter what the conditions, a victory for the capitalists; *or they must topple the capitalist state by force of arms in order to be able to retain the factories they have seized*. Seizing the factories can be an extremely significant step. If, on the other hand, it is seen as a seizure of real power, it puts the advance post of the revolution in a highly dangerous situation. For then the unsuspecting proletariat finds itself confronted by the still unshaken power of the state and is forced to join battle with it on unfavourable terms, terms dictated by the state.

The same applies to the control of production, which was the principal achievement of the 'victory'. Its value for the liberation struggle of the proletariat depends exclusively on how the working class relates to it ideologically. We have already seen that Sr Giolitti sees in it an effective means of integrating the workers into the capitalist system, blunting the class struggle and re-establishing 'production' (i.e. capitalist production). For the workers it may well represent – initially – a moral victory, the capitulation of the capitalists in the face of their power. If, however, it is presented as a 'real achievement', it will soon reveal itself to be something

---

French Socialist Party; Philip Scheidemann (1865–1939), a German Social Democrat, he was head of the government at the time of the suppression of the Spartacus League; Arthur Henderson (1863–1935), one of the leaders of the Labour Party and the English trade-union movement (Editor's note).

illusory. In that case it is vital to exploit what has already been 'achieved' as a *means of intensifying the class struggle*. In part by attempting to exercise a *real degree of control*, which the capitalists will not tolerate under any circumstances. In part, too, by giving the workers an object-lesson in the truth that control within the capitalist framework is meaningless for them; that they *must seize power totally* if they intend to improve their situation and exert *real influence* on production. If the 'victory' is not seen in this light, however – and there are unfortunately few indications that that kind of understanding of the situation is widespread among the Italian proletariat – control in this limited sense represents more of a danger than anything else. For nothing endangers a revolution in its preparatory stages more than illusions. Such illusions are already manifesting themselves clearly: at the FIOM[5] national congress, for example, Comrade Colombino was rapturously applauded for asserting that 'on the day when Kerensky legally handed over control of the factory to the workers, the workers became masters of the factories' (*Avanti*, 23 October). What such notions overlook is that without the – Bolshevik-led – November revolution the Russian workers would not only not have remained 'masters of the factories', but would have been pushed back into Tzarist slavery by the likes of Kornilov or Kolchak. Control on the Italian model could represent a period of Kerenskyism – provided there were Bolsheviks in Italy. If, on the other hand, it goes no further than 'anchoring the factory councils in the constitution', it could well prove analogous to the situation in Germany last year, the period when the social democrats and the independents were preparing the Kapp putsch. The removal of this danger is a matter of ideology, of the consciousness of the proletariat: of the politicization of the movement by the Communist Party (Comrade Garino from Turin put this view very clearly at the same session).

The danger is greatly increased by the masterly conduct of the Italian statesmen. It might even be claimed – not without a tinge of bitter irony – that Messrs Nitti and Giolitti are the only Marxist politicians in Italy. They do at least grasp clearly how important *the ideology of the 'class-neutrality' of the state* is as a weapon for the survival of capitalism. In everything they do they play up to the flawed reasoning of the syndicalists and the political opportunists, who have all – consciously or unconsciously – capitulated to this ideology of the bourgeoisie. The 'state' remains (ostensibly) 'neutral' in the class struggle between capital and labour.

5. FIOM – Federazione Italiana Operai Metallurgici: the engineers' union that organized the campaign (Editor's note).

It 'mediates'; it represents the 'common' interests of 'all' classes, the 'higher' interests of society 'as such'. In this way the politicians of the Italian bourgeoisie ensure that in fact everything happens in accordance with the interests of capitalism and that the section of the working class that does have a revolutionary consciousness never manages to see its deadly enemy in its true colours. That this is conscious politics is demonstrated further by the conduct of the Italian government in relation to Soviet Russia: it managed to obtain a completely free hand for its active support of the counter-revolution, even for possible support for a policy of open aggression against Russia, simply by playing 'world politics' with the Social Democrat Party and not allowing the Italian proletariat to become conscious that *foreign policy, too, is and must be a class struggle*.

The *guarda regia* is on permanent battle alert, ready to mow down the workers the moment the survival of capitalism is threatened. But the workers still cannot see their most dangerous enemy sufficiently clearly. Thus it is that the state, conscious of its tactical superiority, can afford to delay its attack and is able to mediate so as to, at worst, put an end to the crisis of the working-class movement by arranging for it a pseudo-victory (with all that that entails by way of 'morning-after' feelings and confusion); and at best – while still maintaining its 'neutral' pose – help the capitalists to achieve the real victory through a bogus 'settlement'. The real potential threat to such masterfully contrived politics is posed chiefly by those capitalist Hotspurs who see as weakness the conduct of Giolitti and the former syndicalist Labriola (who seems to have a good grasp of his erstwhile comrades' weaknesses) and demand a policy of the 'mailed fist'. If their politics were to gain the upper hand, then clearly the state would be forced to expose itself and provide the workers with the object-lesson which is so necessary.

The really competent organ for this purpose would of course be the party. It alone could bring about a change of front in the movement, confront it with the state, give it political, consciously revolutionary direction. This has not been done so far. True, the majority of trade unionists have consistently adopted a negative attitude towards the idea of leadership by a party. But a party that works on communist lines cannot and must not allow itself to be deterred and restricted by any such resolutions. The 'top organization' in the German boycott campaign against Poland also rejected the participation of the communists. However, the communists exploited precisely this rejection to expose the false tendencies, the betrayals and the apolitical attitude of the campaign's so-called leaders in order to politicize the workers and intensify the class struggle. Our Italian comrades, on the other hand, appear to have accepted an all too passive role throughout the movement; as a result the leadership slipped entirely out of their hands. There is, of course, no lack of encouraging signs pointing in the other direction. The Naples section, for instance, passed a resolution stressing emphatically the political nature of the movement and calling on the party to wrest the leadership of the movement from the trade unions. Similarly, the tendency towards politicization has gained the upper hand in the trade council in Rome.

Therein lies the way out of the crisis which syndicalist ideology has inflicted on the Italian workers and which has developed into the crisis of syndicalist tactics in general. Syndicalism thrives on the disappointment of revolutionary workers with the opportunism of the 'politicians' and their consequent abandonment of politics altogether. Only with the emergence of a political party which has a clearer revolutionary consciousness and hence is not only more revolutionary than the most extreme syndicalists, but is able to point the way to revolutionary action when they have come to a dead end – only then can syndicalism be properly overcome and the revolution carried forward to victory. *Only the Communist Party can really fight the capitalist state*; it alone is able to perceive, recognize and unmask that state as the real enemy of the proletariat. The situation in Italy is revolutionary. The working class is filled with genuine revolutionary spirit. It lacks only this knowledge in order to be properly prepared for the final decisive struggle. The Moscow Congress has provided the necessary theoretical clarification. The crisis of syndicalism can bring about the clarification in practice, provided the party intervenes consciously and energetically.

Unfortunately the revolutionary process of clarification within the party itself has not advanced sufficiently to enable it to fulfil such a mission effectively. It is not simply that, as has been emphasized, the party was unable to seize the leadership of the movement; even the subsequent analysis and self-criticism has contributed precious little to the furtherance of the movement and the overcoming of the syndicalist crisis. (Admittedly the views of the Bordiga group[6] are not yet available at the time of writing.) In so far as they are the consequence of wrong tactics,

6. Amadeo Bordiga and Umberto Terracini: leaders of the extreme left of the Italian Socialist Party; after the Livorno Congress in January 1921 which ended with victory for the centrists under Serrati, they took part in the foundation of the Italian Communist Party in which they played a dominant role (Editor's note).

defeats and mistakes are of course inevitable; on the other hand, however, they can, if relentlessly exposed and thoroughly analysed, even contribute greatly to the strengthening and consolidation of the party and with it the movement as a whole (e.g. the debates in the KPD after the Kapp Putsch). We have to admit quite frankly here that this clarification process has not yet even got off the ground in the Italian party, at least as far as the leadership at the centre is concerned. The debate on the limits and the dangers of syndicalist tactics, a major issue at the Moscow Congress, has not begun, although the delegates have already returned home. It is of course to be hoped – and there are numerous indications in local organizations to reinforce the hope – that the question which the movement has posed to the party in practice will penetrate from the periphery into the centre, there to find its *theoretical, organizational and tactical solution.*

In addition, however, the fact must not be concealed that the conditions for the solution of the question do not yet fully exist. Syndicalism is nothing more than the spontaneous reaction of the instinctively but not yet sufficiently consciously revolutionary masses to the political opportunism of the party. The party, therefore, can only then overcome syndicalism and become the leader of the movement when it has succeeded in *eradicating every trace of opportunism from within its own ranks.* On this, too, the Moscow Congress, has expressed itself unambiguously and has committed all of its sections to carry through such a purging of their ranks. However, while the conditions of affiliation to the Third International have provoked extremely intense ferment among the Independent Socialists and will in all probability lead to a clear-cut divorce between revolutionaries and opportunists, there seems to be a rather marked tendency in the Italian party to blur over the antagonisms. True, at the meeting of the party leadership, victory went to the radical Terracini agenda (albeit by a narrow majority of seven to five), but even this postpones the actual purge until the party congress at the end of December.

So far, then, the conditions for a real clarification of the situation have not been met. It is true that the workers were able to abandon the occupied factories without catastrophic consequences, but the danger that spontaneous movements of the dissatisfied proletarian masses will once more go over the heads of the leaders and either run up against a brick wall or, as a result of repeated futile efforts, lead to demoralization and exhaustion – this danger is by no means overcome. Nor can it yet be overcome, since the only discernible substantial change in the consciousness of the Italian proletariat seems to be a shift from right to left within syndicalism itself. The relationship of the party to the movement remains unchanged; indeed, it cannot change unless the reformists are excluded. Until this change occurs, the situation in Italy will remain critical. The way out of the crisis has been clearly pointed out by Moscow. Apart from formulating the theses, the Moscow Congress also addressed itself directly to the Italian proletariat. It only remains for the proletariat to learn these lessons and establish them as the guiding principles of its actions.

The Question of Educational Work[1]

Methodological and fundamental questions will in all likelihood dominate the coming discussions on the question of education. The theses of the Hungarian comrades have already raised the issue of the predominance of the social and historical sciences over the natural sciences. For this they have been applauded by Comrade Röbig (in no. 6 of the second volume of *Jugend-Internationale*), but they will no doubt also encounter strong opposition. It is therefore perhaps not entirely irrelevant to examine briefly the methodological aspect of the question.[2]

First and foremost, let us remember that if the argument is to be conducted sensibly, it can and must revolve only around priorities of method, rather than subject matter. It must be evident to any intelligent person that the dictatorship of the proletariat, once it has survived the initial critical period, will engender an unprecedented flowering of the natural sciences and technology. Indeed, it is clear that technology cannot be free to realize its full and at present scarcely conceivable potentialities until the profit barrier has disappeared. Given all this, however, the question arises: will and should the method of the natural sciences play the same definitive and omnipotently influential role in the education, thinking, emotions, sciences and philosophy of the new society as it did in bourgeois society? For we have to be quite clear on this point: every aspect of human life in bourgeois society was dominated by that method. The mere fact that – discounting a few (as we shall see later) reactionary exceptions – the knowledge produced by the natural sciences was regarded as knowledge as such, or at least as the ideal type of knowledge; the fact that in this respect the main currents in bourgeois philosophy (materialism *à la* Büchner, Kantianism and empirio-criticism) were all in agreement – this is proof enough, which for lack of space we are neither able nor willing to elaborate upon at this juncture. That this was so is no mere

1. First appeared in *Jugend-Internationale*, II/7, 1921 (Editor's note).
2. Materialistic is not the antithesis of idealistic, as is falsely maintained in the usual accounts of Marxism, but the correlative of formalistic – a fact of profound significance for a proletarian view of history. Unfortunately it is not possible to unravel the consequences of this very important thesis here (G.L.'s note).

coincidence. Not only did the natural sciences make possible the – capitalistic – rationalization of production, etc. for bourgeois society; their methodology also provided it with an excellent ideological weapon in the struggle against both the declining feudal system and the rising proletariat.

The primary function of the laws of nature (for the sake of simplicity we shall centre the issue on this one point) is generally known and easily understood. The personal 'man-to-man' oppression and exploitation characteristic of feudalism needed the ideological sanction of divine revelation and authority. If the nascent capitalist society was to prise the worker 'free' for its purposes, it had not only to remove the economic and political ties of the old order, but also to shatter its ideological foundations. It therefore had to replace the personal god with the impersonal law of nature; the old authority had to be destroyed, but a new one raised to the throne in its stead. This new authority is the law of nature. Its function is twofold. On the one hand it destroys the old authority, shattering the belief among the masses that the feudal form of oppression and exploitation is an eternally valid and divinely ordained order. On the other hand, however, it arouses in them the belief that the capitalist system of production, impersonal and ostensibly conforming to 'the laws of nature', corresponds to the 'eternal' laws of human reason, is independent of human volition and indestructible in the face of human strivings; that it is, in fact, a second nature. We can see here the connection between bourgeois economics and the method of the natural sciences. Just how strong it is is proved by the fact that the political dilution of Marxism at the end of the nineteenth century was accompanied by the infiltration of that very bourgeois 'scientism' into historical materialism. Bernstein began the struggle against the 'unscientific' dialectical method; sociology as 'pure' natural science, Kantianism and Machism followed his lead. And they achieved their objective: among the leadership and large sections of the proletariat there developed the belief in the indestructibility and 'natural' necessity of capitalism. A world-outlook of economic fatalism became widespread which made the idea of a radically new social order, the idea of a revolutionary transformation of society, seem adventuristic, 'unscientific', even un-Marxist. (How deeply this methodological position is rooted in the theory of opportunism cannot be discussed even briefly here. I would just point out that the opportunists, because they operated with unhistorical, 'timeless' criteria of 'the laws of nature', were bent on examining a capitalism as such, a crisis as such, and so on. Consequently they were totally unable to grasp historically new phenomena such as imperialism in all its essential novelty.

In view of this it must be emphasized that the method of the proletariat is a historical one. Marx grasped the essence of capitalism as a historical phenomenon historically – in order to demonstrate its necessary destruction historically. If the proletariat is going to have the support of a revolutionary science for its class struggle, therefore, it must follow the traditions of historical-materialism, the Marxist method. In placing the historical-social method in the forefront, however, we shall have to overcome strong – and understandable – prejudices. For within capitalism the method of the natural sciences was in fact the progressive one and the historical method the reactionary one. Whereas the former was the ideological expression of the rising bourgeois class, feudalism in its desperate efforts to defend itself looked to history for an ideological weapon to safeguard tradition and legitimacy.[3] And again, in the period of bourgeois decadence we find a form of historicism gaining ground as the ideological expression of spiritual exhaustion, indifference, fatalism and craving for sensation. Just as the decadent Romans arrived at a kind of religious eclecticism, so at the end of the nineteenth century there emerged a brand of indiscriminate historical relativism or historicism. To an ever-increasing degree the bourgeoisie abandoned the ideological defence of capitalist society, the proof of its necessity and reasonableness, to their lackeys, the social democrats, who henceforth became the heirs of the bourgeois 'scientific' tradition.

Our conception of history has nothing at all in common with any of that. Above all, it does away completely with all forms of fatalism (the historical as well as that of the natural sciences). 'Men make their own history', says Engels in *Feuerbach*,[4] and Marx in the theses formulates the thought even more pointedly when he stresses that the problem is not to interpret the world, but to change it.[5] However, if that formulation defines the goal and the method of proletarian science, then it follows that the essential object of knowledge is the totality of human society and that the aim of that science is to make conscious what the development of this totality means for the proletariat in terms of tasks, in terms of action.

3. For example the historical school of law. On this see Marx, *Nachlass* I, p. 268 (G.L.'s note) (Marx, 'The Philosophical Manifesto of the Historical School of Law', *Rheinische Zeitung*, no. 221, 9 August 1842, in *Werke*, vol. I, pp. 78ff. – ed.).

4. *Selected Works*, vol. II, p. 354 (Editor's note).

5. *Eleventh Thesis on Feuerbach*, ibid., p. 367 (Editor's note).

Such knowledge, the knowledge of the whole and of the whole as a process – a knowledge which is only the preliminary stage of action – is provided only by Marxism, revolutionary dialectics, historical materialism.

We must of course be clear that such a penetration of all fields of knowledge by the spirit of revolutionary Marxism is today still only a demand posed to science: a demand which can be fulfilled only in and through the revolution. However great the achievements of Marx and Engels and some of their successors are, however much historical development has already wrought certain changes of this kind or at least begun the process in that direction even within bourgeois society (e.g. geography as a social science, as anthropo-geography in conjunction with the theory of location) – we still stand at the very beginning of the road. And the union of all sciences under the aspect of the self-knowledge of the free man living in a free community is a goal in the distant future. We can assume that the individual sciences will retain for a long time to come the abstract isolation, specialization and incoherence which they have inherited from the capitalist division of labour and reification, and from bourgeois individualism. Their transformation into integral elements of an all-embracing totality, which will then include the natural sciences as well, is in itself a process which we have only just begun. The material of the individual fields of knowledge as they exist makes it impossible to offer the fighting proletariat precisely what it is thirsting to learn and what it needs; but this cannot prevent us from attempting even now to make this demand conscious within the proletariat. Precisely because we are at present unable to work through the entire spectrum of the knowable with our method, we must at least put the method itself at the centre of our educational work. For only in this way can our work embrace both the demands of the day and the creation of the future. Only in this way can the ideological sway of bourgeois ideas and prejudices over the proletariat be broken and make way for a fruitful critique that leads to action. This critique of bourgeois society, which only dialectical materialism is able to effect, is at the same time, however, the lever which will be able to set the movement in motion in the direction of the realm of the future.

Spontaneity of the Masses, Activity of the Party[1]

There is no difficulty in making a distinction between on the one hand, the discussion about the correctness or incorrectness of the new 'open' tactics of the United German Communist Party (VKPD)[2] and, on the other, the discussion as to whether or not the March Action[3] was correctly led. This was clearly demonstrated at the meeting of the Central Committee on 7 and 8 April, where Comrade Paul Franken put forward an amendment to Paragraph 12 of the guiding principles[4] of the Central Bureau.

1. First appeared in *Die Internationale*, III/6, 1921 (Editor's note).

2. The United German Communist Party (VKPD) was formed at the end of 1920. It consisted on the one hand of what remained of the KPD after the split of March 1920 and the setting up of the sectarian KAPD following the Kapp Putsch and, on the other hand, the left wing of the USPD (Independent Social Democrats) (Editor's note).

3. The March Action: On 16 March 1921 fighting broke out in the mining district of Mansfeld, a predominantly communist area, when the Social Democrat governor of the province, Hoersing, provocatively ordered the police to occupy the mines. The VKPD, encouraged by Béla Kun and his supporters, thought the time was ripe for revolution and called for an open insurrection (17 March). There was little response and it was followed by a call for a general strike. The subsequent occupation of factories by the unemployed brought the latter and the communists into conflict with workers loyal to social democracy, as well as with police and troops. There were many casualties and thousands of arrests. The action was finally called off on 31 March. The failure had disastrous consequences for the VKPD which, from being a mass party with over 400,000 members, found itself reduced to about 150,000. No less important were the debates on putschism surrounding it. Paul Levi, the chairman of the VKPD, published a pamphlet entitled *Our Road. Against Putschism* condemning the action, and was expelled from the Party. The reverberations were felt also in the International, where Zinoviev, who had been backing Kun, was forced to disavow him. In the debate on the tactical theses at the Third Congress Lenin severely criticized Béla Kun, but took the view that in spite of faulty leadership and the absence of preparation for an offensive, the action marked a great step forward, because hundreds of thousands of workers had fought heroically against the bourgeoisie. Lukács defended the action, describing it in his contribution to the discussion at the thirteenth session of the Third International in July 1921 as 'a great revolutionary mass movement' and by no means a 'partial action' or a 'putschist adventure'. Later, in *My Road to Marx* (1933), he came to regard his earlier stance as one of 'ultra-left subjectivism'. Further information on the action and its repercussions may be found in Jane Degras, *The Communist International, 1919–43, Documents*, vol. 1, London, 1956 (Editor's note).

4. The guiding principles were published in *Die rote Fahne*, 4, no. 160 on 10 April 1921, and in *Die Internationale*, III/4 (1921) (Editor's note).

The proposal was that, from the sentence, 'the Central Committee there-fore approves the political and tactical position of the Bureau', the words 'and tactical' should be deleted. Although the amendment was rejected by the great majority of the Central Committee, paragraph 6 of the guiding principles nevertheless shows, as does Comrade Paul Frölich's essay entitled 'Offensive' in the recent issue of *Internationale* (3, no. 3, 1921), that the March Action was in no sense a classic example of the new tactical line, *but rather a defensive struggle forced on the party in the midst of its preparations for the intellectual and organizational re-orientation demanded by the new tactics.* Which in no way means that the lessons of the March Action are not pertinent to the efforts within the party to develop the new tactical approach and do not have to be made full use of. It means simply that the problem of offensive tactics can be discussed – to some extent at least – independently of the concrete results and concrete criticisms of the March Action.

Those who oppose the new tactics – and they do so for overtly or un-consciously opportunistic reasons – base their arguments essentially on three points. First, they argue that, as long as it is 'correctly' understood, the revolutionary offensive in no respect signifies a new departure for the United German Communist Party; they even set out to prove that the tactic of the 'Open Letter'[5] was itself already an offensive tactic. Secondly, they claim to have exposed the March Action as a putsch launched in the spirit of Bakunin or Blanqui. And thirdly, they are concerned to demonstrate that the theoretical conflict which has now become acute in the United German Communist Party is nothing more than the old con-flict between Rosa Luxemburg and Lenin, which first came to light as far back as 1904 in Rosa Luxemburg's articles dealing with the organiza-tional questions of the Russian party.[6]

5. The Open Letter to German left-wing organizations appeared in *Die rote Fahne*, 4, no. 11 on 8 January 1921; it was sent by the VKPD to the SPD, USPD and the trade unions, proposing joint action on wages, workers' control, trade with Russia, etc. Its author was Radek, whose aim was to reconcile those workers who had been disaffected by the split in the Party by showing them that the VKPD was prepared to join with the other parties in the practical daily struggle; in the course of that struggle they would learn that reformism would not give them what they wanted. Radek drafted the letter with the agreement of Paul Levi, apparently to counter the 'putschism' of a section of the party favoured by Zinoviev. The move had Lenin's support, but the proposal was rejected. It is reprinted in *Der deutsche Kommunismus*, a collection of documents edited by Hermann Weber, Cologne/Berlin, 1963, pp. 168–70 (Editor's note).

6. 'Die neue Zeit' XXI, 2, nos 42, 43 (Lukács refers to Rosa Luxemburg, *Problems of Organization in Russian Social Democracy*) (Editor's note).

We have no intention of entering into a semantic slanging-match armed with quotations from Marx and Rosa Luxemburg. To produce passages from Marx 'for' or 'against' the putschist nature of the March Action would be futile, just as any attempt to protect the reputation of Rosa Luxemburg against charges of opportunistic leanings would be undignified.

Our task is, rather, to clarify – if possible without resorting to quotations and slogans – the nature of the theoretical conflict which has now become insoluble within the United German Communist Party and which the three arguments mentioned above evade rather than bring out into the open. *At issue is the organizational, intellectual and tactical relationship between the party and the masses in the acute stage of the proletarian revolution.* If the question is posed in this way, all appeals to Rosa Luxemburg's theories of mass action become redundant, since they relate to a different, less advanced stage of the proletarian revolution. We must not forget that Rosa Luxemburg was never concerned to pronounce 'timeless', 'eternally valid' truths; on the contrary, she attempted to determine, by concrete analysis of concrete historical situations, the tactics necessary at those particular times. Her observations on mass actions and the role of the party in such actions were written, it must be emphasized, *at the time of the bourgeois revolution* before, during and after the first Russian Revolution; it is therefore wholly inadmissible to apply them as they stand to the present-day situation. Or – more correctly – first we have to raise the question: *does the relationship between the party and the masses remain constant throughout the entire revolutionary process, or is it itself equally a process which is bound to undergo, both actively and passively, the dialectical transformations and sudden changes of direction of the total process?* This is the central question in the discussion; and if the right wing's (mostly covert) response has been negative, the positive answer given by the left wing has often been less than clear.

The minority resolution of the Central Committee, moved by Comrade Clara Zetkin, unintentionally betrays this fundamental theoretical and tactical notion of the right wing. The relevant passage reads: 'The Central Committee of the United German Communist Party condemns most strongly the failure of the Central Bureau to establish the demands posed by the "Open Letter" and the alliance with Soviet Russia as the objectives of a powerful offensive against the bourgeoisie and its state. A campaign on these lines would have lent itself to the mobilization of broad sections of the proletarian masses and the involvement in the struggle of sections of the petty and middle bourgeoisie, thereby strengthening from two sources the power of the revolutionary proletariat and *necessarily* causing it to progress beyond its present state to one where it can confront more ambitious goals.'[7]

I believe that the word I have put in italics (necessarily) constitutes the real core of the controversy. The question is: do mass actions in fact retain throughout the entire revolutionary process this 'necessary' character which they undoubtedly had at the start of the revolutionary period, in the era of spontaneous and elemental mass actions? Or does a decisive change occur in the course of revolutionary development? The conception of the 'inevitability' of mass actions goes back to the classic view – which Rosa Luxemburg also adopted – of the relationship between ideology and economy. It is a view which regards mass action as nothing more than the ideological expression (intellectually and in terms of action) corresponding to the existence and growing acuteness of the crisis in the objective economic process. In this case mass actions arise 'spontaneously' – that is, as more or less automatic consequences of the objective economic crisis. Their 'spontaneity' signifies nothing more than the subjective, ideological aspect of the objective state of affairs. Consequently, the role of the most conscious revolutionary vanguard, the party, is immediately defined. The party is significant in that its tactical activities 'never *lag behind* the actual relations of forces, but rather anticipate them'.[8] In other words, the party is a power which can accelerate and provoke development, but only within a movement which will – in the last analysis – progress independently of what the party decides. The party can therefore in no sense take a real initiative.

Such views clearly derive from the conventional notion of the 'natural laws' governing the necessity of the economic and, subsequently, the political and ideological process. 'Necessity' in the escalation of a revolutionary action means that the 'laws' which govern it must be correctly perceived and applied, just as the natural laws correctly perceived by natural science must be applied in technology. Let us be quite clear: this description of the relationship between economy and ideology (in the broadest sense of the word) and, accordingly, between social events, the scientific perception of those events, and party action, applies without any qualification to *capitalist society*. The question is, though: are we dealing

7. G.L.'s italics; see 'Die vom Ausschuss abgelehnte Resolution Clara Zetkins', in *Die rote Fahne*, 4, no. 193 of 30 April 1921 (Editor's note).

8. Rosa Luxemburg, *Massenstreik*, 2nd edn, p. 38 (G.L.'s note).

here with 'timeless' laws concerning socialized man in general, or simply with laws of capitalist economy and society? The views of Marx and Engels on this question amount to little more than allusions. We can nonetheless assume that expressions used at crucial points in their work, like the famous 'leap from the realm of necessity into the realm of freedom', were intended to be more than mere images and smart turns of phrase. Likewise, their oft-repeated assertion that the evidence provided by the economy and social science can claim to be valid only for certain periods and not supra-historically; that such evidence represents the self-knowledge of certain social circumstances, and hence is evidence of those circumstances not only in the objective, but also in the subjective sense – this assertion seems to me to constitute a crucial element of their total theory (historical materialism as 'ideology' of the proletariat).[9]

Since, then, it is not admissible to assume – as Gorter[10] still does – that the relationship between economy and ideology (taken in its broadest sense) will have the same structure in a socialist society as it does under capitalism; since, likewise, the transition from 'necessity' to 'freedom' cannot under any circumstances be a once-and-for-all, sudden and un-mediated act, but can only be a *process*, the revolutionary, crisis-prone character of which Engels pinpointed with the word 'leap' – we are left simply with the question: *When, where, under what conditions and to what extent does this 'leap into the realm of freedom' occur?* The answer to this question, which, like nearly all questions of fundamental theoretical importance, has unfortunately hardly ever been raised, is of the utmost *practical* importance in determining the tactics of the communist parties. For, assuming that our theoretical standpoint assigns the *beginning* of this process to the period of the final crisis of capitalism, we are obliged to pose extremely far-reaching tactical demands. We are in fact forced to adopt this standpoint – and not only from purely theoretical considerations which rule out the possibility of conceiving of freedom, liberation from necessity, as a gift of fate, a *gratia irrestibilia* which will fall unearned into our laps at the end of our mechanically and automatically conducted struggles. Even a purely empirical study of these struggles and of the milieu in which they are waged will bring us necessarily to the same conclusion. Lenin was absolutely correct in opposing those tendencies which characterized the imperialistic crisis of capitalism (regarded by Lenin

9. Marx, *The Poverty of Philosophy*, op. cit., p. 140 (G.L.'s note).

10. See Hermann Gorter, *Der historische Materialismus*, Stuttgart, 1919 (Editor's note).

himself, of course, as its final crisis) in mechanical and fatalistic fashion as ineluctable. There is no position, he said, which is abstractly and in and of itself ineluctable. *It is the proletariat, the action of the proletariat, which prevents capitalism from escaping from this crisis.* Admittedly, the fact that *it is possible* for the proletariat to be in this position and the fact that the solution of the crisis depends on the proletariat – these are the consequences of economic necessities, of 'natural laws'. But these 'natural laws' determine only the crisis itself; they do no more than make it impossible for this crisis to be resolved in capitalist terms (like the earlier ones). If allowed to work itself out unimpeded, however, the crisis could have quite different consequences: 'the mutual destruction of the warring classes', reversion to a state of barbarism.

The 'natural laws' of capitalist development, then, can only lead society into the final crisis; they cannot show the way out of it. No one who has dispassionately studied the revolutionary period as it has developed so far can shut his eyes to the fact that the most crucial but theoretically and tactically least expected obstacles to the revolution and its victory are not so much the strength of the bourgeoisie as *ideological inhibitions within the proletariat itself.* This is not the place to bring up the whole problem of Menshevism. It must, however, be emphasized that it is a problem which has played virtually no part in pre-revolutionary theory; people were prepared for the common struggle against the bourgeoisie, but not for the struggle among the proletarian parties themselves. Revisionism was treated in non-Russian literature as a problem which has to be solved *within* the party. That it is a problem of world-wide significance, however, perhaps the very problem on which the fate of the entire revolution depends, is demonstrated by the fact that even the most dreadful crisis of capitalism – the rapid succession of revolutionary situations, the ideological confusion of the bourgeoisie to the point where state power is slipping from its grasp – *has by no means succeeded in necessarily generating a revolutionary ideology in the proletariat.* From this state of affairs, however, we must draw more than mere tactical conclusions with which to prevent Menshevist ideology from slipping into the comfortable position of concluding that, because there is a lack of widespread revolutionary determination in the proletariat, the total situation is not objectively revolutionary. The task is rather to revise – above all theoretically – those premisses of Menshevist vulgar-Marxism from which such conclusions follow. In other words the situation just mentioned, which Menshevism designates symptomatically as counter-revolutionary, *must be made into the problem, and the root causes of this – let us be quite honest about it ! – surprising ideological crisis of the proletariat, thoroughly investigated.*

This crisis has of course been frequently identified and its causes analysed in detail. Far be it from me to doubt the correctness of such analyses, with their references to the economic stratification within the proletariat, the privileged position of the labour aristocracy, the bourgeoisification of their life-style and ideology, and so on. I merely doubt whether such analyses satisfactorily explain the *totality* and hence the *crux* of the matter. In the first place, the so-called privileged position of the labour aristocracy is already in many respects so problematical that on its own it cannot adequately explain the Menshevism of the broadest masses. Moreover, it is by no means proved that the revolutionary determination of individual strata of the proletariat is absolutely proportionate to their depressed economic position and vice versa. Even more important, though, is the fact that the revolutionary experiences of recent years have demonstrated clearly the *limits of revolutionary spontaneity.* That is to say, the mass actions of the revolutionary period – considered by themselves – have exhibited essential characteristics basically very similar to those of the pre-revolutionary period, even if they are *quantitatively* far more pronounced. They erupt spontaneously, almost without exception as a defence against an economic (or, more rarely, political) offensive on the part of the bourgeoisie, and cease spontaneously when their immediate objectives appear to be realized or unattainable. They have thus kept to the pattern in terms of 'natural laws'.

There is no longer any doubt among communists that, in view of this state of affairs, the party assumes a role that is not only decisive, but will in fact determine the outcome of the struggle. The question is, simply; how is this role of the party to be conceived theoretically (and, accordingly, tactically)? Is merely propagandistic enlightenment of the masses on the part of the party sufficient to instil into this spontaneity a constantly increasing degree of consciousness which will then at some point carry the actions of the masses over and beyond the dead-point alluded to above? Or is the party obliged to take the initiative by actively intervening and engaging *the entire proletariat* directly in their own immediate interests in a way designed to overcome this inertia by 'necessary' escalation of the action and in constant interaction between the masses and the party? The earlier discussions between the KPD and the USPD revolved essentially around this point, and the tactics of the United German Communist Party before the March Action, the tactics of the 'Open Letter' and the alliance with Soviet Russia, were based on this position. They seemed all the more attractive, all the more clearly to be the only ones which were – theoretically – consistent, since they were based, not only on the established classic theory of ideology, but also on the experiences of the Russian Revolution. To take just one example: the slogan of peace was indubitably the best means in 1917 of bringing the broadest masses, almost the majority of the working population, into action under the banner of Bolshevism, or at least of binding them to a benevolent neutrality towards such action. The question arises, however: will that same position be the position of the proletariat in all cases immediately before the decisive struggle? Did particular, not necessarily recurring historical circumstances (and the skill with which the Bolshevists exploited them) help the Russian Revolution to overcome the inertia? *Or is it of the essence of the proletarian revolution that these inhibitions are dispelled automatically and with the necessity of natural laws?*

Posed in this way, the question must be answered negatively. The opportunists, of course, are anxious to avoid posing the question like this: the entire statistical material in Paul Levi's pamphlet,[11] for instance, has no other purpose than to exclude it a priori from any discussion and to denounce any conception of the revolution which does not proceed from an affirmative answer to it as a relapse into putschism. However, if we are to avoid further confusion, we must reject such sleight-of-hand attempts to shift the focus of discussion on to the question of putschism. For neither the negative response to the question posed above nor the tactical consequences of this response give rise to a situation which has anything at all to do with putschism. As the Central Bureau of the United German Communist Party correctly emphasized, what is at issue is not an organizational measure by which the Communist Party (i.e. a 'well-organized minority' in Blanqui's sense, however large it might be) can seize state power. The question, rather, is *how, through independent initiatives on the part of the United German Communist Party, the ideological crisis, the Menshevistic lethargy of the proletariat, the dead-point of revolutionary progress, can be overcome.* The putsch and the Marxist-communist action of a section of the proletariat or its vanguard differ not only by virtue of the numbers who participate in them – although one particular quantitative difference, the existence of the mass party, in this respect

11. A reference to Paul Levi's pamphlet *Unser Weg. Wider den Putschismus* ('Our Road. Against Putschism'), published with an appendix, 'The Lessons of an Attempted Putsch' by Karl Radek, Berlin, 1921 (Editor's note).

acquires decisive qualitative significance. The fundamental point of difference is rather this: on the one hand, the action being planned is designed to achieve a concrete objective (seizure of state power) by virtue of organized preparation, regardless of the level and maturity of the class-consciousness of the proletariat; on the other, the immediate objective of the action is *only a means* of influencing decisively the class-consciousness of the proletariat, and, *through this influence*, of bringing about the seizure of state power.

The necessity of such tactics follows not merely from the fact that waiting for spontaneous mass actions indicates – as the Youth Congress resolution[12] on the world-political situation puts it – 'a quietistic belief in miracles', but from the fact that it is not possible, even when all 'objective' conditions are present, to rely on the 'inevitability' of spontaneous mass actions in the acute phase of the revolution, neither as regards their breaking out in the first place, nor as regards their potentiality for being escalated sufficiently to realize the necessary goal. In the first place, it is quite possible that a succession of 'ineffective' spontaneous mass actions will produce, on the one hand, a marked preparedness for action and aggressiveness on the part of the bourgeoisie, and on the other, a certain tiredness and lethargy on the part of the proletariat. Consequently, the existence and growing acuteness of the objective conditions would not meet with an appropriate reaction from the proletariat. (This seems to have been the case in Italy as a result of the tactics of Serrati and his followers.[13]) Secondly, there is no experimental and theoretical guarantee

12. Lukács probably has in mind here the 'Resolution on Point 1 of the Agenda: The World-Political Situation and the Tasks Confronting the Communist Youth Organization'. This was put forward at the Second Congress of the Communist Youth International (7-11 April 1921) in Jena, which was not recognized by the Moscow executive committee. It is reprinted in *Jugend-Internationale*, 2, no. 9, May 1921, see especially p. 247 (Editor's note).

13. Giacinto Menotti Serrati (1872-1926), one of the leaders of the 'Maximalist' left wing of the Italian Socialist Party. From 1915 he was the chief editor of *Avanti* and was a delegate of his party to both the Zimmerwald and Kienthal conferences during the War. An ardent supporter of the Third International he was elected a member of the executive committee (July-August 1920). He then came into conflict with Lenin and the Comintern on the issue of national autonomy for the Italian Party at the time of the debates on Lenin's Twenty-one Points. Serrati argued that the rise of Fascism in Italy made it inopportune to proceed with the immediate expulsion of all reformists (Turati, Modigliani, etc.), and that a gradual purge was preferable. This conflict ended with the expulsion of Serrati along with the entire Italian Party with the exception of Bordiga's extreme left-wing faction, which constituted itself as the Communist Party in 1921 (Editor's note).

at all that masses who go into action as the result of external prompting or simply under the *intellectual influence* of communist slogans, *without having detached themselves organizationally from their Menshevistic leadership*, can be driven essentially any further in their action than such Menshevist organizations see fit. It is, for instance, more than questionable whether the Spartacus League, even had it been clearer about its objectives and more determined in pursuing them, could have succeeded in the struggles during and after the Kapp Putsch in prevailing against the calls to retreat issued by the SPD and USPD, as soon as the 'objective' of the joint action had been achieved and the republic saved. Herein lies the great danger of the 'Open Letter' line *as the sole tactic* of the United German Communist Party. To be sure, the party can and must extend the area of its intellectual influence by means of this and similar slogans just as it must attempt to exploit for its purposes any action which arises spontaneously (or as a result of such influence). But it will not do to *stake the fate of the proletarian revolution in Germany exclusively on this one card*. If the progress of the revolution is to avoid the danger of stagnating, another answer has to be found: the action of the United German Communist Party, the switch to the offensive. Which means: rousing the proletarian masses from their lethargy through independent party action, undertaken at the correct moment and with correct slogans, wrenching them free from their Menshevistic leadership *through action (that is, organizationally and not merely intellectually)*, severing the knot of the ideological crisis of the proletariat with the sword of action. This statement of our objectives effectively refutes the claptrap of the opportunists about the putschist nature of such minority-initiated activity. Besides, 'majority' and 'minority' of the proletariat are *not statistical, but historical-dialectical concepts*. They do not exist ready-made for computing before action begins, but they emerge in and during action, through action itself. In spite of all our possible reservations about the March Action as a real example of the intended new tactical approach, in spite of all the criticisms which we can and must level against the tactical mistakes made during it – its effect in this sense (at least in some parts of Germany) is beyond dispute. We have at last begun to move along the road which will lead the German proletariat to real revolutionary action. The important thing now is to achieve complete clarity about the road itself and the way in which we have to move further along it. The lessons of the March Action are essentially and above all organizational ones. Tactical clarification will produce little that is new; its function will be rather to make the motives which led to the party's decision to go over to the offensive wholly conscious for the party itself and fully intelligible to the masses. Organizationally, however, decisive conclusions will have to be drawn at every point.

Organization and Revolutionary Initiative[1]

It has already been frequently pointed out – and certainly correctly so – that the crisis of the United German Communist Party, beginning with the Serrati conflict and going up to the acute Levi crisis after the March Action,[2] is nothing more than the repercussion in reality of the terms of affiliation laid down by the Second Congress. For it was bound to become evident that these terms – assuming that they are taken seriously – cannot in any sense be fulfilled simply by voting on one occasion to accept them, nor even by resolving to put them into effect organizationally; but rather, that they do no more than *set in motion the process at the end of which stand the real communist parties*. All opportunists in the Third International, from Serrati to Levi, therefore acted instinctively correctly in rebelling against them and adding their voices and support – albeit at first cautiously and pianissimo – to the centrists' howls of rage. The demand of all the centrists and opportunists, that affiliation be tied to political conditions only, means in effect that no steps be taken towards the formation of communist parties, but that 'mass parties' of pseudo-communists should emerge instead. (Parties, that is of working-class masses with revolutionary feelings but lacking revolutionary clarity, and led by opportunists in accordance with all the rules of 'autonomy'.) Although the resolutions of the Second Congress definitively blocked off that particular deviation, they could do no more than begin to steer the process in the correct direction. The party crises which have broken out everywhere between the two congresses demonstrate that the process of clarification has already advanced a long way, but is by no means yet completed. It will be the task of the Third Congress to summarize the experiences of all these crises and to further the development which has so auspiciously got under way.

Among such experiences that of the March Action occupies a very crucial position, principally because both party and revolution are most highly advanced in Germany. What must strike even the outside observer

---

1. First appeared in *Die Internationale*, III/8, 1921 (Editor's note).

2. i.e. the period from July 1920 (Second Congress of the Comintern) to April/May 1921. For further details see the preceding essay, 'Spontaneity of the Masses, Activity of the Party' and the notes on it (Editor's note).

at once is, on the one hand, the failure of centralization during the Action, the revelation that the party was centralized only on paper, and on the other, the fact that this organizational defect was understood immediately and with correct revolutionary instinct by the mass of the party members, and was placed at the centre of the subsequent discussions of the Action. As a result, there can be no doubt that the prospects of recovery are well-founded.

At the same time, however, it is somewhat surprising that this organizational defect, which without a doubt already existed earlier, should not have come to light so conspicuously until during the Action itself. The reason, in my view, lies in the fact that *organizational centralization and tactical initiative on the part of the party are mutually determining concepts.* This interaction is in the first instance technical. For, on the one hand, every attempt of the party somehow to seize the initiative must necessarily remain at the level of mere intention – or, indeed, even turn into empty phrase-making – unless an organization exists which is so perfectly centralized that all the parts of the party, men no less than institutions, are capable of acting in unison like the limbs of a single body. On the other hand, centralization which has actually and effectively been accomplished will and must, simply by virtue of its inner dynamics, drive the party forward in the direction of activity and initiative. Just as, at the time of the Kapp Putsch, the feeling and the consciousness of organizational weakness had a paralysing effect on the Spartacus Group and was largely responsible for its tactical wavering and irresoluteness, so an organization which is properly developed – in a revolutionary sense – is bound through the way it functions to drive the party on in a tactical sense as well.

However, to see things in this context is at once to indicate the *intellectual* (*geistigen*) point of contact between tactics and organization, initiative and centralization. Being organized in a revolutionary fashion and having an awareness of the significance of revolutionary organization – this presupposes a very high degree of class-consciousness. Not merely in the sense that the simple, emotional readiness for – instinctive – revolutionary action is inadequate; even the clear realization that we find ourselves in the final crisis of capitalism is not enough. What must be present is the unshakeable knowledge that the moment for action has come, that we are in the midst of the decisive phase, in which the devotion, selflessness and utter self-subordination of every single individual have become the issues on which the fate of the revolution hangs. For a revolutionary organization cannot be contrived mechanically. And until its intellectual conditions are met, the finest resolution (acceptance of the terms of affiliation) remains a mere resolution. Indeed, those concerned may well pass the resolution with the noblest intentions and the best will in the world, yet still fail to understand its significance and its consequences. This was the case almost everywhere with the terms of affiliation. However much, therefore, the decision of the United German Communist Party to go on to the offensive deserves to be welcomed; however correct the view of those who initiated the move that that is the only way in which the vanguard can expect a really decisive and impelling influence on the whole of the proletariat class, it is necessary to point out at the same time that the very vanguard itself was not organizationally equal to the task. Which in turn also revealed that it was not sufficiently prepared for its task in intellectual terms either.

Such criticism cannot and must not be interpreted as disapproval of the tactics of the offensive. In an earlier essay ('Spontaneity of the Masses, Activity of the Party', *Die Internationale*, no. 6) I substantiated my basic agreement with such tactics in a sufficiently clear and theoretical manner. When it comes to drawing practical conclusions from the Action, however, it would be wrong to suppress any aspect of it at all. More: not only must we not conceal a single 'mistake', but we must initiate the discussion on precisely what is *symptomatic* about each and every mistake. Without going into details here, it ought to be pointed out that the criticism of the March Action from both sides (not counting Paul Levi, of course) is motivated by correct instincts. On the one hand, the Central Bureau is perfectly correct both in pointing to the lack of discipline during the action as the most important source of failure and in its intention to change things in this respect by draconian measures. No less correct, however, is the charge levelled by the other side, namely that the statements issued by the Central Bureau of the party, both in the preparatory stages and during the action itself, were totally inadequate. Both criticisms are aimed at the same target. For although there can and should be no reservations about insisting on discipline, discipline can only become effective, even with the best will in the world, when the central agency which does the insisting is not only united in itself and clear about its objective, but at the same time possesses the necessary ability to express that clarity clearly for others. It would be wrong to hush up the fact that in this respect serious deficiencies have come to light. There can be no doubt that the central leadership was motivated in the action by clear and conscious intentions. To assert the contrary is not only to distort the facts maliciously but to divert attention from the relevant organizational questions – from which much can and should be learnt. It can do nothing but give rise to futile arguments about the personal abilities of individuals. On the other hand, it is legitimate to doubt whether the Central Bureau possessed the organizational means which would have made it at all possible for its intentions to be conveyed unambiguously to the whole party (this being a *sine qua non* of discipline).

There is a great deal of talk nowadays to the effect that the United German Communist Party has advanced beyond the propagandist stage and has entered the period of action. If this is not to become empty phrase-making, it can be understood only in the sense that propaganda and its proper organization have acquired a greater significance. For as long as the party is on the defensive, circumstances will see to it that the organizational defects of the propaganda machine remain concealed. What does it ultimately mean to be on the defensive? It means that the real starting-point and incentive for the party's activities, no matter how strong the revolutionary feeling and consciousness which sustain them, is not to be found in the party itself, but is, rather, determined by the conduct of the bourgeois or social-democratic counter-revolution. The boundary between voluntary initiative and imposed reaction is of course fluid. The actions and decisions of even the most powerful mass party, irrespective of how resolutely committed it is to the offensive, are partly determined by the conduct of the groups it opposes. On the other hand, how far even the weakest and smallest of groups is prepared to pursue the lines of action 'imposed' on it depends very largely on its own will and determination. In spite of this fluid boundary, however, the difference expresses itself precisely *in organizational terms*. As long as the conduct and the position of the party remain defensive – 'determined', that is, in the sense just mentioned – the essential task of its propaganda is to unmask the commissions and omissions of all overtly or covertly counter-revolutionary forces. Its object in this is to accelerate the process of development of revolutionary class-consciousness in the proletariat, and, by exploiting the economic and political situation, to contribute to the outbreak of spontaneous mass actions. To achieve this it is absolutely necessary that the party be both intellectually and tactically united; yet even the fulfilment of this condition does not get to the root of fundamental organizational inadequacies. The very fact that the nature of defensive tactics is determined from 'without' introduces a certain element of diffuseness, dissipation and indiscriminateness into the propaganda and actions of the party (even where it seems to be well organized). As long as the party remains at the stage where it is merely gathering forces, moreover, it is difficult to overcome the diffuse nature of its work. It is obliged to turn in different directions, to recruit indiscriminately forces of extremely varied strength and maturity; to seize every available opportunity to make itself known and to unmask the enemy. It is forced to make substantial concessions to movements which have arisen spontaneously, with the result that, in this phase, there is no possibility of judging sufficiently clearly how much of this particular mode of extensive and diffuse work is deliberate tactics and how much is simply organizational weakness. It may well be the case, especially where propaganda is concerned, that party organs acting quite 'independently' are in a position to achieve excellent results: simply by pursuing the tactical line of unmasking the counter-revolution or sparking off spontaneous uprisings, they can provide a tremendous impetus to the movement – albeit, of course, within certain limits.

That kind of organization, characteristic for almost all non-Russian communist parties in their initial phase, is far from ideal, even for that particular period. It becomes *catastrophically dangerous*, however, the moment the movement and the party have become so strong that an active initiative on the part of the party is not only possible in the light of the balance of forces but is actually necessary if the revolution is to be advanced. Even then, it is true, propaganda will relate *to the same topics as before, but its function will have undergone a decisive transformation*: it will have to become systematic internally. Which is not to say that the party is in a position to lay down the exact course and tempo for the revolution. Through its propaganda *it must create the intellectual conditions for an appropriate, united and concerted action on the part of the Communist Party vanguard itself.* Not simply by reacting in a revolutionary manner to the practices of the counter-revolution, but by seizing every opportunity which the party regards as suitable for an advance *to push forward in tactical and organizational solidarity.* This means that the preparation and intensification of propaganda becomes a primarily organizational task. The apparatus must be so firmly under the party's control that its entire propaganda functions like the parts of a single instrument. And this is precisely where, in my view, so much of the criticism of the March Action is wide of the mark. It is incorrect to assert that the United German Communist Party's action was wrong because it was not understood by the mass of the proletariat and therefore led the party into renewed isolation. In the first place, this is not true of all areas of Germany, and secondly, even if it were, it would still not constitute a conclusive objection to the action. It is indeed quite possible that such an action on the part of the party will not be understood at the time it is initiated and will therefore be condemned to defeat. But such a defeat can subsequently turn into a source of new strength for the party if the economic consequences of the defeat (wage cuts and increased working hours in Central Germany) which the party attempted to prevent by their offensive action actually materialize. The belief that purely propagandistic preparation of the entire proletariat is a sufficient prerequisite to such an action is both opportunistic and utopian. Only through the object-lesson provided by a whole series of actions – including, of course, partial failures – can the entire class be made to understand their situation and the subsequent mode of action which it makes necessary. The weakest aspect of the March Action (not so much the 'idea' as such, but the execution) was, rather, *that it was not understood sufficiently quickly and adequately by the revolutionary vanguard itself.* A large proportion of the slogans came 'out of the blue'. This is not to imply that they were unintelligible in terms of the situation and therefore objectively incorrect. But the propaganda apparatus was neither attuned to them nor practised in putting them across. Consequently they stuck out like sore thumbs in the party's publications, where the leading articles, commentaries on topical events, etc., clung largely to the old familiar approach. To be sure, there was a great deal of sabotage to contend with. Even so, it goes without saying that not every such failure can be attributed to sabotage; and, on the other hand, the fact that such extensive sabotage was possible merely emphasizes that the organization was intrinsically defective, *that the party's propaganda apparatus was functioning more or less automatically and 'independently' and was not controlled organizationally by the Central Bureau.* Nor was it merely a question of 'technical' defects (tenuous or intermittent contacts with the provinces, and so on); what was lacking was the principle of intellectual organization. This is shown by the fact that the party's central organ was almost as ineffectual during the action as the provincial organs. (It must be self-evident that all the foregoing remarks about the propaganda apparatus are intended to be symptomatic and apply to an even greater degree to the other organs of the party.)

The task, then, is not only to produce an iron code of revolutionary discipline, but *to create at the same time the intellectual and organizational conditions for such discipline in the building of the party.*

On the way in which this proposition is put into effect in concrete terms will depend whether the United German Communist Party emerges strengthened or weakened from the March Action. If the party succeeds in grasping the idea of revolutionary organization in all its magnitude and drawing all the necessary conclusions from it, it will have emerged victorious from the crisis. If it fails to do so, the 'switch to the offensive' will remain a mere good intention, which is bound to entail even worse crises the next time an attempt is made to put it into practice.

Every communist party is by nature a higher form of organization than any opportunistic or centrist party. This new organizational form, however, cannot be brought about simply by taking over the old apparatus and re-directing it towards new objectives; it can only be achieved through a process which initially dissolves, indeed, in some senses smashes the old organizations, and provokes a spontaneous rebellion of the masses against their former party discipline. Hence every communist party is bound to achieve its new and higher organizational identity only by undergoing serious crises. The affiliation conditions of the Second Congress have engendered many such recuperative crises. But these crises cannot bring about true regeneration unless and until the conditions are not only accepted but actually put into effect. This means at the same time, of course, that they should not simply be conceived of as demands of the International and 'conscientiously' carried out, but that at least the revolutionary vanguard should grasp their essential underlying spirit in all its significance. Within the United German Communist Party this process has undoubtedly *begun*. Everything now depends on not allowing it to falter but rather helping it to become fully effective.

The decisive organizational feature which distinguishes Bolsheviks from Mensheviks had already manifested itself clearly by the time of the first split in the Russian movement. The difference lies in the *demands which are made on the members of a Bolshevik party*. Even at that time, Lenin had already formulated the concept of the professional revolutionary, a term which was completely misunderstood by the entire non-Russian public. Without being in the least irreverent towards the memory of Rosa Luxemburg, it can fairly be claimed today that even her opposition to Lenin in 1904 was based on total non-comprehension of his proposals; that even she had in mind nothing but the old-style party structure (which she saw very largely – and in the central and western European context correctly so – as an inhibiting factor in the revolution) when she made her counterclaim that the spontaneity of the masses was the real driving force of the revolution. It was from this point of view that she fought Lenin's demand for absolute centralization. In so doing, she overlooked the salient feature of the new form of organization, namely *the increased demands made on the individual party members.* It is no coincidence that all opportunists – most recently Paul Levi in a statement of rare clarity – constantly appeal to the lowest instincts and the all-too prevalent weaknesses of the proletarians. They adduce the fact that such 'earthly ties' still have great sway over the proletarians as an additional pretext for their passivity, their condemnation and denunciation of each and every revolutionary action. True, the revolution has to be made, in Lenin's words, with the people who are available. But that is a very different matter from deciding which people should be allowed to join the vanguard of the revolution, and above all what, in terms of work and sacrifice, should be required of those who consider themselves entitled to belong to it. At least in this respect, the question of the ethical demand, Gorter[3] and company grasped correctly the Bolshevik concept of organization. However, they thoroughly corrupted this correct understanding straightaway by developing it mechanically and applying it even more mechanically. To sit back and wait for some such firm nucleus to emerge and – by example – expand its influence, thereby educating the (in Gorter's view) as yet non-revolutionary proletariat towards the revolution, is no less utopian than to believe, as the opportunists do, in those 'mass parties' which are likewise supposed to unite gradually the whole or at least the majority of the proletariat and thus achieve the revolution. *For although it is true that the development of the communist party and that of the proletarian revolution are mutually determining, their growth is by no means a homogeneous process; indeed, they do not even run along consistently parallel lines.*

The separation of these two lines of development is therefore of the utmost *practical* importance, because it is here that opportunism, which always manages to concoct a 'theory of evolution' that can be adapted to fit any conditions, erects its *organizational line of defence.* Its tactical premiss is that the worsening economic crisis will bring about the

3. Hermann Gorter was the leader of a dissident group of Dutch communists who emphasized the differences between conditions in Russia, where the nature of the party was determined by the preponderance of peasants among the population, and in western Europe and America, where the proletariat was a majority. The proletarian party in the west should have no truck with the petty-bourgeoisie, parliaments or reformist unions. Gorter put forward his views in an 'open letter' to Lenin in which he took issue with *'Left-wing' Communism,* and urged the separation of the Comintern from Russian state policy. He left the Communist Party in the autumn of 1921 and formed the Communist Labour Party of Holland on the lines of the German KAP (see Degras, op. cit., p. 67) (Editor's note).

revolutionizing of the entire proletariat as a matter of course (*naturgesetzlich*) and that all the communist party needs to do is to exploit the crisis propagandistically and then work its way up to the leadership of the – independently – erupting movement. Similarly, its organizational premiss is that the emergence and growth of the communist party is a mere endorsement of the revolutionary situation in the relevant countries. Such organizational opportunism is far more dangerous even than the tactical kind, because so far not nearly enough theoretical attention has been devoted to the connection between organization and revolutionary action. The significance of the connection has therefore not yet adequately penetrated the consciousness of the masses, with the result that the concealed opportunism which is at work has rarely been recognized and even more rarely been unmasked as such.

Just as the opportunists obscure the real problematic in the tactical question of the putsch, so here too, in the matter of organization, the false dilemma of mass party or sect is posed. In such circumstances the organizational opportunists are very adept at exploiting the one-sidedly ethical, chimerical and unhistorical notion of the party propagated by Gorter and his supporters; the aim is to represent the question as if the only possible choice were between two types of organization, type KAP or type PSI.[4] That would doubtless apply if the problem were actually such that two solutions were possible: either an organizational grouping, divorced from the unclear masses, of those communists who are already fully conscious and determined; or a 'revolutionary evolution' of the masses themselves towards communism. Clearly, however, this kind of 'either-or' has nothing to do with either historical reality or the dialectical method. The coming into being of the 'realm of freedom', the historically decisive effect of the determined vanguard which clearly recognizes and is prepared to accomplish the course of history – this occurs rather *in the midst of historical reality, in uninterrupted dialectical interaction with the objective economic crisis and the masses revolutionized by that crisis.* I have already indicated the tactical implications of this in the previously mentioned essay. In organizational terms the lesson is that the formation of the consciously revolutionary *nucleus*, of the real vanguard group, from among the ranks of the proletariat is a *process* which, although it is accomplished in constant interaction with the subjective and objective

4. The Communist Labour Party of Germany (KAPD) as the type of a sectarian party; the Italian Socialist Party (PSI) as the type of the large mass party (Editor's note).

revolutionary development of the class, *is nevertheless the conscious and free act of the vanguard itself.* Since the setting up of the Russian Bolshevik party, the whole principle of organization has constantly been clarified; one of the major objects must be the intellectual and organizational strengthening of this conscious nucleus. In Russia the vanguard was able to work its way up to full clarity and consciousness between the two revolutions; in Hungary it took the collapse of the dictatorship of the soviets to create the intellectual and organizational conditions for such a party. The problem in Germany – and presumably in most Western European countries – is that large sections of the masses have already been so moved by the spirit of the revolution that they are even joining the Communist International on an organizational basis, long before those conditions have established themselves sufficiently clearly in the consciousness of the vanguard itself. The question is therefore not the static, unhistorical and undialectical question: mass party or sect; but the dynamic question which emerges from the revolutionary process and flows back into it: *how is the revolutionary mass party to be transformed into a truly communist party?*

Here again it would be crassly opportunistic to separate the organizational from the tactical question, for instance by refraining from active politics until this organizational work has been completed. On the other hand it would be a new kind of putschism to pose the question so one-sidedly (likewise by wrongly separating tactics from organization) as to concentrate exclusively on the revolutionary offensive. As always, the crucial thing is the indissoluble unity of tactics and organization. It is essential that every member of the United German Communist Party feel in his very bones the fateful importance of revolutionary organization; that every single comrade who is resolved to fight the decisive battle and to risk his life in it should understand clearly what is at stake in the solution of this question; *that organization should no longer be treated* – as in the old-style party – *as a technical question, but as the supreme intellectual (geistig) question of the revolution.* The debates which have followed the March Action show that this process has already begun. For instance, the way in which individual districts have of their own accord dealt with every breach of discipline; the way in which they have begun instinctively correctly by punishing the indiscipline of functionaries and others in authority more severely than that of ordinary party members – these and other moves indicate a growing awareness of what is involved here. The all-important thing, however, is not simply to 'put one's house in order' in a once-and-for-all fashion, but to ensure that this spirit of revolutionary discipline is constantly developed and intensified.

This is where the central leadership above all must take the initiative consciously and actively. On the one hand, it must create the apparatus without which revolutionary discipline is not possible; on the other hand, it must ensure that the theoretical working-through of this problem makes consistent headway, to the point where the consciousness of its importance takes a real hold on the masses. For no matter how important the role of the centre is as initiator in this respect, *the centralization of a revolutionary party cannot possibly be achieved by bureaucratic and technical means*. The centralized organization of the party is of course a prerequisite for the revolutionary discipline of its members. But the fully developed consciousness of the party members in this question is in turn a prerequisite for the feasibility of any such centralization. Thus the question of organization reveals itself to be an intellectual (*geistig*) question. The inhibitions to be overcome here are intellectual, the ideological remnants of capitalist reification in the thinking and feeling of the communists themselves: bureaucratic routine, individualism with its insistence on 'freedom' and disdain for 'day-to-day work', and so on. That such shying away from day-to-day organizational work conceals an even more dangerous form of individualism and an even more ossified form of reification – that has not yet been generally recognized. Which is why it is so urgently necessary that the problem of organization be properly worked through intellectually and practically.

Only if the question is so posed does it become quite clear that it is the self-same problem which underlies both the tactical principle of revolution and the question of centralized organization: namely, the approaching 'realm of freedom', the historical necessity to intervene consciously in the world-crisis, in the course of world history. Objectively the situation is ripe for revolution. The principal obstacles to the victory of the revolution are ideological. To the vanguard in its revolutionary initiative falls the task of overcoming the Menshevik crisis of the proletariat. The revolutionarily centralized organization of the communist party is not merely designed to make such an offensive possible, however; it has at the same time the duty thoroughly to purge the vanguard, the task force, of all the dross of capitalist reification, to make it worthy and capable of its historic mission.

The Politics of Illusion – Yet Again[1]

The illusory politics of the former opposition, now the central committee of the Hungarian Communist Party,[2] cannot simply be characterized as the inability to take real circumstances and possibilities into account. Even the most honest and well-intentioned (not to mention the most gifted) of politicians are liable to misjudge the situation from time to time. What we are concerned with here is something quite different; namely, the fact that *these people have a mentality which precludes from the outset the possibility of judging the situation correctly*. In the first place, neither in their thinking nor in their analysis of the situation do they take as their *starting-point* the real position, the position of the Hungarian proletariat. Moreover, their *objective* is not oriented towards goals that proceed out of that position – towards, that is, the liberation of the Hungarian proletariat.

What follows is a platitude, but the politics of the present central committee of the Hungarian Communist Party force us to spell it out in detail: the Hungarian Communist Party's sphere of activity is Hungary; its goal is to lead the liberation struggle of the Hungarian proletariat; its organization and its tactics are determined by the actual economic and political situation in Hungary. Everything else – whether it be the whole problem of the émigrés or the position which individual comrades occupy (rightly or wrongly) in the international movement – must be considered exclusively *as a means by which to achieve this, the only serious goal.*

It is disgraceful that such commonplaces need to be written down at all, even more so that they have to be specially emphasized. Disgraceful it may be, the fact remains that it is not the situation in Hungary, nor what can be done there, which determines the central committee's entire politics, but rather *speculations about the possible impact of their actions on the mood of the émigré masses and the consequences they might have for the international standing of individual comrades.*

1. First appeared in Ladislaus Rudas, *Abenteurer- und Liquidatorentum. Die Politik Béla Kuns und die Krise der KPU*, Vienna, 1922 (Editor's note).

2. Lukács is referring here to the central committee headed by Béla Kun, which the executive committee of the Comintern set up provisionally in October 1921 (Editor's note).

A typical example was the first proclamation which went out from the central committee to the workers of Baranya. (Fortunately it only appeared in the Berlin *Rote Fahne* and never reached the Baranya comrades.) It contains a detailed set of instructions as to how the communists of Baranya should conduct the politics of a 'loyal opposition' *vis-à-vis* the bourgeois republic. They should not support it, but neither should they overthrow it; they should demand freedom of assembly, freedom of the press, all the right and proper things – but not, at least not just for the present, soldiers' soviets. It was no use the minority[3] on the central committee pointing out (although even they were ill-informed, since the proclamation was sent off to Vienna before their arrival) that, according to all the signs, the Baranya Republic was nothing serious. No matter: the proclamation was necessary. It was no use the Baranya republic collapsing meantime. No matter: the proclamation had to be published. Why? If its author[4] had given even a moment's thought to the proletariat of Baranya, he would not have pressed for its publication. But he did, for the simple reason that he wrote the proclamation not for Baranya – but *for Moscow*. He was so anxious to clear himself in Moscow's eyes from the suspicion of leftist tendencies dating from the March Action that he forgot amidst all his blind efforts to advance his own career – *that the people in Moscow are not fools*. Of course they will appreciate that he is concerned to move to the right, but at the same time they will also observe that *he is attempting to play 'rightist Realpolitik' in a non-existent situation and with non-existent forces*. The most important thing here is not the fact itself, nor even its immediate consequences, but *the political tendency of which it is an expression*. And the minority on the central committee committed a grave mistake in not exposing there and then the political manœuvres of such people, who, far from concerning themselves with their proper field of activity, merely use the whole working-class movement for their own personal advantage. It was a grave mistake on the part of the minority of the central committee that they did not there and then force the situation in the party to breaking-point, that they sanctioned this – relatively – innocent expression of what amounts to the *politics of illusions and adventurism*.

3. The minority included Albert Király, Jenö Landler and Lukács himself; they had originally constituted the majority, which had however been overturned by the Third Congress of the Comintern (June 1921). Rudas and Lengyel were in sympathy with this group (Editor's note).

4. Presumably Béla Kun or one of his supporters (Editor's note).

Further: in the issue of *Proletár* dated 10 November, pride of place is given to a five-column statement from the central committee. One sentence reads exactly as follows: 'Under the leadership of the Communist International the Hungarian Communist Party *will become a strong mass party in Hungary in the near future.*'

Anyone whose view of the Hungarian situation is the least bit sober and whose politics are directed towards results which can and should be achieved there, knows full well that the announcement that a communist party of the masses is about to materialize is, as an idea, *a fantastic illusion,* and, as an objective, *irresponsible political adventurism.* If we ask ourselves now how it is possible for such attitudes to rule the thoughts of the central committee, we are bound to conclude that when it put those lines to paper, *it was not thinking about Hungary at all and never even dreamt of making a serious effort to realize the stated objective.*

On the other hand, the central committee was certainly thinking seriously about those comrades who now enjoy the status of international celebrities and whose position would doubtless be strengthened if they could claim to represent, not a small illegal party, but a powerful mass party. A further serious consideration in the eyes of the central committee was the mood of the exiles: that nervous impatience which finds its outlet in cries such as 'When can we go home?' or 'Nothing's happening at home!'; that inability to understand the demands of the illegal work in Hungary and to subordinate their own feelings and wishes to those demands. In many respects, such people cannot be regarded as the really communist, or at least not as the *consciously communist* ones among the exiles generally. Besides social democrats and anarchists they include many workers who, *given lengthy and persistent schooling,* could be educated to become communists. In its present state, however, this group is in no sense one whose views should be allowed to govern the politics of the Hungarian Communist Party on any issue whatever.

Unfortunately the central committee has now become the slave of those illusions which it so frivolously and irresponsibly nurtured and exploited when the movement to 'build up'[5] the party was in its infancy. At that stage the movement derived its slogans from the impatient mood of the exiles. Now that it has won control of the official apparatus of the party it can do nothing but concentrate its organizing activity and its tactics on fulfilling the very pretensions it itself nurtured, instead

5. A term used by the Kun faction to describe its own policy in opposition to that of the rival 'liquidators' (Editor's note).

of on the possibilities and demands of the real work to be done in Hungary.

It is an organization built on sand; just how hollow it is is shown by *the soullessness of its bureaucracy*, which becomes daily more blatant. In the atmosphere created by the central committee it is impossible to put the accent on real work. They have to be able to *produce results immediately* if the expectations of the exiles are not to rebound on the selfsame central committee which nurtured and encouraged them. But the only organizations which can be created immediately, even in the most favourable circumstances, are skeleton organizations. The central committee, bent on producing immediate and impressive results for Moscow and the exiles, however, has gone far beyond the necessary evils this entails, and is now hurtling forward towards the abyss. It has not even set up skeleton organizations which could at a later stage (perhaps!) be filled out with a meaningful content, but rather organizations *which from the very outset are so designed that they can never become anything more than impressive façades with nothing behind them.* Two primary factors have combined to produce this state of affairs: on the one hand, the policy of arousing illusions out of deference to the understandable impatience of the exiles; on the other, the whipping up of all individual feelings of inferiority and base passions. *And now, of course, these personal ambitions have got to be realized*, services rendered in the faction fighting have got to be rewarded. *Which straightaway excludes the possibility of solving objectively the personnel problems of the organization.* Moreover, not only are gigantic apparatuses created to cope with non-existent tasks (e.g. the 'mass party' in exile with its district secretariats and so on); they are orientated in such a way that *they are absolutely useless as far as real work, i.e. work relevant to Hungary, is concerned.* (E.g. the frivolous, indiscriminate way in which members are recruited, the destruction of the illegal apparatus, etc.) Such organizations can therefore never develop meaningfully. They are machines which operate only in neutral gear; consequently, they can produce results only by fabricating reports, questionnaires, statistics, news-cuttings, archives and so on. Hence, of course, the impression that their idle impotence is really feverish activity – which in turn provides in their own eyes 'objective' reasons for their self-aggrandizement and thus a convenient – albeit provisional – means of satisfying the unfulfilled personal ambitions that are already becoming evident.

There is a further important factor: the degeneration of the central committee's mode of organization into empty bureaucracy. The basis for this is the mutual – and, let it be added, quite justified – *mistrust* between leaders and party members. A section of the leadership knows full well that its policies are built on sand. But it knows at the same time what means it has employed (misleading information, encouragement of un-realizable illusions, job promises, etc.) to acquire supporters. And it also knows *what kind of people it has acquired as supporters.* All of which rules out from the very start the possibility of cooperation on the basis of com-radely communist trust. In such a situation witnesses are required to attend every conversation to make sure that what was agreed is not subsequently denied. Similarly, every order has to be transmitted in writing; not simply to ensure that it is actually carried out, but – in the not infrequent event of its proving impossible to carry out – to provide appropriate documentary evidence of its having been issued. In so far as the bureaucratic apparatus produces anything at all, then, it produces dossiers, material for accusations and counter-accusations between com-rades that can one day be turned to account in the personal battles which are bound to develop.

In such an atmosphere, charged as it is with mutual (and, I repeat, wholly justified) mistrust, *the authority of the central committee can only be asserted* – even superficially – on the basis of blind and slavish submis-siveness. The more so since membership of the central committee was granted as a reward for services rendered in the faction fighting, with the result that most of its members do not occupy a position in the working class movement, either as theoreticians or as organizers, which would allow them to maintain their authority in any other way. It is significant, for example, that a member of the central committee, a so-called theoreti-cian, had to resort to the disciplinary protection of the central committee because a theoretically educated member of the party had dared to register for his seminar in the party school. There can be no doubt that such arti-ficial and illegitimate cultivation of authority serves only to make the party bureaucracy even more hollow and soulless; it turns it into an *office*, with bosses and subalterns, not a communist organization which is centralized but based on comradely cooperation.

Such an organization was obviously bound to sever links with all the traditions of the Hungarian Communist Party's previous – modest but real – organizational work. It did so out of instinctive hatred and contempt for any kind of consistent work. But it also did so because it is only by destroying and declaring null and void everything the Hungarian Com-munist Party has produced so far that *it can provide itself with an alibi for not itself achieving anything in Hungary*. And since the central committee knows very well that it will never be in a position to produce any real work in Hungary, it has planned its work of destruction in such a way that it is armed with a long-term justification for its inability to achieve anything. And the bureaucratic apparatus, the powerful central bureaucracy of the 'mass party' in exile, even if it prevents any real work being done, can at least produce the occasional dossier as an apparent justification of its idleness.

But only for a time. And since the excessive expectations which they have fostered cannot always be satisfied by promises and accusations, *sham results are necessary*. And herein lies the greatest danger of the central committee's organizational principles. *Such an organization is by its very nature susceptible to corruption*. Whenever illegal work is being carried on, the difficulty of checking what has really been achieved represents a great danger. Reports which do not tally with the real situation are very often received from even the most honest comrades engaged in illegal work; this is not a consequence of malevolent intentions, but rather of exaggerated hopes and over-estimation of the importance of their own work. It is the duty of the central apparatus, not only to distinguish the wheat from the chaff in such reports, but to *educate* the comrades engaged in illegal work to the point where their activity is governed by absolutely objective factors and not by illusions. I repeat: even a central committee which is utterly dedicated to working soberly and stands at the head of the best of parties, is forced to fight against such tendencies. If, however, the central committee itself is committed to obtaining sham results, if it even lends its support to such tendencies, then those comrades who are working illegally are bound to arrive at the conclusion *that the centre does not expect a sober assessment of reality from them, but that they themselves are expected to represent illusions as facts*. Add to these factors the central committee's basic principle in terms of organization, the total lack of discrimination in selecting party members, and the abyss towards which the central committee's illusory and unreal policies are necessarily being driven immediately becomes apparent.

For there is no turning round on the path of lies. Once I have given my word to Moscow and the exiles that I shall produce this, that or the other within a short time, I can only talk myself out of trouble for a short time by blaming everything on the impotence of the previous central committee, sabotage by the minority, etc. Sooner or later I must be able to point to some tangible result. And if I have judged the situation on the basis of illusions, if my organizations are so orientated that they are incapable of accomplishing any real work at all, then *there is no other way out except the false report : the representation of illusions as if they were reality*. And then, to corroborate the first lie, a second one becomes necessary, and so it goes on inevitably until the final collapse.

No honest communist can follow the central committee along this path. There are many among the serious communist elements in exile who have already recognized this fact. What is certain, however, is that the Hungarian workers will not allow themselves to be used as tools. And when the 'party-building' bubble has finally burst, every communist worker will realize that we were right. If he reproaches us, it will only be because we did not take up the struggle against the politics of adventurism and illusions even sooner.

Reviews
1924–1925

Bernstein's Triumph: Notes on the essays written in honour of Karl Kautsky's seventieth birthday[1]

> The main thing, however – as I've already said to you – is to do something like this, but not to say so (Ignaz Auer: *Letter to Bernstein*).

The man who did it without saying so, the man who did not preach but actually practised the revision of Marxism, the transformation of revolutionary dialectics into a form of peaceful evolutionism, was none other than Karl Kautsky. It was, therefore, only fitting and logical that the reformists of every country should come together to celebrate his seventieth birthday. The *Vorwärts* report on the celebration in London was equally true to form in its – correct – emphasis on the real climax of the proceedings. 'It was only when the ageing *Eduard Bernstein* finally rose from his place to the right of Kautsky, the man who, like Kautsky, has faithfully preserved and administered the enormous intellectual heritage of Marx and Engels throughout his life, that the celebration acquired its peculiar, deeper significance. . . . The words that Bernstein uttered were words of friendship. Adler once quoted, in a different context, the saying that *what divides people* is insignificant beside the *multitude of factors which unite them*. For Kautsky and Bernstein, this saying took on a new and special meaning. When Bernstein had finished speaking and the two veterans, already legendary figures in the eyes of a young third generation – embraced and held each other for several seconds, it was impossible not to be deeply moved. Indeed, who would have wished it otherwise?'

Kautsky himself does not dispute such harmony with Bernstein. On his attitude to the World War he writes: 'I was very close to Bernstein at that time. It was in the war that we rediscovered each other. Both of us maintained our theoretical individuality, but in our practice we were now almost invariably at one with each other. And so we have remained ever

---

1. This review appeared in *Die Internationale*, VII/21–22, 1924 (ed.). The essays in honour of Kautsky appeared as follows: *Die Gesellschaft*, Special number with contributions by Max Adler, Boudin, Chernov, Bernstein, Stampfer; *Der Kampf*, XVII, 10–11, Special number with contributions by Ellenbogen, Helene Bauer, Friedrich Adler, Abramovich, Bracke, Hillquit; *Der lebendige Marxismus*, Jubilee issue in honour of Karl Kautsky's 70th birthday (Jena); *Die Volkswirtschaftslehre der Gegenwart in Selbstdarstellungen* ('Self-portraits by Economic Theorists of the Present'), vol. I, articles by Bernstein, Diehl, Herkner, Kautsky, Liefmann, Pesch, Julius Wolf (Leipzig) (G.L.'s note).

since' (*Self-portraits*, p. 26). These words indicate the spirit in which the Kautsky jubilee took place. While the struggles concerning Marxist 'orthodoxy' which occupied Kautsky's early period and culminated in the Bernstein debate are fading increasingly into the past as an insignificant episode, those disputes which he waged after the first Russian revolution – initially with Rosa Luxemburg, Pannekoek and others, later with Lenin and Trotsky – are developing into the central concerns of his life's work.

Hence it is no coincidence that appreciation of Kautsky should be based chiefly on his latest sizeable work, *The Proletarian Revolution and its Programme*, a book in which all his reformist tendencies manifest themselves clearly in the guise of a new 'theory of revolution'. Karl Kautsky is acclaimed by all reformists as *the great theoretician* of revolution. And rightly so. For their sabotaging of revolution, their *fear* of revolution, their frantic efforts to *prevent* revolution – all this has found its clearest theoretical expression in the life's work of Karl Kautsky.

Precisely therein lies Bernstein's triumph. The isolated 'differences of opinion' have in any case long since been forgotten. The really crucial question even then was whether, in the period leading up to the decisive power struggles between bourgeoisie and proletariat, social democracy would become the leader of the revolutionary class, or whether it would hurry to help the bourgeoisie to survive this, the severest crisis in its history. Bernstein expressed his preference for the latter course in a premature, overly frank and tactically clumsy fashion. Had his arguments been *really* discussed and their consequences properly and thoroughly analysed, the Social Democrats would inevitably have been split. This would have left the bourgeoisie facing a party which, though numerically weakened, took a clear and determined revolutionary line. It was Karl Kautsky's historic mission in that situation to thwart the clarification of such problems, to prevent the development of any such tension, and to preserve at any price the unity of the SPD (and with it that of the Second International). He has fulfilled this mission faithfully. Instead of calling openly for the liquidation of the revolutionary theory of Marxism, as Bernstein did, Kautsky argued for a 'development', a 'concretization' of the Marxist theory of revolution. This new approach, while apparently rejecting Bernsteinian reformism, in fact provided the theoretical underpinning for precisely what is *central* to Bernstein's conception of history, namely the notion of *peacefully evolutionary progression towards socialism*. L. Boudin has summarized this vocation of Kautsky's quite clearly: 'Not until the smoke of battle (the allusion is to the Bernstein debate. G.L.)

had cleared somewhat and *this* battle had been practically won could Marx's great successor – Karl Kautsky – write the series of masterpieces which for the first time explained Marxist theory as an evolutionary conception of the coming social revolution' (*Die Gesellschaft*, p. 44). Z. Ronais puts it in similar terms: 'In Kautsky's struggle with reformism, where the theoretician proved to be better at *Realpolitik* than the short-sighted, merely practical, day-to-day politicians, history has decided in Kautsky's favour' (*Der Kampf*, p. 423). In *The Proletarian Revolution and its Programme*, which his admirers have consequently and quite rightly hailed as his greatest achievement, Kautsky expresses this equivocal and ambiguous theory with the utmost possible clarity. He claims that he is not intent on liquidating the revolution. Quite the reverse, in fact: he attempts to grasp its essence, the essence of the proletarian revolution, quite clearly, and to protect the proletarian revolution from any possibility of being confused with the bourgeois revolution. But it is precisely this 'pure' proletarian revolution which, in Kautsky's exposition, acquires a form which objectively is such as to make it essentially equivalent to Bernstein's notion of peaceful progression towards socialism.

For this revolution takes place within democracy. And the significance of democracy is precisely 'that it brings the greatness of this power (of the proletariat, G.L.) clearly to light while obviating the need for a confrontation of armed forces' (*The Proletarian Revolution and its Programme*, p. 82). The advantage of this kind of revolution over the bourgeois variety is precisely that a counter-blow, a counter-revolution does not usually follow it (ibid., p. 96) – provided, of course, that the principle of 'pushing the revolution forward' (ibid., pp. 85–94) which Rosa Luxemburg erroneously took over from the bourgeois revolution is not applied. Under such circumstances, clearly, to talk of democracy as being a 'dictatorship of the bourgeoisie' is to employ 'one of the most ludicrous slogans produced in modern times' (ibid., p. 112). And so on.

It is not our intention at this point to write a critique of Kautsky's theory of revolution, the crowning thesis of which is the notorious notion of the coalition government as a transitional form between capitalism and socialism. We have been concerned only to demonstrate the method with which Kautsky 'transcended' Bernstein's fundamental tendencies – the struggle against dialectics in the theoretical domain and against 'Blanquism' in the practice of the working-class movement. On the one hand he seemed to refute them, but on the other he turned their objective content into a permanent element of the theory and practice of the SPD.

Bernstein was naïve enough to imagine that it was possible to turn a continental workers' party quite openly into an ally of the bourgeoisie, that it was possible to talk a continental working class into believing that the age of peaceful democracy had arrived. Where Kautsky scores over Bernstein is in his apparent recognition of the revolutionary moments in the world situation, although, of course, he puts a theoretical construction on this recognition which – unintentionally – leads to the same ultimate consequences *in practice* as Bernstein's approach. For instance, Kautsky sees quite clearly that democratic means are useful only *within* democracy, and that the struggle *for* democracy has to be waged with other means (op. cit., p. 82). But since, on the one hand, he does not concretize what these 'other' means should be, and since, on the other, he is concerned to attune the proletariat exclusively to the notion of the peaceful 'proletarian' revolution, he arrives *in practice* at the same results as he would have done if he had decided to apply the democratic means exclusively and in all situations. With the difference, however, that he has meanwhile succeeded in diverting workers, who though instinctively revolutionary, do not yet think clearly, from the real problem: the power struggle between bourgeoisie and proletariat. It is this diversionary strategy: this *deliberate attempt to prevent a clear and correct split* between revolutionaries and reformists in the workers' party, or – when a split has already become inevitable – the engineering of *a false split* – it is this which constitutes the historic mission of Karl Kautsky as the theoretical leader of the Centrists in the Second International. The Serbian, Topalovich, in a very characteristic essay, explains the necessity of this sort of diversionary theory for reformism. He agrees with Kautsky that in Western countries 'only a modified form of class hegemony, but not a dictatorship, is possible' (*Der Kampf,* p. 419). But 'in Eastern Europe, in contrast to the West, the power of capitalism has increased, whereas the power and class situation of the proletariat has remained unchanged. Which is why the proletariat in the East does not grasp the new constructive rise to power of the rejuvenated West European proletariat. This blindness to the necessity of such development and its various stages drives it to look towards anarchism as a salvation for revolutionary socialism' (ibid.). He goes on to emit a sigh of nostalgia for 'Vienna', for the late lamented Two-and-a-half International.[2] 'Those Western comrades who perhaps find these con-

2. The International Union of Socialist Parties, usually referred to as the Vienna Union or the Two-and-a-half International, was founded at a conference held in Vienna from 22 to 27 February 1921. The impetus leading to its foundation had come from the

siderations petty should bear in mind that we have to do battle, not merely with our immature bourgeoisie, but also and especially with an immature working class, which is more susceptible than its Western counterpart to those forms of demagogy which appeal to the basest instincts' (ibid., p. 421).

This antithesis between 'east' and 'west' is by no means a merely *geographical* distinction (although Kautsky himself also represented it in this way; cf. the remarks in his piece on Liebknecht-Luxemburg-Jogiches about the 'English' and 'Russian' types of working-class movements). Even in the West it can happen that the proletariat is not sufficiently 'schooled' to be able to realize properly the Kautskyan ideal of the pure proletarian revolution, where the struggles to gain political power (as Kautsky sees it!) are waged 'by great organizations which have existed for decades, rich in experiences, fully schooled, with carefully thought-out programmes, and leaders who are as renowned as they are experienced' (*The Proletarian Revolution and its Programme*, p. 77). In those cases where a conflict does arise in this respect, Kautsky exploits this self-same antithesis *tactically* or *historically*. Tactically, for instance, in the debate with Rosa Luxemburg on the question of the mass strike. Unlike the unsubtle and outspoken trade union leaders he did not directly oppose the mass strike movement, nor did he reject the mass strike out of hand; he merely offered a 'strategy of attrition' as an alternative to what he called the 'strategy of violent overthrow' propagated by Rosa Luxemburg (*Neue Zeit*, XXVIII, 2). The most fatal historical consequences of this approach manifested themselves at the decisive moments of the World War, in the theory according to which imperialism is *not* a necessary stage of capitalist development but a more or less 'chance' episode of development as a whole. Consequently, this theory maintains, it is as mistaken to fight

---

Swiss Socialist Party and the English Independent Labour Party. It claimed a following of 10 million members and included, in addition to those mentioned, the Austrian and French Socialist Parties, the right wing of the German Independent Socialist Party (the left having merged with the Communist Party), the Russian Mensheviks and a number of smaller groups, who had left the Second International, but were reluctant to join the Third. However, after The Hague conference of December 1922, the Second International and the Vienna Union agreed on fusion. The Tactical Theses of the Third Congress of the Third International claimed that the Two-and-a-half International was 'trying to hover between democracy and proletarian dictatorship. In fact it is helping the capitalist class in every country by encouraging a spirit of irresolution among the working class' (Degras, op. cit., pp. 209–10 and 256) (Editor's note).

imperialism from a revolutionary position (Luxemburg-Lenin) as it is to support it (Cunow-Lensch). The fight should be for peace, for the establishment of the *normal* preconditions of the proletarian revolution. Even today, ten years after the outbreak of the war, Helene Bauer – who has learnt nothing from history – is still preaching the same gospel according to Kautsky. 'It is not imperialistic war as a salvation from total collapse, but much rather monopolistic domination of the world by what Kautsky calls international "ultra-imperialism" and Hilferding a "general cartel", which is latent in the imminent economic tendencies of capital. But of course it can also be forced in the direction of war through the power of the pre-capitalist factors . . .' (*Der Kampf*, p. 389). The inevitable practical consequence of this perspective is that those sections of the proletariat which are instinctively too revolutionary to give their support to Cunow and company but are not able to grasp the situation properly and draw the correct conclusions, turn into an 'appendage' of western democracy. The one-sided emphasis on German-Austrian war 'guilt' also serves this two-fold purpose: diversion from the real revolutionary central issue (imperialism and civil war) on the one hand, blind allegiance to 'western democracy' on the other (cf. Friedrich Adler's essay in *Der Kampf*). No, it is certainly no coincidence that Bernstein and Kautsky came together in the World War and that they have remained 'almost invariably at one with each other ever since'.

This is why, in my view, Kautsky is historically important. Lenin's greatness consisted in consciously shaping the unity of the revolutionary proletarian movement from a consistently *revolutionary standpoint*, removing those elements antagonistic to the revolution and seeking an alliance with all objectively revolutionary forces. Kautsky, on the other hand, has been utterly consistent in attempting at all times *to blur theoretically the decisive problems of revolution*; he was never prepared to sacrifice organizational unity with the reformists for a single moment, and he was always willing to pay any price to preserve that unity. Hence, even as early as the first split in the Russian party he *was bound* to support Martov against Lenin. The jubilee issue of *Der Kampf* has published a very typical letter of his on precisely this question. He writes: 'Should every party member be forced to join the secret organization? Or, to put it another way, should the scope of the party be limited to match that of the secret organization? German Social Democracy was faced with the same question at the time of the Emergency Law; its answer was no. It does not serve our cause to admit to the party only those elements capable of organizing themselves secretly. Nor does it serve our cause to take all those who support it into the secret organization. A secret organization should not grow beyond certain minimal limits if it is to remain viable and undetected. We have no cause to expand it beyond those limits (at a given place), and they are determined by practical considerations. The expansion of the party, on the other hand, should know no limits' (p. 471). This passage illustrates Kautsky's basic idea only too clearly. His prefatory remarks to the effect that he has 'never been an organizer in the practical sense' and therefore is 'none too competent' in this matter merely reinforces our view: namely, that Kautsky sees the question of organization purely from a *technical-cum-mechanical* point of view. Just as he conceives of the bourgeois revolution as 'purely elemental' and the proletarian revolution as 'organized' (in the sense of a rigid organization of big-wigs); just as he never seriously examines the *dialectical interrelationship* between elementality and organization (i.e. in the final analysis: between class and party); so, too, he regards the entire historical process. He, the 'orthodox' pupil of Marx, consciously rejects the very crux of the Marxist method: the inner, dialectical connection between all '*spheres*' or '*fields*' which, viewed in the reified terms of bourgeois thinking, necessarily appear as separate and independent of one another. (The most typical example of this is the rigid separation of economics and politics in *The Proletarian Revolution and its Programme*.) However, it is precisely this turning away from dialectics (again, a triumph for Bernstein!) which enables him to fulfil his historic mission. Which is: to cling to the *entire vocabulary* of the Marxist method and yet to derive conclusions from it which amount *objectively* to the elimination of the class struggle and to the cooperation between bourgeoisie and proletariat. Objectively, then, it was Bernstein who was victorious in the struggle between Kautsky and himself. But his triumph was possible only in the *form* of victory for Kautsky. Only *Kautsky's theory* could manage to transform the substance of Bernstein's reformism into the theory of a large part of the working class.

The most valuable thing about these laudatory pieces is that they bring this connection very clearly – albeit unintentionally – into the open. They enable every thinking worker to appreciate how correct Lenin was to see in the Centrists and in their theoretician, Kautsky, the most dangerous enemies of the revolutionary proletariat, and how correct he was to fight them. Apart from that, they consist – with very few exceptions – of more or less diligent examinations of single issues or short articles on Gandhi, Freud, Spann and other topics of 'current interest'.

N. Bukharin : Historical Materialism[1]

Bukharin's new work serves the long-felt need for a systematic Marxist summary of historical materialism. Nothing of this kind has been attempted within Marxism since Engels's *Anti-Dühring* (except for Plekhanov's small volume). Summaries of the theory have been left to the opponents of Marxism, who have generally only understood it very superficially. Therefore Bukharin's attempt is to be welcomed even though its methods and results must be criticized. It should be said that Bukharin has succeeded in drawing together into a unified, systematic summary that is more or less Marxist all the significant problems of Marxism; and further, that the presentation is generally clear and easily understood, so that the book admirably fulfils its purpose as a *textbook*.

As Bukharin's aim is only to produce a popular textbook, the critic must be indulgent towards particular statements especially in rather obscure areas. This, and the difficulty of obtaining the relevant literature in Russia, also excuses the fact that in his handling of art, literature and philosophy, Bukharin draws almost completely on secondary sources, ignoring most recent research. But this intensifies Bukharin's risk of *simplifying the problems themselves* in the effort to write a popular textbook. His presentation is brilliant and clear, but at the same time it obscures many relations rather than explains them. But we must never accept a simplified presentation that simplifies the problems and solutions themselves, rather than the historical constellations of problems and solutions, especially as Bukharin's tendency to simplification is not confined to marginal ideological creations, but encroaches on central questions. For example, Bukharin sets out a precise parallel between the hierarchy of power in the structure of economic production on the one hand and that of the State on the other (pp. 168–70). He closes with the remark: 'Thus we see here that the structure of the state apparatus reflects that of the

1. This review of Bukharin's *Theorie des historischen Materialismus. Gemeinverständliches Lehrbuch der marxistischen Soziologie*, Hamburg, 1922 (English translation, *Historical Materialism. A System of Sociology*, London, 1926), appeared in *Archiv für die Geschichte des Sozialismus und der Arbeiterbewegung*, vol. XI, 1925; page references are to the original edition. This translation, by Ben Brewster, was first published in *New Left Review*, no. 39, September/October, 1966 (Editor's note).

economy – i.e. *the same classes* occupy the same positions in both.' This is undoubtedly correct as a developmental tendency. It is also true that a long-run, major contradiction between the two hierarchies usually leads to a revolutionary upheaval. But concrete history will not fit into Bukharin's over-schematic, simplified formula. For it is perfectly possible that a balance of economic power between two classes in competition may produce a state apparatus not really controlled by either (if it must secure many compromises between them) so that the economic structure is by no means simply reflected in the State. This is true for example of the absolute monarchies at the beginning of the modern era. A class may even reach economic power without being in a position to mould the state apparatus completely to its own interests, or to stamp it with its class character. Mehring has convincingly demonstrated that the German bourgeoisie was so afraid of proletarian assistance in its bourgeois revolution that, even in the energetic struggle for bourgeois reforms at the time of its most rapid economic advance, it left the Junkers' state apparatus alone and quietly accepted the survival of its feudal-absolutist power structure. Of course, a textbook cannot be expected to deal with these questions in depth. But the absence even of a hint of the importance of such exceptions to the model makes Bukharin's presentation somewhat suspect. Plekhanov and Mehring have frequently demonstrated in more specialized works how a popular presentation is compatible with a basically scientific approach. Bukharin has accepted the timely and important task of summarizing all the problems of Marxism; but in many respects he does not attain the standard reached by Plekhanov and Mehring.

But we must not confine ourselves to details. More important than such oversights, Bukharin deviates from the true tradition of historical materialism in several not inessential points, without thereby proving his points or improving on the highest level reached by his predecessors; indeed, he hardly even reaches that level. (It goes without saying that we consider his achievement, remarkable even in its errors, to partake of the best tradition of Marxism; popularizers rarely deal with such matters.) This remark applies particularly to the introductory philosophical chapter, where Bukharin is suspiciously close to what Marx aptly called bourgeois materialism. Bukharin apparently does not know of the critique of this theory by Mehring and Plekhanov, not to mention Marx and Engels themselves, which sharply restricts its validity for an understanding of the historical process because of the particular place of history in historical, dialectical materialism. When every 'idealist' from Bernstein to Cunow has inverted this real centre of Marxism, it is understandable and, in the last analysis, healthy, that there should be a reaction. But in his philosophical remarks, Bukharin rejects all the elements in Marxist method which derive from classical German philosophy, without realizing the inconsistency this involves. Of course, Hegel is mentioned from time to time, but the essential comparison of his and Marx's dialectic is absent. Characteristically, the only reference to Feuerbach is to note that with him 'matter came to the fore'; 'his influence on Marx and Engels assisted the development of the true theory of dialectical materialism' (p. 56). He completely ignores the problem of the relation between Feuerbach's humanism and the Marxist dialectic.

This point has been particularly stressed because it clearly reveals the essential error in Bukharin's conception of historical materialism. The closeness of Bukharin's theory to bourgeois, natural-scientific materialism derives from his use of 'science' (in the French sense) as a model. In its concrete application to society and history it therefore frequently obscures the specific feature of Marxism: that *all economic or 'sociological' phenomena derive from the social relations of men to one another*. Emphasis on a false 'objectivity' in theory leads to fetishism.

The discussion of the role of technique in social development highlights these remnants of undissolved quiddity (*unaufgelöster Dinghaftigkeit*) and false 'objectivity'. Bukharin attributes to technology a far too determinant position, which completely misses the *spirit* of dialectical materialism. (It is undeniable that quotations from Marx and Engels can be found which *it is possible* to interpret in this way.) Bukharin remarks: 'Every given system of social technique *determines*[2] human work relations as well' (p. 150). He attributes the predominance of a natural economy in classical times to the low level of technical development (p. 158). He insists: 'If technique changes, the division of labour in society also changes' (p. 164). He asserts (p. 206) that 'in the last analysis' society is dependent on the development of technique, which is seen as the 'basic determinacy' of the 'productive forces of society', etc. It is obvious that this final identification of technique with the forces of production is neither valid nor Marxist. Technique is a *part*, a moment, naturally of great importance, of the social productive forces, but it is neither simply identical with them, nor (as some of Bukharin's earlier points would seem to imply) the final or absolute moment of the changes in these forces. This attempt to find the underlying determinants of society and its development in a principle

2. G.L.'s italics.

other than that of the social relations between men in the process of production (and thence of distribution, consumption, etc.) – that is in the economic structure of society correctly conceived – leads to fetishism, as Bukharin himself elsewhere admits. For example, he criticizes Cunow's idea (p. 132) that technique is bound to natural conditions, that the presence of a certain raw material is decisive for the presence of a certain technique, on the grounds that Cunow confuses raw materials and the subject of labour, forgetting 'that there must be a *corresponding technique* for which wood, ore, fibres, etc., can perform the role of raw materials. . . . The influence of nature in the sense of material requisites is itself a product of the development of technique' (pp. 132–3). But should we not apply this valid criticism to technique itself? Is the conclusion that the development of society depends on technique not just as much a false 'naturalism' as Cunow's theory, just as much a somewhat refined version of the 'environmental' theories of the 18th and 19th centuries? Naturally, Bukharin avoids the crude error of this 'naturalism': the attempt to explain change by a fixed principle (p. 133). For technique indeed changes in the course of social development. His explanation of change is thus correct from the point of view of formal logic, in that it explains change by a variable moment. But technique as the self-sufficient basis of development is only a dynamic refinement of this crude naturalism. For if technique is not conceived as a *moment* of the existing system of production, if its development is not explained by the development of the *social* forces of production (rather than the other way round), it is just as much a transcendent principle, set over against man, as 'nature', climate, environment, raw materials, etc. Nobody doubts that at every determinate stage of the development of the productive forces, which determine the development of technique, technique retroactively influences the productive forces. Bukharin emphasizes this in reference to all ideology (Engels's later theoretical insights are relevant here); but it is altogether incorrect and unmarxist to separate technique from the other ideological forms and to propose for it a self-sufficiency from the economic structure of society.

This is a serious error, for if technique is seen as even only mediately determinate for society, the remarkable changes in the course of its development are completely unexplained. Take for example the difference between classical and medieval technique. However primitive medieval technique may have been in performance, however much it may have represented a retreat from the well-known technical achievements of antiquity, medieval technique's principle was development on a higher level: i.e. the rationalization of the *organization* of labour as compared with classical society. Labour performance remained un-rationalized, and the rationalization of the organization of labour was achieved rather through the 'door of social violence'[3] than through the development of technical rationality. But this laid the basis for the possibility of modern techniques, as Gottl has clearly demonstrated for the water-mill, mines, firearms, etc. This crucial *change in the direction* of technical development was based on a change in the economic structure of society: the change in labour potentialities and conditions. One of the essential co-determinate causes of the breakdown of classical society was, of course, its inability to support the social basis of its productive organization: the wasteful exploitation of inexhaustible slave material. The Middle Ages laid the general basis of the new form of social organiza-tion necessary. Max Weber[4] has convincingly demonstrated that the coexistence of slaves and freemen in antiquity hindered the development of guilds and hence of the modern state – another contrast between the Orient or Antiquity, and modern society. Medieval social organization arose in quite opposite circumstances (shortage of labour, etc.) which then determined the essential course of technical development. So when Bukharin asserts (p. 153) that 'a new technique made slave labour impossible; as slaves ruin complex machinery slave labour no longer pays', he turns the causal relation on its head. Slavery is not made possible by a low level of technique; rather slavery as a form of the domination of labour makes the rationalization of the labour process, and hence a rational technique, impossible. Little work has yet been done on slavery as a relatively isolated enclave in a world economy based on wage labour, so we know little about the modifications it introduces.[5]

This inverted relationship appears even more clearly if we turn to the transition from medieval production to modern capitalism. Marx explicitly stresses that the transition from guild handwork to manu-factures involved no change in technique: 'With regard to the mode of production itself, manufacture in its strict meaning is hardly to be dis-

3. *Gottl, Wirtschaft und Technik. Grundriss der Sozialökonomik*, vol. II, pp. 236–9 (G.L.'s note).

4. *Wirtschaft und Gesellschaft. Grundriss der Sozialökonomik*, vol. III, pp. 584–5 (G.L.'s note).

5. See, however, Marx's notes on slavery in the Southern States of the USA where the purely technical aspect is seen only as a moment of the overall socio-economic process (*The Poverty of Philosophy*, op. cit., pp. 124–5) (G.L.'s note).

tinguished, in its earliest stages, from the handicraft trades of the guilds, otherwise than by the greater number of workmen simultaneously employed by one and the same individual capital. The workshop of the medieval master handicraftsman is simply enlarged. At first, therefore, the difference is purely quantitative.'[6] It is the capitalist division of labour and its power relations which give rise to the social preconditions for a mass market (dissolution of the natural economy), which produces a qualitative change. The *social* preconditions of modern mechanized techniques thus arose first; they were the *product* of a centuries-long social revolution. The technique is the consummation of modern capitalism, not its initial cause. It only appeared after the establishment of its social prerequisites; when the dialectical contradictions of the primitive forms of manufacture had been resolved, when 'at a given stage of its development, the narrow technical base on which manufacture rested came into conflict with requirements of production that were created by manufacture itself'.[7] It goes without saying that technical development is thereby extraordinarily accelerated. But this *reciprocal interaction* by no means surpasses the real historical and methodological primacy of the economy over technique. Thus Marx points out: 'This total economy, arising as it does from the concentration of means of production and their use *en masse* ... originates quite as much from the social nature of labour, just as surplus-value originates from the surplus-labour of the individual considered singly.'[8]

We have considered this question in some detail because of its *methodological* importance. This importance does not only derive from the central position it has for Marxism, but also from the fact that Bukharin's solution is typical of his false methodology. We have already referred to his attempt to make a 'science' out of the dialectic. The externalization of this tendency in scientific theory is his conception of Marxism as a 'general sociology' (pp. 7–8). His leanings towards the natural sciences and his frequently acute dialectical instinct are here inevitably in contradiction. Engels reduced the dialectic to 'the science of the general laws of motion, both of the external world and of human thought'.[9] Bukharin's theory of sociology as a 'historical method' is in conformity with this view. But, as a necessary consequence of his natural-scientific approach,

6. *Capital*, vol. I, p. 322 (G.L.'s note).
7. ibid., p. 368 (G.L.'s note).
8. ibid., vol. III, p. 79 (G.L.'s note).
9. Marx/Engels, *Selected Works*, vol. II, p. 387 (G.L.'s note).

sociology cannot be restricted to a pure method, but develops into an independent science with its own substantive goals. The dialectic can do without such independent substantive achievements; its realm is that of the historical process as a whole, whose individual, concrete, unrepeatable moments reveal its dialectical essence precisely in the qualitative differences between them and in the continuous transformation of their objective structure. The *totality* is the territory of the dialectic. A 'scientific' general sociology, on the other hand, if it does not surpass itself into a mere epistemology, must have its own independent substantive achievements allowing only one type of law. Bukharin wavers between various conclusions. On the one hand he realizes that there is clearly no such thing as society 'in general' (p. 270), but he does not see what necessarily follows from this, as his theory (his applications of his theory are often much better than the theory itself) sees historical variation merely as a 'determinate historical *shell*',[10] a 'uniform' (ibid.). On the other hand, his attempt to establish a distinction between 'theory' and 'method' makes sociology a unified science – inevitably, given the confused posing of the question. The basically incorrect theory of the primacy of technique which we have analysed is merely the substantive result of Bukharin's attempt to create a general sociology. It is not an accidental oversight, but the necessary consequence of superficially examined premises.

This confusion emerges particularly clearly in Bukharin's conception of a scientific law. It is fortunate that he usually forgets his theoretical presuppositions in his concrete analyses. For example, he derives a general type of law for equilibrium and its disturbance in determinate systems, whether these belong to inorganic or organic nature, or to society (pp. 73–81). Marx and Hegel are thereby linked in a fairly inorganic way. But in spite of this theoretical position, Bukharin admits that these relationships 'can only be applied to complex systems such as human society *at best as analogies*.'[11] Thus he fortunately forgets his theory in concrete analyses, with the result that his conclusions are frequently very interesting in defiance of his starting-point. His attacks on the various 'organic' social theories, and so on, often lead to remarkable critical comparisons (e.g. pp. 31ff.).

But his preoccupation with the natural sciences is crudest where he examines the *theoretical purpose* of sociology. 'Everything we have said indicates that prediction is possible in the social sciences *just as it is in*

10. G.L.'s italics.
11. G.L.'s italics.

the natural sciences.[12] At the moment we are unable to predict the point in time when this or that phenomenon will appear. . . . This is because we are still not sufficiently informed of the laws of social development to be able to express them in statistical terms. We cannot tell the *speed* of social processes, but we know their *direction*' (pp. 44–5). Bukharin's bias towards the natural sciences has made him forget that our knowledge of directions or tendencies rather than statistical predictions is not a result of the difference between what we actually know and what there is to be known, but *of the objective, qualitative difference in the object itself.* Marx and Engels knew this perfectly well. I only need refer in passing to Engels's intelligent and thoughtful methodological remarks on the impossibility of understanding the immediate present through statistics.[13] Marx, of course, in his equally basic theory of the average rate of profit, drew a sharp methodological distinction between certain statistical facts and the social tendencies of the process as a whole. 'As concerns the perpetually fluctuating market rate of interest, however, it exists at any moment as a fixed magnitude, just as the market price of commodities. . . . On the other hand, the general rate of profit never *exists* as anything more than a tendency.'[14] Lenin himself repeatedly stressed this notion of the tendency of development, whose tendential character is not the result of our ignorance, but is based on the type of objectivity of social events whose structure also, on the other hand, founds the theoretical possibility of social relations and the reality of 'revolutionary praxis'. In his critique of the *Juniusbrochüre*[15] Lenin stressed the unmarxist character of the thesis that national wars are impossible in the era of imperialism. He argues that, though they may be very unlikely, an analysis of developmental tendencies cannot absolutely exclude their possibility. *A fortiori*, it is methodologically impossible to know the timing of any historical event. In his speech to the Second Congress of the Communist International on the international struggle he gave even more emphasis to this methodological impossibility: 'Here we must first of all note two widespread errors. . . . Revolutionaries sometimes try to prove that there is absolutely no way out of the crisis. This is a mistake. There is no such thing as an absolutely hopeless situation. . . . To try to "prove" in advance that there

12. G.L.'s italics.

13. In the introduction to Marx's *Class Struggles in France* (*Selected Works*, vol. I, p. 119) (G.L.'s note).

14. *Capital*, vol. III, p. 359 (G.L.'s note).

15. 'Against the Stream', in *Collected Works*, vol. 22, pp. 305ff. (G.L.'s note).

is "absolutely" no way out of the situation would be sheer pedantry, or playing with concepts and catchwords. Practice alone can serve as real "proof" in this and similar questions.'[16]

Marx, Engels and Lenin are not just quoted here as authorities. Our purpose is to point out that Bukharin's theoretical aim is different from that of the great tradition of historical materialism, which descends from Marx and Engels through Mehring and Plekhanov to Lenin and Rosa Luxemburg (it is, incidentally, unfortunate, but methodologically consistent, that Bukharin hardly refers to Rosa Luxemburg's essential economic theses at all). A really thorough discussion of this theoretical aim would exceed the space of a review. It would have to show how Bukharin's basic philosophy is completely in harmony with contemplative materialism; that instead of making a historical-materialist critique of the natural sciences and their methods, i.e. revealing them as products of capitalist development, he extends these methods to the study of society without hesitation, uncritically, unhistorically and undialectically. But although Plekhanov's work on Holbach, Helvétius and Hegel has provided some of the groundwork for such a critique, it has not yet been attempted, so we can only note those *consequences* of Bukharin's conception which confuse his concrete sociological results and lead them into dead ends.

This short criticism cannot consider many details of the book. It has been limited to demonstration of the methodological source of the errors. It should be stressed that these errors remain in spite of Bukharin's worthy goal of systematically organizing into a popular form all the results of Marxism. Perhaps we may express the hope that in later editions many of these errors will be corrected, so that the whole work may achieve the level of its – many – excellent sections.

16. *Collected Works*, vol. 31, pp. 226–7 (G.L.'s note).

Karl August Wittfogel:
The Science of Bourgeois Society[1]

The value and merit of this book lie more in the problems it raises than in the positive answers which it offers. The attempt to subject contemporary scientific activity to a Marxist analysis and critique is both important and timely. Equally important and timely is the attempt to indicate, on the basis of that analysis, the directions in which the hierarchy and organization of scientific life will – probably – move in the course of the proletarian revolution. But Wittfogel's[2] book – and this we must concede straightaway – does more than merely pose this initial question: in many detailed respects its correct and subtle analysis goes right to the heart of the matter. For example, his sociology of the trend towards popularizing in the various fields of learning rightly traces it back to the class interests of the bourgeoisie. Further, he makes the telling point that the lack of hierarchy, structure and organizational coherence prevents bourgeois scientific activity – particularly the humanities – from achieving even the level which the bourgeois class itself would regard as possible and attainable.

However, since Wittfogel's book is the first attempt to formulate this kind of critique and summary, it seems more essential to me to indicate its *methodological* faults and ambiguities, thereby taking up and developing most fruitfully the discussion generated by its publication. The book's basic weakness derives, in my view, from the fact that its author has neither thought nor argued through consistently his critical attitude towards

1. Malik Verlag, Berlin, 1922. This review of *Die Wissenschaft der bürgerlichen Gesellschaft* first appeared in *Archiv für die Geschichte des Sozialismus und der Arbeiterbewegung*, vol. XI, 1925 (Editor's note).

2. Karl August Wittfogel, born 1896 near Hanover. Studied philosophy, history and philology, 1928, took his doctorate at Frankfurt. 1925–33, worked at the Frankfurt Institute for Social Research. He published articles in the Institute's own journal and also in other left-wing publications, including *Die rote Fahne*, *Die Internationale* and *Die kommunistische Internationale*. Member of the German Communist Party, 1930–2, wrote a series of important theoretical articles on literature and Marxism for the magazine *Die Linkskurve*, 1934, emigrated to the USA and was naturalized in 1941. Became an expert on Chinese affairs (he had visited China first in 1932 at the instigation of the Marxist Workers' School in Berlin). From 1934 onwards he pursued an academic career specializing in Chinese history at Columbia and in New York (Editor's note).

bourgeois science and scientific activity. For instance, he claims repeatedly that the methodological standpoint of Avenarius and Mach represents the highest achievement of bourgeois science. This seems to me to be a highly questionable assertion, to say the least. But even if we were to admit that Wittfogel was right, he would still be faced with the task most relevant to his investigations: that of establishing clearly, convincingly and unambiguously the relation of such a standpoint to that of Marxism. This Wittfogel utterly fails to do, however. He operates with a concept of Marxism that is totally uncritical. Small wonder, then, that his comparisons frequently strike us as over-simplified, even distorted, and that they are bound to do violence to the very important complications which arise out of what are often extremely involved ideological problems. To give just one more characteristic example: in his discussion of Darwin, he terms him simply a 'social democrat of the natural sciences', without investigating more closely Darwin's by no means coincidental connections with the reactionary philosophy (Nietzschean variety) of the capitalism of the period. Similarly, what Wittfogel – on the basis of his Mach-Avenarius theories – seems all the time to be envisaging as an ideal is a kind of intellectual Taylorizing. This likewise ignores the fact that this entire school of thinking and its epistemological foundations are a product of capitalistic, class conditioning.

Which brings me back to my central objection to Wittfogel's book: namely that Wittfogel adopts a sociologically uncritical attitude towards the method of the natural sciences. True, he points out that the activities of the natural sciences, their research interests, the manner in which they are popularized, and so on, are very largely influenced by the interests of capitalism. But he does not touch at all upon the sociological problem of the connection between the rationalizing method of the natural sciences and the economic development of capitalism – something which even bourgeois investigators like Tönnies have already very clearly formulated. As a result, there is something erratic and – from a Marxist viewpoint – inconsistent about his whole approach. For the Marxist as a historical dialectician both *nature* and all the forms in which it is mastered in theory and practice are *social categories*; and to believe that one can detect anything supra-historical or supra-social in this context is to disqualify oneself as a Marxist.

In saying this, of course, we are at the same time postulating a more thorough-going analysis of the economic *structure* of society and its ideological consequences than Wittfogel himself has undertaken. Such an analysis must not stop at the – relatively – simple analogies with large factory and small factory, accumulation, etc.; rather, it must proceed from the methodologically fundamental chapters of Marxist theory, beginning with commodity fetishism, to discover the *structure* of the various sciences. This in turn makes it possible to ascertain the class-determined sociology of their formations and their methods. Only then would it be possible to elucidate the typical problems of modern bourgeois science, its 'formalism', the specificity of its 'division of labour' (the problems of the rigidly divided and, at most, eclectically combined 'individual sciences'), and so on, as concrete sociological problems. Wittfogel's failure to perceive this problematic is strikingly exemplified by his analysis of the individual humanities (*Geisteswissenschaften*): jurisprudence is not mentioned at all (and it is only in passing that he talks of the class character of legal practice). And that in spite of the fact that it is precisely the analysis of the genesis of modern juridical formalism, theories of state, natural law and so on, which would provide the best key to a sociological study of 'formalism' and 'specialization' as characteristics of bourgeois science.

Wittfogel, then, poses the question in a grossly over-simplified manner, and a further consequence is that his account makes it seem as if the entire ideological apparatus of the bourgeoisie were something homogeneous. This fails to account for two things: on the one hand, the fact that the modern ruling strata are objectively and in class terms heterogeneously constituted, and that this in itself very often gives rise to a penetrating and correct critique of bourgeois society. (It is sufficient here to allude to Sismondi's place in the history of economics.) On the other hand, there is the fact that the antagonism of the capitalist system of production, which is of course reflected in all its ideological expressions, very often forces bourgeois science to state the true situation clearly (Ricardo), and in some instances even drives it beyond the limits of bourgeois methodology (Hegel). And this does not only occur at the beginning of such developments. In the reactionary critique of natural law (Bergbohm), in isolated historical accounts (Delbrück's history of the war, and so on) – in these and many other cases it is possible to observe similar (albeit, on the part of the authors, obviously unconscious) tendencies.

But let us not get too bogged down in details. The essence of our objections to Wittfogel's book will by now be sufficiently clear to the reader: namely, that it fails to provide a really critical (really historical) and hence really concrete analysis of the phenomenon under discussion. In this respect, his work will and must be frequently corrected. But this of course does not prevent us from welcoming it warmly as a very commendable attempt to raise these questions at long last as problems, nor from expressing at the same time our warm appreciation of Wittfogel's excellent individual analyses and observations.

The New Edition of Lassalle's Letters[1]

With the conclusion of this monumental work – it is planned to run to five or six volumes – the entire material relating to Lassalle's development will at last be available. Even then, of course, it will not be in a readily usable form, except for those trained in academic, scientific work. Various factors, such as the conditions in the publishing world, the nature of contemporary scientific work, cost considerations, etc., will prevent the inclusion in this edition of material that has already appeared elsewhere (e.g. the correspondence with Heine). With the result that, even after publication of his entire posthumous writings, the material relating to Lassalle's development will still have to be culled from an enormous number of different sources (many of them scattered in newspapers and periodicals). The correspondence between Marx and Lassalle provides the only, but nonetheless very welcome exception: here Gustav Mayer has unearthed fresh material, thereby completing Mehring's edition (vol. IV of the posthumous edition),[2] and in some respects (especially in the dating of letters) correcting it. Consequently everything available has been published in context. This makes Mehring's edition of the letters redundant, although his excellent commentaries still retain their great value as aids in understanding the relations between Marx and Lassalle. It is to be hoped that these commentaries will soon be republished in what would be a most welcome collection of Mehring's essays.

1. First appeared in the *Archiv für die Geschichte des Sozialismus und der Arbeiterbewegung*, vol. XI, 1925 (Editor's note). The edition of letters under review is Ferdinand Lassalle, *Nachgelassene Briefe und Schriften*, ed. Gustav Mayer, vol. I – Letters to and from Lassalle up to 1848; vol. II – Lassalle's correspondence from the 1848 Revolution up to the start of his agitation on behalf of the workers; vol. III – Correspondence between Lassalle and Marx; vol. IV – Lassalle's correspondence with Gräfin Sophie von Hatzfeldt; Stuttgart/Berlin, 1921–3. (Two further volumes complete the edition: vol. V – Lassalle's correspondence from the years of his agitation on behalf of the workers, 1862–4; vol. VI – Posthumous writings and the correspondence with Karl Rodbertus – Stuttgart/Berlin, 1925 – ed.) This edition is referred to as Bf, the Marx–Engels correspondence as Bw, Wk refers to F. Lassalle, *Gesammelte Reden und Schriften*, ed. E. Bernstein, 12 vols, Berlin, 1919–20 (G.L.'s note).

2. Mehring's edition, *Aus dem literarischen Nachlass von Karl Marx, Friedrich Engels und Ferdinand Lassalle*, vol. IV: Letters from Ferdinand Lassalle to Karl Marx and Friedrich Engels, 1849–62, Stuttgart, 1902 (Editor's note).

The regret expressed above is not intended to imply even the slightest criticism of the present learned and conscientious editor, Gustav Mayer. After all, it is only thanks to his unceasing efforts that Lassalle's post-humous writings (or, at least, those which have not been irretrievably lost through vandalism and negligence[3] on the part of his family and Lothar Bucher) have become accessible at all. In his foreword to volume one, Mayer provides a very engaging account of how he salvaged the manuscript material, a story which ends on a thoroughly romantic note with his finally smuggling it out of the Hatzfeldt castle in Sommerberg during a brief interlude in the French occupation. But this is by no means all we have cause to be grateful to him for. Not only has he prepared the frequently intractable text in exemplary fashion; he has also succeeded by virtue of his short, precise and unfailingly pertinent notes, in bringing the personalities with whom Lassalle was connected into a clearer and more familiar light. More than that, his forewords to the individual volumes are as lucid as they are telling in their description of the back-ground to such relationships. Having already, it can be said, discovered the young Engels[4] for us, Mayer has now laid the foundations for a truly scientific understanding of Lassalle.

It is of course impossible in a review such as this even to attempt a scientific assessment of such basic work. Quite apart from the fact that it would not be feasible before the entire work has been published, a task of that nature will have to be the prerogative of a – Marxist – biography of Lassalle. We must limit ourselves here to a few allusive remarks, without claiming for a moment that they in themselves even outline the general scope of the problems under discussion.

Even given this limited frame of reference, however, it seems fairly clear that Mayer's work – just like his one on Engels – throws the youthful development of his subject into far sharper relief than was previously the case. I intend to pass over completely the very interesting personal prob-lems involved (the young Lassalle's friendships and love affairs) and refer simply to the problem which is crucial to his entire development: namely, his relationship with Hegel. Even on this matter, of course, we shall have to suspend any kind of definitive judgment until we have access to the manuscript (mentioned in Bf. 1, p. 37) entitled 'Grundzüge

3. See Mayer's introduction to Bf, 'On the History of Lassalle's Posthumous Writ-ings,' pp. 1ff. (Editor's note).

4. Cf. Gustav Mayer, *Friedrich Engels, Eine Biographie*, vol. I (with a supplementary vol.), 'The early Friedrich Engels, 1820–51', Berlin, 1920 (Editor's note).

zu einer Charakteristik der Gegenwart mit besonderer Berücksichtigung der Hegelschen Philosophie' ('Foundations for a characterization of the present, with special reference to Hegelian philosophy'), in which Lassalle also takes issue with Heine, and to the other philosophical fragments, notably the later *Philosophie des Geistes* ('Philosophy of Mind') mentioned in Bf. 1, p. 161.[5] However, volume one of the present edition already contains, among other things, two lengthy and detailed letters of Lassalle's (to his father, 9 September 1844, and to his friends, mid-September, 1845) which can perfectly well be regarded as treatises and which even at this early stage provide material for a study of the young Lassalle's relationship to Hegel.

And that is all the more important in that Lassalle in our view never ceased to be a Hegelian. The dominant feature of Marx's early development is his struggle with, and his inner conquest of, Hegel. This, in fact, is accomplished so thoroughly that Marx in later years never again takes up the matter in any detail, although there are occasional references to a plan to provide a short account of the usable kernel of Hegelian logic, and although the kernel of Hegelian philosophy 'sublated' by Marx in his thinking is both bigger and more important than the vulgar Marxists are wont to assume. Lassalle, on the other hand, remains an orthodox Hegelian throughout his life – as is shown, for example, by his late (and, of its kind, excellent) treatise on Rosenkranzian and Hegelian logic, and by the structure of his *System of Acquired Rights*. Not in a pedantic sense, of course; indeed, we could almost go as far as claiming – however paradoxical it may at first appear – that the relationship of the young Lassalle to Hegel is to some degree freer, both in detail and in general content, than that in which the young Marx finds himself before he finally settles accounts with the master. (The comparison, needless to say, has objectively nothing at all in common with the similar one made by F. A. Lange between the *mature* Lassalle and the *mature* Marx.) However, even this medal has its reverse side, in that Lassalle never comes to grips decisively with the idealistic dialectic. As far as we know, the young Lassalle conceives Hegelianism *immediately* as revolutionary. He does not see Hegelianism as the philosophical expression of bourgeois society, containing *for that very reason* within itself the elements of the dissolution, overcoming and supersession of that society; nor as entailing *for that very reason* the necessary liberation of those elements striving beyond the given system turning them against their author. No, Hegel appears to him as the

5. Both MSS were included in vol. VI of the edition under discussion (Editor's note).

discoverer of *the* method of thinking, thinking which if it is to be correct and scientific, can only be revolutionary thinking. This the young Lassalle naïvely and without any evidence simply takes for granted.

In other words, Lassalle is not concerned in the least with reforming Hegelian philosophy from within. His aim is merely to eliminate tacitly from Hegel's categories the meaning which underlies the philosophy of history elaborated by the master himself: reconciliation with bourgeois society, the culmination of the system in idealized bourgeois society Of course, even Hegel himself took this last step quite unconsciously. And since Lassalle does not criticize Hegel's premisses, he passes over the matter in silence – in striking contrast to Marx, who in this respect is the first to perceive the *historical conditionality* of classical German philosophy. But it is only thus that Hegel can be truly overcome in fact. Marx writes: 'The political state is as spiritual in relation to civil society as heaven is in relation to earth. It stands in the same opposition to civil society and goes beyond it in the same way as religion goes beyond the limitation of the profane world, that is, by necessarily recognizing, re-establishing, and allowing itself to be dominated by it.'[6]

These words are apparently nothing more than the application of Feuerbach's critique of religion to society. But only apparently. In reality they also entail the overcoming of Feuerbach's unhistorical standpoint: the concrete social condition now appears as the basis of the categories in which we express our particular conception of reality; the seed of Marx's theory of categories has already been planted – that theory which, in the foreword to the *Critique of Political Economy,* identifies categories as 'forms of existence, determinates of existence'.

The young Lassalle does not see this problem at all. For him, as for most of the radical young Hegelians of the time who were attempting to transform the dialectic into a philosophy of revolution, Fichte's activism is the tool which they can use for their projected revamping of Hegelian philosophy. True, the letters in this collection do not contain any documentary evidence that Fichtean philosophy did in fact play this role. But in this context, such evidence is not absolutely indispensable. In the first place, Lassalle's later development shows it was quite possible for Fichte and Hegel to coexist peacefully and harmoniously in his thinking. And the inner development of his thinking gives us no reason to assume that it was only in his later years that he recognized Fichte's significance and

6. *On the Jewish question,* in *Writings of the Young Marx on Philosophy and Society,* ed. L. D. Easton and K. H. Guddat, New York, 1967, p. 225 (Editor's note).

succumbed to his decisive influence. Secondly, we have to take into account the analogous development of his contemporaries – this, admittedly, is merely indirect evidence, but it is by no means insubstantial. Marx and Engels were the *only* exceptions to the general tendency, which saw the inner revolutionizing of the Hegelian dialectic being carried out through the active influence of Fichtean concepts. To what extent this should be seen as a general trend of the time; to what extent it is possible to provide documentary proof that Fichte actually influenced such thinkers (Moses Hess, say, or Bruno Bauer) directly; to what extent Hess or Bauer exerted this kind of influence on the young Lassalle: these are more philological questions than anything else. Unfortunately, the correspondence provides less evidence than we might expect. Bauer is not mentioned at all; nor is Marx. No new light is shed on the relationship with Feuerbach and Ruge. On the other hand, the young Lassalle's most intimate friend, Arnold Mendelssohn, mentions Weitling's *Garantien der Harmonie und Freiheit* ('Guarantees of Harmony and Freedom'; 13 July 1845, Bf. 1, pp. 189–90), and calls Hess's *Die letzten Philosophen* ('Recent Philosophers'; letter to Lassalle on 18 November 1845, Bf. 1, p. 245) 'a not unimportant pamphlet'. He also writes in glowing terms of Grün's *Die soziale Bewegung in Frankreich und Belgien* ('The Social Movement in France and Belgium') and quotes the passage concerning the Hegel studies of the French that Marx, in a review in *Neue Zeit* (XVIII/1, p. 8), makes particular fun of (29 October 1845, Bf. 1, pp. 240–1). Mendelssohn further alludes to Engels's *Condition of the Working Class in England* as 'a highly commendable, painstaking work', citing Engels in the same letter as, 'one of the fathers of the *Holy Family*' (4 November 1845, Bf. 1, p. 242). Since Lassalle's replies are missing, however, it is difficult to make anything of these clues. The fact that Grün is praised, however, does tend to indicate that in Lassallean circles even Hess's critique of Stein in the *21 Bogen*[7] was hardly known or its full import grasped, let alone the essays by Marx and Engels in the *Deutsch-Französische Jahrbücher*. All Lassalle's early letters demonstrate what Mendelssohn states explicitly (Bf. 1, p. 241): that Lassalle believed that in his version of the Hegelian dialectic he possessed the absolute means by which order could be created out of the chaos of those 'manifold forms of consciousness' thronging round 'the 'birthplace of the Lord, that is, the concept'. Hence, he considered himself exempt from the need to gain a proper understanding of dialectics and

7. Moses Hess, 'Socialism and Communism', in *21 Bogen aus der Schweiz*, ed. by Georg Herwegh, Pt I, Zürich/Winterthür, 1843 (Editor's note).

history, or to undertake a thorough critique of the various revolutionary theories. Perhaps the clearest illustration of this mixture of self-certainty and lack of thorough penetration into his material is his sketch of the development of communism, to be found in a letter to his father (Bf. 1, p. 132): 'It (communism) appears in its crudest form immediately after property has been represented as a prerequisite of state freedom, in the constitution of 1795; it develops further in 1796, in the shape of the conspiracy of Babeuf and his comrades; is elaborated into the socialist theories of Saint-Simon and Fourier, both of whom must be counted as communists by virtue of their basic thinking; turns into communism proper; divides once more into various sects such as the *travailleux égalitaires* and the *réformistes*; and finally emerges in its highest form so far, that of Icaric communism,[8] founded and represented by Cabet (even in this form, however, and in spite of its manifestly profound and true significance, it remains abstract and one-sided).'

Nevertheless, the importance of such philosophical problems diminishes if we bear in mind that this kind of reversion to Fichte was the only *objective philosophical possibility* of retaining the inner structure of the Hegelian dialectic and yet at the same time imparting a revolutionary accent – that is, directed towards action – to the philosophy of history. This is neither the time nor the place to discuss even in outline all the ramifications of this question. Let us merely discuss a few of the ideas involved. The activist character of Fichtean philosophy already mentioned is very closely connected with the fact that in Fichte, the methodological position of the present, the necessary pivotal point of every philosophy of history, is not the conclusion, not the achieved goal of the historical process, as it is with Hegel, but *the middle*. Fichte, too, is intent on grasping and explaining the present through his philosophy of history; unlike Hegel, however, he does not see this present as the perfect realization of the idea, but on the contrary as the age of absolute sinfulness. This present must therefore be judged in thoroughly negative terms. Its significance and function consist in its being a necessary *point of transition* towards the perfection of the idea, towards the utopian vision of the future. (This is most clearly set forth in Fichte's 'Characteristics of the Present Age'.) At first glance this philosophical idea may seem to indicate a stage beyond Hegel – and in fact it did go beyond Hegel in terms of effectiveness, even

8. Étienne Cabet (1788–1856), one of the outstanding representatives of utopian communism in France. 'Icaric communism' refers to the utopia depicted in his novel *Voyage en Icarie* (1840) (Editor's note).

though to this very day its actual consequences have been largely neglected by research. But it must not be forgotten that the Hegelian notion of 'reconciliation', the culmination of the philosophy of history in the present, implies – for all that it is politically reactionary and ends up philosophically and methodologically in pure contemplation – a more profound connection between the logical categories and the structural forms of bourgeois society. And that precisely because it is a 'reconciliation' (Hegel himself was, of course, largely unconscious of this connection, which consequently remained unexploited by him). Hence, it signifies *a closeness to reality greater than anything Fichte could ever achieve.* Fichte's *views* may have been much more revolutionary than Hegel's, but they remained merely *utopian,* whereas Hegel is able to take into his system of categories the inner social structure of the present (*including* its self-transcending tendencies). In other words, the logico-methodological sequence of Hegel's categories is *far more dependent* on the historical progression of real development than is that of Fichte's categories.

True, the problem is not solved in Hegel's work either. But in reverting to Fichte in order to overcome the conservative elements of Hegelian thinking, the radical and revolutionary young Hegelians – and that includes Lassalle – necessarily fall short of Hegel's own achievements. This they do by loosening the methodological connection between category and history, instead of rooting the categories in history and making them grow out of historical reality. In some cases – especially with Bruno Bauer and Stirner – this gives rise to a kind of philosophical subjectivism, partly influenced, it is true, by the young Hegel, particularly his *Phenomenology of Mind.* Lassalle himself, even in his early youth, adhered to the objectivism of the mature Hegel. But he is unable to prevent a loosening of the relationship between category and history finding expression in his own work. For even he is not able to do more than merely *apply* a – logical, timeless, ready-made – system of categories to history. The relationship between logico-methodological sequence and historical progression thereby remains, as it must, *contingent.* The strength of this tendency in Lassalle is shown by the lecture he held as late as 1861 on the difference between Hegelian and Rosenkranzian logic: not only does he stick to this duality, but in response to other Hegelians (e.g. Cieszkowski) who tried to solve the problem by drawing *mechanical parallels* between category types and historical epochs, he emphasizes expressly that the categories are independent of history. It is a tragic irony in Lassalle's development that, at the very point where he shrewdly exposes Rosenkranz's relapse into the Kantian duality of thinking and being, he himself should return via Fichte to the problem of the 'Critique of Judgment', the problem of the real applicability of the categories, the subsumability of the particular (historically real) under the general (logical category).

But Lassalle himself never became conscious of this retrogression. On the one hand, his strict adherence to Hegelian logic made him feel justified in regarding the problem of thinking and being as definitively settled. On the other hand, he believed that the wealth of empirical material which he worked up in his mature works and ordered strictly in accordance with the orthodox Hegelian categories had enabled him to bridge the gulf from the empirical side, too. Now, of course, we do not intend to belittle the significance of this latter aspect of Lassalle's work. In fact, we even believe that it was not merely by virtue of his intellectual superiority, but chiefly because of this circumstance, namely because he immersed himself so consistently in empirical, social material that he was able to escape from the blind alley of revolutionary Young Hegelianism. But in doing so, Lassalle did not *bridge* the methodological gulf *philosophically*; he merely concealed it *psychologically*. Marx and Engels were always very keenly conscious of this, the weak aspect of Lassalle's thinking. Discussing Heraclitus in a letter to Engels dated 1 February 1858, Marx stresses that 'the fellow is even less inclined to betray any kind of critical thoughts on the dialectic itself. . . . He will realize to his own cost that there is a world of difference between using criticism to raise science to the level where it is possible to represent it dialectically, and applying an abstract, ready-made system of logic to vague notions of precisely such a system.'[9]

That the 'idea' will in this way acquire an *autonomous existence vis-à-vis* history, is obvious; it is simply the *necessary logical consequence* of this kind of starting-point. Any such self-development of the concept which is *methodologically uninhibited* by real historical matter (no matter how richly illustrated it is by empirical material) is bound to be reflected as a *straight-line development* in which the idea becomes conscious and penetrates reality. This, in fact, is how Fichte constructs his philosophy of history. (Of course, we ought to ask whether, in so doing, he is not merely systematizing and schematizing the infinite progress of Kant's philosophy of history – but that is a question which we cannot even begin to discuss here.) And Lassalle's philosophy of history as expounded in the 'System of Acquired Rights' (Wk. IX, pp. 390–400) – which is a work of his most mature period – continues essentially along the same lines. His critique of

9. Bw. II, p. 243 (Editor's note).

the relationship between history and the timeless In-itself in the Hegelian philosophy of right culminates in merely the demand for a structure 'like the one Hegel developed in writing his philosophy of religion'. Behind the change in the historical process, there is an Identical-with-itself which remains in existence 'in the generally formal essence of the philosophy of right (property, contract, etc.)', 'but which is to be conceived as a mere In-itself'. The relationship between this In-itself and historical reality could only be demonstrated in a 'system of the philosophy of mind' (ibid., pp. 140–1). Whether such a system of categories, the In-itself itself, is not likewise a product of history, or how – if that question is answered in the negative – a history is to be made methodologically intelligible at all: these are things which Lassalle never raised as problems. Very revealing is the remark (quoted by Bernstein) which Lassalle made to Marx when Marx visited him in 1861: 'If you don't believe in eternal categories, then you must believe in God' (Wk. VI, p. 9). From the methodological standpoint, then, Lassalle's progress beyond Hegel is only apparent. The contents of his work are revolutionary, and this gives rise without his being conscious of it to a more incisive formulation of the question. This in turn means that he advances *as far as the threshold of the real problem*. But since he is never at any point able to cross this threshold, it makes no decisive difference to the overall situation. On the contrary: Hegel, for all his limitations, discovers unintentionally far more important connections between philosophical categories and the structural forms of concrete historical epochs than Lassalle, whose 'clarity' forces him back in the direction of Fichte.

The higher the value put on the 'idea', and the more timelessly and independently it reigns over the concrete historical process, the less able it is to give any guidance in the concrete. If, as in Marx and Engels, it is the concrete historical process itself which is understood as the origin and seat of the dialectic and which our thoughts merely summon into consciousness, then it is from *that process itself* that the decisive tendencies of social happening can be gleaned and thus made into the object of science. The science thus attained can guide practice *as a science*: it makes *methodologically* possible a *Realpolitik* in the *world-historical sense*. Lassalle, however, cannot derive any criteria for correct action from *his* dialectic or *his* philosophy of history, and so he is bound to become a practitioner of *Realpolitik* – in the usual sense of the word. He himself repeatedly expressed this limitation in his conception of history – albeit without being aware of the full implications of what he was saying. The clearest example occurs in his discussion with Marx and Engels about his 'Sickingen' play (17 May 1859, Bf. III, p. 188):[10] 'If one starts from the Hegelian constructive conception of history, which is after all what I myself essentially believe in, then one must of course reply with you that Sickingen's downfall would in the last instance have happened of necessity anyway, and that it *had* to happen because, as you say, he represents what is at heart a reactionary interest; and that he *had* to do this *again of necessity* because the spirit of the age and his class position made it impossible to adopt consistently a different position. . . . But this critical-philosophical conception of history, in which one iron necessity leads to another, and which for that very reason leads destructively over and beyond the efficacy of *individual* decisions and actions, is – for those self-same reasons – no kind of foundation, either for *practical-revolutionary action*, or for the *dramatic action portrayed*.'

This conception of necessity does more than indicate the unbridgeable gulf which separates it from Marx's conception of history. (Oncken also quotes it enthusiastically in his biography of Lassalle[11] as a refutation of historical materialism.) It signifies at the same time a profound relapse from the Hegelian dialectical unity of freedom and necessity in history to the Fichtean duality of 'absolute being' and 'absolute freedom'. (We cannot discuss here to what extent Spinoza and Kant, too, are implicated in this problematic.) It is not only the Hegelian theory of tragedy (to touch briefly on the concrete, but in this context not crucial occasion for the discussion) which is based on a unity of freedom and necessity: such a unity constitutes the core of his entire philosophy of history. The theory of passion, by means of which the – in Hegel's eyes very important – role of the great individuals in history is mediated, shows this most clearly. Idea and passion form the 'thread of the tapestry of world history'. They

10. Lassalle's historical drama *Franz von Sickingen* was written in 1858-9 and published anonymously. It deals with the rebellion of the Swabian and Rhenish knights at the time of the Reformation. Sickingen together with Ulrich von Hutten was the chief leader of the knights against the princes, above all the Archbishop of Trier. Abandoned by his allies he fell during the siege of his castle, Landstuhl. Lassalle sent a copy of the play together with an account of the tragic idea it contained to Marx on 6 March 1859. Marx and Engels both subjected the play to severe criticism and Lassalle defended himself energetically. The entire correspondence on this matter is of great interest and Lukács returned to it in 1931 in an essay *Die Sickingen-Debatte zwischen Marx/Engels und Lassalle*, published in *Karl Marx und Friedrich Engels als Literaturhistoriker*, Berlin, 1948 (Editor's note).

11. Herman Oncken, *Lassalle*, 2nd edn, Stuttgart/Berlin, 1912 (Editor's note).

are 'the extremes; the middle which binds them together and in which both compete, is moral freedom'.[12] Since Lassalle was so thoroughly and expertly acquainted with Hegel, we can rule out from the outset the possibility that he could ever have overlooked any of the essential points of the Hegelian system. Indeed, he quoted this particular theory of Hegel's at length in a number of court speeches and described the Hegelian conception of passion as his own.

In other words, what he is doing here is going *consciously* beyond Hegel, *correcting* Hegel by means of Fichte, because the Hegelian notion of necessity does not satisfy his activism. And it is in fact true that the Hegelian conception of history, for all its greatness, is much too abstract and much too contemplative to be capable of giving directions *for individual actions*. Only the historical dialectic in its Marxist form can do this. But since Lassalle on the whole never advances beyond orthodox Hegelianism, he is unable to find the way to action except by moving in the direction of Fichte, except, that is, in the irrationality of the purely individual decision and – in political terms – in *'Realpolitik'*.

That Lassalle on many individual issues showed admirable political perspicacity is attributable to his personal genius. His method, his philosophy of history could not provide him with *any guidelines* in that respect. This, of course, is not to deny their significance for his agitational work in other ways. On the contrary: in many cases they prevented him from being able to achieve a proper understanding; for example, his position on the trade union question, the problem of the State, etc. There is a frequent tendency to attribute individual crass blunders made by Lassalle in his politics – such as his dealings with Bismarck[13] – to nothing more than his 'personality', his temperament, and so on. But it is only just, particularly when dealing with such a great admirer of Fichte as Lassalle, to regard his method of thinking as the clearest expression of his personality, and since his thought determines his attitude towards reality, we must use it to comprehend his actions in their conformity with the innermost

12. *Die Vernunft in der Geschichte. Einleitung in die Philosophie der Weltgeschichte* ('Reason in History. Introduction to the Philosophy of World History'), ed. G. Lasson, Leipzig, 1917, p. 61 (G.L.'s note).

13. Shortly before his death Lassalle entered into some abortive negotiations with Bismarck (October 1863–January 1864), in which he attempted to win the latter's support for some of his plans, such as universal suffrage. In exchange he offered to enlist the nationalist feelings of the proletariat on the side of Bismarck's endeavours to unite Germany under Prussian hegemony. For tactical reasons Bismarck expressed his interest, but he had no intention of making concessions (Editor's note).

core of his being. (Which does not, of course, preclude the observation that this entire method and its substantial fulfilment in Lassalle's world view are for their part ideological forms of the development of the German proletariat, signifying a stage in the emergence of its class-consciousness.) The connections between all these factors become most apparent in Lassalle's greatest and most significant experience, his relationship with Countess Hatzfeldt:[14] not only in the way in which he took up her cause and fought for her, but also – and chiefly – in his understanding of what constituted the essence of the whole matter.

This is not the place to talk about the actual events in the Hatzfeldt affair. Not simply because the available correspondence does not provide much material upon which to base a new assessment of the details (the affair of the stolen casket, etc.), but above all because we consider that an analysis – no matter how short – of Lassalle's attitude to the Hatzfeldt case will tell us more about his essential self than the individual events of the case themselves could do. The correspondence with the Countess provides a great deal of interesting information on this point. Above all, there is a long essay-cum-letter (Bf. IV, pp. 12–48) in which Lassalle expounds in detail his view both of her actual trial and – intimately bound up with it – her as a person in terms of his philosophy of history. In his eyes she is the incarnation of a principle. The reserved, even reticent attitude of her friends and acquaintances is to be attributed to their sensing this. 'What women experience in your presence is that uncertain feeling of fear and hatred, that vague, trembling realization that comes over a person who finds himself in the vicinity of the principle from which he is to receive his death blow. In nature, as in history, indeed, even in the lives of individuals there is an abundance of such cases, in which an existence brought into proximity with the principle through which it is destined to meet its end, is seized *unconsciously* by an uncanny fear and hence even more intense hatred' (ibid., p. 13). It does not matter whether or not the countess Hatzfeldt herself always realizes this. 'You sometimes forget

14. Lassalle met Countess Sophie von Hatzfeldt (1805–81) in 1845 when he was twenty. She had long been separated from her husband, and was embroiled in a complicated legal struggle with him over her property rights and custody of the children. Lassalle took up her cause and this led him into a ten-year legal battle fought out before thirty-six courts of law and involving a great deal of publicity. The case ended in victory for the Countess, who rewarded her defender with a handsome annuity and became his devoted political supporter. The casket referred to was stolen from the Count's mistress, because it contained a deed required to establish the Countess's claims (Editor's note).

that what seems to you to be merely your own individual suffering contains within it something quite different: that is, a world-historical idea has borrowed your body in order to express and represent itself for the first time in reality. Hence, your fate, whether good or bad, is nothing other than the practical (actually occurring) consequence of that idea and its antagonistic attitude towards the hitherto existing world' (ibid., p. 14). We do not at this point want to discuss the various historical stages in the philosophy of the liberation of woman and love, which leads from the eighteenth century via Goethe, F. Schlegel's *Lucinde,* Schleiermacher's *Vertraute Briefe* ('Intimate Letters'), Saint-Simonism, George Sand and so on right down to the case of Sophie Hatzfeldt. What is more important is that Lassalle saw this struggle as the struggle for a principle, for *the* principle of revolution. And this is how he wants to have his relationship to Sophie Hatzfeldt regarded – by her, too. 'The most powerful and victorious proof that woman in her lone struggle will yet find such help is the fact that she is not fighting for her mere pleasure, nor even for any *purely* personal element, however excellent – but has been suffering and struggling for a real and absolutely universal idea of the time, for the truly universal principle of the free personality itself. Such help, however, will be accorded to that individual, not on account of her individual relations with others, but on account of the principle actively emanating from the individual herself. It is not, therefore, a question of one lover, who does what he does because he loves her, but of three men at once, who do not have a personal love relationship with her but are destined purely by the inner might of the principle to put themselves at the service of the personality struggling to assert itself. And it is precisely because this help has not sprung from personal relations or personal sympathy that it does not limit itself to a greater or lesser effort to be helpful, but rather, brought into being as it is through an identity with the principle, it bears within it the fanaticism of the principle and is help until death! ... Obviously, however, such help could only emerge from the ranks of those who had in every respect sworn allegiance to the flag of free fulfilment of the personality – in other words, the social revolutionaries. Further, it could only develop at a point in time where the idea of the absolute fulfilment of the free personality had already worked its way deeply enough into the world and had developed sufficiently to be resolved to accomplish itself in violent practice – that is, shortly before the outbreak of a general social revolution' (ibid., pp. 40–41).

Marx wrote disparagingly about Lassalle's role in the Hatzfeldt business to Engels:[15] 'As if a really significant person would sacrifice ten years for such a trifle.' And when, writing about Lassalle's 'pretext for death', he remarked that it was 'one of the many indiscretions which he committed during his life',[16] we can be sure that the Hatzfeldt affair was one of the indiscretions – *vis-à-vis* the workers' movement – which Marx had in mind. For Lassalle, however, the position he took up – the act itself, together with the motives which induced it and which it induced in him – was not an 'adolescent aberration', to be overcome later in his maturity, but the most important and certainly the most characteristic, expressive and symbolic act of his life. This is why what he wrote to Sophie Hatzfeldt on 20 January 1863, makes such perfect sense – even if it was perhaps penned in a moment of depression: 'Oh, how much better it was when I still had my trials on your behalf! You at least knew what I was doing for you! This people doesn't even know or understand' (Bf. IV, p. 329.) I should like to mention here simply in passing that what these words express – even though, I repeat, they may well have been the product of a temporary depression – is precisely that fundamentally wrong attitude of the bourgeois 'leader' towards the proletariat, an attitude which shows complete ignorance of what the workers' movement essentially is, an attitude which Bebel characterized so precisely and tellingly when talking about Schweitzer: 'He is the chosen champion of their demands, the interpreter of their longings, their hopes and their wishes. As long as the leader remains true to this task, he will retain the party's trust. . . . A party does not exist for the leader, but the leader for the party. . . . The masses, in other words, are *never* ungrateful. . . . He who accuses the masses of ingratitude should accuse himself.'[17] It is perhaps unnecessary to add that it is not our intention to compare Lassalle with Schweitzer at all, let alone with the Schweitzer of Bebel's memoirs. But it cannot be denied that such utterances of Lassalle's express a world-view which regards the leader, the 'great personality', as the true bearer of the

15. Letter of 5 March 1856, Bw. II, p. 99 (G.L.'s note). (*Selected Correspondence*, Moscow, n.d., p. 109 – ed.)

16. Letter of 7 September 1864, Bw. III, p. 181 (G.L.'s note). (Lassalle's death at the age of 39 was as sensational as anything in his life. It arose out of a love affair with a woman nearly twenty years his junior, who had first promised to marry him and then, under pressure from her aristocratic parents, had renounced him for another. Lassalle was outraged both by the behaviour of the parents and by the thwarting of his own passion. He challenged his rival to a duel and was killed. The incident was used by George Meredith in *The Tragic Comedians* – ed.)

17. August Bebel, *Aus meinem Leben*, vol. II, pp. 133–4 (G.L.'s note).

events of world history, and the masses as the *means* of achieving the goal – even if the goal itself may well lie in the interest of the masses. From his early youth onwards, Lassalle rightly regarded himself as a revolutionary socialist. For his *goals* were socialist, and so, too, were the ways in which he strove to achieve them. But the *nexus* between the workers' movement, the activity and awakening to self-consciousness of the proletarian masses, and socialism – this was something which remained external for him. That is the theoretical basis for his frequent bouts of depression concerning the slow pace of progress and his reluctance to adjust inwardly to the tempo at which the proletariat's consciousness develops. Sometimes these bouts reached such an intensity that he wished to withdraw completely from the movement. It cannot be decided, of course, to what extent such wishes would have been translated into action, and hence even today we cannot judge how deep or superficial his attacks of depression actually were. What we *can* say is that Marx, Bebel and Lenin (to pick out three completely different personalities of the opposite type) never knew such moods at all.

In another letter to countess Hatzfeldt (28 July 1864) Lassalle writes: 'Ah, how little you know about me! I long for nothing more fervently than to be rid of all this politics and to withdraw into science, friendship and nature. I am sick and tired of politics! True, I would flare up as passionately as ever if serious events were happening, or if I had power or could see the means to seize it – a means that would be appropriate for me. For nothing can be done without supreme power. But I'm too old and too big for childish games. Which is why I was so reluctant to take over the presidency! I was only making a concession to you! Which, in turn, is why it now oppresses me so powerfully. If I were free of it, this would be the moment when I would be determined to take off with you to Naples! (But how can I free myself of it?!)' (ibid., p. 370).

I repeat: it is *not* the psychological, but the *philosophical* problem involved here which is crucial in our eyes. Manifested in such outbursts – regardless of how profound they may or may not have been – is the very conception of the relationship between the masses and leader which even the young Marx opposed in his controversy with Bruno Bauer. Its *philosophical basis,* Hegel 'radicalized' *à la* Fichte, is what Marx finally and radically defeated when he turned the Hegelian dialectic 'right side up' by means of historical materialism. (Here, too, it is not our intention to compare Lassalle with Bruno Bauer; Lassalle's Fichteanism is of a totally different kind. They have only two things in common: on the one hand, they were contemporaries – although Lassalle concerned himself hardly at all with Bruno Bauer; and on the other, they represent related, albeit quite differently constituted philosophical tendencies to radicalize Hegel in idealistic fashion.)

It seems as if these remarks have taken us a long way from our analysis of the significance of the Hatzfeldt case for Lassalle. But it must be borne in mind that concealed behind this conception of the problems of the relationship between leader and masses, lies precisely this whole problem of 'idealism'. It is not for nothing that Marx, even as early as in his initial polemics against Bruno Bauer, emphasizes the connection between Hegelian 'idealism' (one could also say formalistic philosophy of history) and over-estimation of the role of the great 'individual'.[18] And what he stresses as the very characteristics of the coming age, the world-historical period of the proletarian liberation struggle, is in fact the real coincidence of 'idea' and 'mass', that genuine growth of the 'idea' out of the real interests of 'the masses'.[19] The formalism of a Hegel 'revolutionized' by Fichte does not allow Lassalle to perceive what is *radically new* in the revolution which he is experiencing and helping to create. For him – although he does not recognize it – there is a *hiatus irrationalis* (to use Fichte's expression) between 'principle' and 'empirical reality'. Therefore, the only way he can bridge this hiatus is symbolically, mythologically: somehow or other, and in some empirically given situation or other, the 'principle' becomes embodied in one human being and its fate. The Hatzfeldt case represents for Lassalle just such an embodiment of the total problematic of bourgeois society, in exactly the same way – and in our view these are the correct parallels to Lassalle's action – as the Calas case and the Dreyfus affair embodied the situation for Voltaire and Zola. At one time during his youth, in the famous letter to his friends, Lassalle explained the crisis of bourgeois society theoretically in two ways: on the one hand, by an abstract dialectics of the idea; on the other, by reference to individual figures such as Diderot's Rameau, Cagliostro, Casanova, etc., in whom the fate of that society is crystallized (Bf. I, pp. 222ff.). Now, in just the same way, the Hatzfeldt case represents for him the quintessence of the entire struggle for revolutionary emancipation. The individual and the whole, his fate and the historical crisis: in part, they are connected in an emotional, immediate way – that is, symbolically, rhetorically, poetically; and in part – as a necessary complement – they

18. *The Holy Family*, Marx/Engels, *Werke*, vol. II, pp. 89–90 (G.L.'s note).
19. ibid., p. 83 (G.L.'s note).

are mediated in abstract juridical terms. For whereas the collective fate of a class is only the *expression* in terms of consciousness of its socio-economic situation and is conditioned *simultaneously* by its correct totality-relationship to the whole society and to the historical process both really and cognitively (remember how in Marx's work the ratio of the relation of V to C[20] expresses the fate of the proletariat in capitalist society), no individual fate can be posited as simultaneously coexistent in the totality with the 'idea'. The infinite ramifications of real-causal relations between social totality and individual fate are bound of necessity to remain so full of elements which cannot be rationalized that no really general connection is possible in this respect. (In their historical analyses, too, Marx and Engels always concretized to perfection the socio-historical, economic, class-determined, *real scope and limits of possible actions*, but they did not derive, either 'causally' or 'deductively', the 'personalities' from these conditions.) But if – as is the case with Lassalle – the totality is not grasped in this economic concreteness; and if even the economy appears merely as one of the many phenomenal forms of the 'idea', the 'idea' being the essence and the truth of the whole process; then the individual person and the individual's fate acquire far too much significance in that process, since they are then the only true 'concrete' embodiments of the 'idea' remaining. On the other hand, however, this gives rise to the difficult problem already mentioned: that of their necessary and manifest connection with the 'idea'. There are two possibilities: first, the 'idea' in its merely conceptual-mythological concreteness is connected in a concrete and immediate way with the fate of an individual. However, since the concreteness of the idea is merely mythological and that of an individual's fate merely sensuous and immediate, such a connection can only be of a symbolic poetic nature. The second possibility is that the abstract character of the 'idea' comes to light in the course of the connection, in which case the individual fate of the abstract 'idea' can only be subsumed as an abstracted individual case. And the natural, socially given form of such a subsumption is – in bourgeois society – the juridical relationship. It is, therefore, not accidental that in Lassalle's work these two

---

20. In the Marxist theory of surplus value, V = variable capital, i.e. capital used for paying wages, which produces surplus value and is therefore variable; C = constant capital, i.e. all other capital invested in production. Constant capital creates no surplus value, but simply reproduces itself. Marx used the formula $sv/C + V$ to express the rate of profit, i.e. the relation between the profit and the invested capital as a whole (Editor's note).

moments of the Hatzfeldt case should appear as necessarily connected with each other. 'You provided Westphalen[21] with that supreme proof of the power of free personality over that which stands in absolute opposition to it. A real victory was thereby achieved, for the absolute opposite itself was overcome; the very estate which represented the old principle par excellence and was being attacked – namely, the nobility – was made to acknowledge the truth of the new principle. Such an admission – the admission that one's own life-principle has been overcome and that the free personality represents the true principle – could of course only come (as it also did, for example, in the case of the French Revolution) from the intellectually cultured section of the old nobility. You must beware, however, of regarding Westphalen and his like as mere exceptions. Westphalen, Oppenheim, Mendelssohn, I and others, we are none of us *exceptions*, but only the *representatives of the different classes* of society, hurrying hither to render homage to the newly dawned principle of the female personality. . . . The free personality struggles for general acknowledgement and validation of its inner truth, its principle. The principle which has attained general acknowledgement and outward validity is – the principle of right. The free personality therefore struggles for its *rights*, and it does so on the path of right' (Bf. IV, p. 44).

This kind of formalistic/systematic necessity is of course not sufficient in itself to explain fully the priority accorded to right in Lassalle's conception of society – even though its role is certainly greater than is usually assumed. We must add here that right, apart from fulfilling this formalistic/systematic function (as the principle of the subsumption of the individual under the general), also appears in substantial fulfilment: as *natural right*. For right is 'at the same time the expression translated into reality, of the old society and its principle. The law therefore stands everywhere in opposition to the new truth' (ibid.). What Lassalle does at this point is not only to bring this antagonism to a theoretical head, thereby making right dialectical in itself, but also to draw out all the ensuing practical consequences. In the process, it becomes manifest that Hegel is being 'corrected' by the revolutionary proponent of natural right, Fichte. Natural right emerges as the principle of justice, freedom and human progress in the struggle against, and as triumph over, the ossified principle of merely positive right. What this entails, however, is the forfeiture of

21. Ferdinand Otto Wilhelm von Westphalen (1799–1876), an arch-conservative Prussian statesman, was Minister of the Interior at the period of the Hatzfeldt lawsuit (he was also Marx's brother-in-law) (Editor's note).

Hegel's achievement, which was to have overcome – at least partially – the stumbling block of natural right. Hegel's reduction of right to the forms of 'society' (Hegel's state is essentially far more social than juridical) may well be extremely conservative, even reactionary, in character. Nonetheless, the forms of right – both those which are abstract-formal and purely juridical in form, and those which take the form, inspired by the notion of natural right, of a rebellion against them – are at least sublated in the higher moments of the dialectical process (even though, of course, this latter is primarily a logical-dialectical-systematic process, and not a real historical one). With Fichte and Lassalle, on the other hand, it is precisely in its revolutionary victory over the old principle that the natural-right version of the 'higher' principle of right *perpetuates systematically the continuity of right*. Lassalle, incidentally, admits as much explicitly in his 'System of Acquired Rights': 'The substantial idea underlying my thesis is, conceived in its highest and most general form, none other than the idea of *transforming an old state of right into a new one* – such a transformation issuing from, and corresponding to, the idea of right itself' (Wk. IX, p. 113). Thus, however emphatically Lassalle elsewhere stresses the historical character of natural right itself, the fact nevertheless remains that his understanding of it is totally different from Marx's. For Marx (and – albeit inconsistently and only partially – for Hegel), right itself represents only a stage of the historical process and hence arises and disappears in and through that process. What we find in Lassalle, however, is *a history of individual forms of right developing within a general philosophy of right that is both timeless and supra-historical.* The culmination of Lassalle's theory of revolution is therefore: on the one hand, a proof in terms of natural right of the 'right to revolution'; and on the other, the theoretical establishment of the 'Revolutionary System of Right'. Lassalle thus fails to perceive properly that the notion of right in general is rooted in class society, and that of our present form of right in particular, in capitalism. Consequently his whole conception of revolution remains – for all its individual proletarian elements – within the ideological confines of bourgeois society. It is the conception of a *bourgeois revolution*. A revolution, let it be added, though, that is so comprehensive, so thorough and so profound, that bourgeois society as it stands cannot possibly carry it out and will have to cede it as a heritage to the proletarian revolution. In this respect Lassalle stood intuitively on the brink of a discovery the meaning of which has only now become clear to us – primarily as the result of Lenin's work. But he was unable to recognize the correct conclusion: that only the proletariat can carry through such a revolution.

True the proletarian revolution in its initial phase is concerned with problems of this kind; true, it also solves them in the course of its radical advance; but it is in a position to do so only because it is here and nowhere else that the *specificity of the proletarian revolution* has achieved totally clear consciousness. But this entails above all complete understanding of the class-determined, economically-determined nature of *all* forms of right (including, of course, the right which the dictatorship of the proletariat establishes for itself). Whence it necessarily follows that, even in questions that are bound to appear as questions of right if looked at formally, the nature of the proletarian revolution is concerned with right merely from a technical, formal point of view. Right 'as such' has precious little to do with the essence of the matter. On the other hand, it is of the essence of the bourgeois revolution that, in and in spite of the revolution, *the continuity of right should be maintained* – that, in other words, any revolutionary changes should be justified in terms of right. Some kind of natural right (de lege ferenda) is therefore indispensable in order to bring about a continuity of right (de lege lata). Hence, revolutionary natural right overthrows the existing, positive form of right – but without decisively changing the fundamental character of society. The result is that the new right which thus emerges (natural right which has become 'positive') forms a continuous link with the former right. For the bourgeois class, even in its revolutionary period, such a structural connection is a vital necessity. It is concerned to impose on the whole of society its own form of existence, which is already an economic reality and is to some extent even legally sanctioned (in the shape of 'privileges' and so on). Two forms of right are involved in its revolution: natural right in the struggle, positive right in victory. And both are integrally connected with their vital economic interests. Not so for the proletariat, which strives to establish a radically new social order, and hence, even though for technical and other reasons it creates forms of right as transitional forms – and indeed sometimes deliberately maintains the continuity with the old form of right – must always regard any and all such measures as nothing more than minor aspects of the revolution. Lassalle, therefore, may well have been extremely disappointed when Marx showed so little interest in the conclusions that his meditations on the philosophy of right had led him to on the subject of expropriation. But the very fact that he expected a reaction demonstrates that he never really got to grips with the theoretically and practically central question posed by the proletarian revolution: the question as to which *economic* forces lead to the necessity and possibility of expropriation, and which *real means of power* are able to realize this necessity; the question which was the only essential one for Marx in this context.

If, however, even the victorious revolution is related to the development which preceded it by the continuity of right, then clearly the victory of the 'principle' can only be the victory of 'right', victory in the struggle for right. Just as right was the *formal* mediating instance connecting the purely individual Hatzfeldt case with the destiny of the revolution, so now victory in the struggle for right appears as the only possible *substantial* method of raising the 'principle' embodied in the individual to historical stature, to a historical power.

Of course, this Lassallean conception of bourgeois revolution far surpasses all the possibilities – both real and conceptual – which were available to the bourgeoisie of that time. The only support Lassalle could find was in the working class, just as the German working class, which at the time was taking its first tentative steps as an autonomous class, did the only consistent thing it could in choosing him as its first leader. However, we are more interested at this point in what the resultant relationship meant for Lassalle than in what it meant for the proletariat. And now finally, having considerably clarified matters by virtue of this 'detour', we can revert to the problem of Lassalle's '*Realpolitik*', to find confirmation of our earlier assertion that Lassalle's philosophy of history was by its very nature unable to provide him with a practical guideline to action. It was not a matter of personal 'loneliness' or lack of companions of the same 'calibre'. Marx and Engels also lived in profound isolation, surrounded by an atmosphere that was anything but understanding. But whatever they thought politically, they always had their criterion: the class situation of the proletariat and the proletariat's class-consciousness deriving from that situation. And this criterion was to remain constant even when, in individual instances, it happened that not a single proletarian actually attained the level of class-consciousness.[22] They could err in individual instances, but they could not stray from their path. Lassalle, on the other hand, could not find any criterion for his action except in *himself*. The proletariat was – at best – a faithful ally for his actions, and such a thing as the bourgeois class, whose great revolutionary theoretician he was,

22. For the Marxist concept of class-consciousness see my book *History and Class Consciousness*, Berlin, 1923 (London, 1971) (G.L.'s note).

existed only in his mind. What Lassalle did was to reduce the problems of the French Revolution to their real conceptual meaning and to think them through to their proper conclusion. In this he performed the creditable feat of bringing German classical philosophy to perfection. But he in no sense went beyond it, and hence he found himself from a world-historical point of view in a vacuum. The relationship of his ideas to reality was truly that between 'idea' and 'reality'. And if we are to understand his personal *Realpolitik*, his 'vanity' and so on, it is only by reference to this tension. Moreover, the many instances where his revolutionary temperament and his genuine alliance with the proletariat enabled him to represent the proletariat's class interests correctly, demonstrate his political genius all the more clearly – especially in view of the fact that the essence of his philosophy did more to bar than to point the way forward.

At the same time, however, we can understand why he should have got involved in the hazardous game he played with Bismarck, and why he should always have felt drawn – as Marx puts it – to the Koblenz of the revolution (to Rüstow, Herwegh, etc.).[23] At the end of his life he may well have sensed that his chosen path had led him into a blind-alley, but the fate which finally befell him – however grotesque and undignified a death it was – saved him from recognizing the blind-alley truly as such. Which makes it understandable that posterity should remember him most vividly for those episodes where the ethical emotionalism of his Fichteanism was able to express itself most appropriately.

The letters of Lassalle's youth, particularly the lengthy letters-cum-treatises already mentioned, are interesting mainly because they show us how early his *essential* development came to an end. He later worked an enormous amount of empirical material into his method, and his conception of history became even richer and more mature; and yet all his later work was never in fact anything more than a *flowering*, a development (in

23. Friedrich Wilhelm Rüstow (1821–1878) was an officer and writer on military affairs, a democrat who lived in Switzerland as an émigré; in 1860 he served as Garibaldi's chief-of-staff. He was friendly with Lassalle and acted as his second in the fatal duel. Georg Herwegh (1817–1875) was a radical political poet, who had attempted to lead an army to invade Germany in the 1848 revolution. The invasion was doomed from the outset (despite the encouragement of the French government who were anxious to export the large numbers of German émigrés in France back to Germany). For an account of Herwegh see E. H. Carr's *The Romantic Exiles*, Harmondsworth, 1968 (Editor's note).

the literal sense) of those youthful ideas. It would really be very interesting to discover precisely when and how he absorbed the consequences of Marxist thought, for in terms of real influence they never actually affected him. It is very characteristic of Lassalle that, even in his Hatzfeldt correspondence, he did not make a single reference to Marx's theory. This may of course be coincidental – at least in part: for example, Countess Hatzfeldt was also in Berlin at the time of Marx's visit to the city. Nevertheless, the fact that even the problems involved are not dealt with at all must be regarded as typical. Lassalle clearly appropriated for himself only those aspects of Marx's writings which could be organically integrated into his own interpretation of Hegelian philosophy.

His philosophy is a philosophy of freedom, as it was for Fichte and Hegel. And like them, he sees the way as leading from Greece and Rome via Christianity to bourgeois society. Christianity introduces the principle of 'the absolute justification of the personality' into history (Bf. I, p. 116). And the French Revolution, through which bourgeois society became the dominant form, is nothing other than the secularization and hence the true realization of that principle (ibid. and pp. 120–21). In holding this view, Lassalle demonstrates that he has a far more acute sense of history than his near-contemporary, Bruno Bauer. But it is precisely those passages where he seems to be closest to the arguments in *On the Jewish Question* which demonstrate most clearly the profound difference between Marx's and his own mode of thinking. True, Lassalle's critique of bourgeois society also takes the merely formal notion of freedom as its starting-point. But in his case, any advance made remains purely speculative and ideological. The material fulfilment of formal freedom can only be ownership, property; they alone can give the individual real, material freedom (Bf. I, p. 123); and it is from this state of affairs that the essence of the present, the system of free competition, is derived (ibid., p. 125). Just how artificial and ideological this whole argument is is shown, for example, by the way in which Lassalle substantiates his perception – in itself quite correct – that industry nowadays far surpasses trade in importance: 'Trade revolves around the *objective* substratum of trade, the thing itself, the commodity. It is in industry, on the other hand, that the principle of the *free* subjectivity of the personality finds its appropriate realization and validation. Industry does not revolve so much round the objective substratum, the *material* itself, as rather around the personality which forms and processes the material. In trade, value is determined by the material itself, whereas in industry it depends rather on the processing. In industry, subjectivity and its free spirituality (*Innerlichkeit*) – that is, talent – can show and assert themselves; in industry the subject acquires the objective – ownership – precisely by virtue of the activity and exploitation of a personality, a spirituality, a subjectivity: in other words, by virtue of what it itself is, what is most subjective of all in itself – its skill, taste and talent' (ibid., p. 129). And then there is Lassalle's dictum on the social role of money: 'There exists the dreadful situation that I see the reality of my *being-for-itself*, that most inward, most personal property, in the power of the other (money). Being-for-itself has thereby come outside itself (out of itself), it sees itself dependent and in the power of the other' (ibid., p. 125). Both arguments concerning money as the 'alienated essence' of the individual and the parallels drawn between such material alienation and the spiritual alienation existing in the relationship with God, are strongly reminiscent of Feuerbach and Moses Hess. (For the moment, however, we are not in a position to establish the precise connections.) The personal and practical consequences which Lassalle drew from such reasoning are, of course, entirely his own (ibid., p. 221, pp. 230ff.).

It would be a mistake to regard such utterances simply as expressions of young Lassalle's 'naïveté'. On the contrary, they contain the germ of nearly all his later, fundamental attitudes and the germ of his deviations from Marx and Engels. One example is his blurring of the difference between bourgeois and proletarian revolution. Communism, he argues, has 'its ideal justification', it will 'surely prevail, as every stage of the concept has done; besides, it is by no means such a harsh matter – much harsher transitions have occurred before now' (ibid., pp. 133–4). This extreme formulation is especially characteristic because in it the Fichtean-cum-Hegelian limitations of Lassalle's thinking find their clearest expression: *as a result of the supra-historical nature of his system of categories,* as a result of his basing the dialectical method in the realm of pure logic and not in real history, what he achieves is an historical equalization of the events of the different historical epochs. How little Lassalle *really* developed later on in this respect is also shown in the discussion he had by letter with Marx and Engels in 1859 concerning his Sickingen play (Bf. III, pp. 148–58 and 175–211). The essential difference between the two sides is that Marx and Engels, even when dealing with the substance and form of a tragedy, are constantly thinking of the *specific* problems of *one particular* historical epoch, whereas Lassalle's intention is to write *the* tragedy of *the* revolution (ibid., p. 187). Even more significant, however –

especially for the later controversies – is the fact that Lassalle repeatedly abandons the extremely important distinction which Hegel made between state and society. This distinction is one of the levers which helps the young Marx to accomplish his revolutionary 'inversion' of the Hegelian dialectic. In what is for him the decisive sentence, 'Communism first grasps anew, albeit still obscurely and vaguely, the idea of the state or of society as being *an organic whole*' (Bf. I, p. 134), Lassalle uses state and society as synonyms. To point this out is not to engage in hair-splitting – for two reasons. In the first place, for Lassalle, a ratiocinating dialectician if ever there was one, the relation of concepts to one another is systematically crucial. And secondly, that is the only way in which he can substantiate systematically his philosophy of history – to which he remained true even later – concerning the relationship of the proletariat to the state. It is, too, the only possible basis for the theory he propounded in his most mature period, namely that 'above all, the fully-developed idea of the state should be called the idea of the working class'.[24] That Lassalle on several later occasions rigorously separates state and society does little to change matters basically, for his concept of society never advances beyond that of Hegel's, and in fact as often as not does not even measure up to it.

Admittedly, sometimes even Lassalle has vague inklings of the self-sublation (*Selbstaufhebung*) of right (Bf. I, p. 220), but in the main he sticks to the supra-temporal character of the idea of right and state. This idea necessarily leads in part to a blurring of, and in part to an undialectical and crude emphasis on, this decisive difference. What this does in practical political terms, however, is to *determine his relationship to bourgeois liberalism*. In the passage referred to above (Bf. I, p. 134), Lassalle stresses that the communist should direct his fiercest polemics against the radical democrats and the republicans. It is not possible to go into the implications of this position at this point; but anyone who is the least bit familiar with the history of the German working-class movement will know that precisely this conceptual legacy of Lassalle's lay at the root – politically speaking – of the breach in later years between Marx and Engels, and Lassalle's successor Schweitzer.

Clearly, a review of this kind cannot claim to delineate, even in the most sketchy way, the philosophical personality of the young Lassalle.

---

24. 'Science and the Workers.' Speech made before the Berlin criminal court (on 16 January 1863), defeuding himself against the accusation that he had publicly incited the poor and needy to hatred and contempt of the well-to-do; in Wk. II, p. 241 (G.L.'s note).

Even so, the foregoing remarks provide sufficiently clear evidence that, on the one hand, Lassalle's development was unbroken and rectilinear, and, on the other, that even those points where he seems to have come close to the Marxist position signify nothing more than that he was a more coherent and consistent Hegelian than the other young Hegelians. We can, for example, find intimations of the later Marxist theory of 'false consciousness' in statements like the following: 'None of these industrialists themselves is capable of grasping the *concept* of industry and its true significance; and when they talk of the power of industry and tell us that it is the soul of our time, their words remain empty, futile chatter. Of course industry is the soul of our time, but how this comes to be so is something beyond the comprehension of all the German manufacturers and the Paris commission together, irrespective of their expertise in matters of detail. In this respect they are every bit as unconscious as the very cog-wheels of their machines, totally unconscious of what they are and what they are doing' (Bf. I, pp. 115–16). But when he goes on straightaway to say that this consciousness is to be found in the *philosopher*, we realize that all he is doing is applying Hegel's 'cunning of reason' to a new domain, but certainly not propounding the *historico-social concretization and elaboration* of that theory which it underwent in Marxism. (Incidentally, we can also detect here the nucleus of Lassalle's later duality – albeit a duality that has become an alliance – between science *and* working class. This, too, has its methodological roots in his Fichteanism.) The same applies to Lassalle's absolutely correct remark to the effect that materialism is 'also a product that has been brought into being for the first time by this modern age. It has *never* appeared before on the stage of history. It is a product of this most modern age, for it is a product and a stage of the new idealism and spirit' (Bf. I, p. 129). Lassalle thus quite clearly perceives the connection between bourgeois development, the development of capitalism, and materialism; in this he proves himself infinitely superior to those historians of philosophy who were unable to see anything in materialism except a revival of the ideas of the ancient materialists. (That those ideas themselves developed in a context that was – in some respects, but only *some* – similar to that of modern bourgeois progress, and hence were able, *on account of that analogy*, to exert influence on the course of modern philosophy, does not affect our argument.) But here, too, we must not forget that this assessment of materialism was likewise introduced by Hegel himself and given special emphasis by the Young Hegelians (e.g. in Bruno Bauer's 'The Trumpet of the Last Judgement'). It is therefore quite consistent with revolutionary orientated Hegelianism, with adherence to the essence of Hegelian philosophy and the tendency of his own ('Heraclitus'), when Lassalle, in the company of the Berlin Hegelians, rallies wholeheartedly to the defense of Moleschott – together, of course, with Michelet (Bf. IV, p. 196).

The reason for our discussing Lassalle's early philosophical ideas at such length is not simply that they are of great importance as an aid to understanding his later development, but also because it is here, in our view, that the objective basis for the relationship between Marx and Lassalle is to be found. In his extremely interesting foreword to their correspondence, Gustav Mayer concerns himself more with the personality differences and the various clashes they had. Mehring, who in his history of the party and his notes to vol. 4 of his posthumous edition[25] finally disposed of the myth that Lassalle was a mere pupil of Marx's, alludes to the problem only occasionally. Nor is it mere chance that this should be so; for it is in this respect that it is most difficult to assess the relationship. For a long time even the material was incomplete; after all, Mehring himself was largely ignorant of the existence of Marx's and Engels's letters to Lassalle. But it will also remain incomplete forever, for Marx and Engels never *really* took issue with Lassalle. The dispute is no more contained in the letters published by Mayer than it is in the correspondence with Engels or in *The Critique of the Gotha Programme*. The latter, however, does make short shrift of the repercussions of Lassalleanism. The letters to Engels contain some very caustic and telling remarks – but they are no more than remarks which show where a proper debate with Lassalle *could have* begun. The debate itself, however, never took place. And as for the letters to Lassalle: they are so diplomatically worded, and the criticism they contain is so guarded, that the only possibility throughout of divining Marx's real opinion lies in reading between the lines or studying the letters he wrote to Engels at the same time. Which is not to say that the newly published letters do not contain an extraordinary number of interesting things. It is sufficient to refer to the polemic against *The System of Acquired Rights*, in which Marx provides a description – as profound as it is exact – of the real scope and context in which ideological formations are effective in history: 'You have convincingly proved that the adoption of the Roman form of testament was based originally on

25. Cf. Franz Mehring, *Geschichte der deutschen Sozialdemokratie*, vol. II, 5th edn, Stuttgart, 1913, pp. 139ff., especially p. 153; and also his preface to 'Letters from Lassalle to Karl Marx and Friedrich Engels', op. cit., pp. XII–XIII (Editor's note).

misunderstanding (and as far as the scientific insight of the lawyers is concerned, still is even today). But it by no means follows that the testament in its modern form is the *misunderstood* Roman testament – even though the modern lawyers may have rationalized it to themselves in terms of various misunderstandings of Roman law. Otherwise you could say that every achievement of an older period that is appropriated by a later one is *the old thing misunderstood*. It is certain, for example, that the three unities as theoretically construed by the French dramatists under Louis XIV are based on a misunderstanding of Greek drama (and of Aristotle as their foremost exponent). It is equally certain, on the other hand, that they understood the Greeks in a way which corresponded precisely to their own aesthetic needs and therefore remained true to this so-called "classical" drama even long after Dacier and others had correctly interpreted Aristotle for them. Or again, it could be argued that all modern constitutions are based largely on the *misunderstood* English constitution and take up as essential precisely those aspects – e.g. a so-called responsible *cabinet* – which appear to mark the decline of the English constitution and which today cling on to *formal* existence only *per abusum*. The misunderstood form is precisely the general one and the most suitable one for general use at a certain level of social development' (Letter of 22.7.1861 – Bf. III, p. 375).[26] But it is very significant, on the one hand, that he does not react at all to Lassalle's reply, in which Lassalle urges him especially to read the sections of the book on the philosophy of right ('Sections 7 and 10 concern you above all others' – 27/28.7.1861; Bf. III, p. 381). And on the other hand Marx takes care in his criticism to suppress his real views; it is only in his letter to Engels[27] that his out-and-out rejection of Lassallean dialectics is expressed really bluntly: 'Ideologism is gaining ground, and the dialectical method is being *wrongly* applied. Hegel never called the subsumption of a mass of "cases" under a general principle dialectics.' (Marx's opinion of Lassalle is expressed most openly in his letter to Kugelmann of 23.2.1865, which Kautsky published in *Der Kampf* [vol.

26. Lassalle's *System of Acquired Rights* set out to show that the inheritance of property rests on quite different bases in different civilizations. Ultimately the reason for these differences is to be found in the differing *Volksgeist* of those civilizations. Hence, the adoption by the Germanic peoples of the Roman form of testament can only result from a misunderstanding, since the spirit of the two peoples is essentially different. The aim of the entire argument is to discredit rights and legal forms that have been accepted in the past but which no longer conform to the spirit of the people (Editor's note).

27. Letter of 9 December 1861, Bw. III, p. 44 (G.L.'s note).

XVI, p. 3].[28]) However, a public debate centring on these issues never ensued. Although Marx and Engels made theoretical mincemeat of the Proudhon and Dühring tendencies, they never openly settled accounts with Lassalle. (Only Engels knew that the article on Proudhon in the *Sozialdemokrat* of 1865[29] was directed at Lassalle, and *The Critique of the Gotha Programme* was not published until very late on, either.) To the considerable detriment of theoretical clarity in subsequent developments.

Marx and Engels made it quite clear why they behaved in this way towards Lassalle. For example, Marx wrote to Engels:[30] 'Lassalle really has too great an interest "in the cause" not to stick with us, come what may. . . . So, if we manage things cleverly, he'll be with us through thick and thin, no matter how many "last-straw" antics he gets up to.' This hope later diminished more and more; in fact, after Lassalle's death, Engels wrote to Marx as follows:[31] 'Even as things were he was a very unreliable friend for us, and in the future he would have pretty certainly been our enemy.' And yet the diplomatic stance was maintained right up to Lassalle's death, and was even carried over – in spite of the temporary open breach – into the relationship with Schweitzer. Marx and Engels obviously considered an open debate with Lassalle to be a waste of time; it must have seemed an absolutely impossible task to win him over genuinely and completely to their point of view. On the other hand, the situation of the workers' movement and the position he occupied in it did not allow them to settle accounts with him as they had done with Proudhon and Dühring. Moreover, he was too important and influential a figure to be simply ignored like Moses Hess. Clearly they were working on the assumption that the German workers' movement would get over the 'infantile disorder' of Lassalleanism as well. But their hopes were only partially realized. In their very own lifetime, above all, it took far longer to complete the recovery than they had hoped. It was not a great deal of use pointing out, however subtly and incisively, the wrong consequences of Lassalleanism (e.g. his theory of the state in *The Critique of the Gotha Programme*), as long as even the closest supporters of the movement were not clear about the fundamental theoretical differences of principle. True,

28. Marx's letter to Kugelmann can be found in *Selected Works*, op. cit., vol. II, p. 413 (Editor's note).

29. Cf. Marx to J. B. Schweitzer on Proudhon, in *The Poverty of Philosophy*, op. cit., pp. 218–28 (Editor's note).

30. On 25 February 1859, in Bw. II, p. 308 (Editor's note).

31. Letter of 4 September 1864, in Bw. III, p. 179 (Editor's note).

the living movement has gradually – and without much theory – managed to cope with and settle many of the problems involved. But it was precisely because Lassallean theory ceased to be a definite intellectual tendency within the party *gradually* – without any real attempt being made to clarify and thereby surmount the basic differences between it and Marxism – that it was able to survive underground in a variety of guises, only to re-surface later in a more up-to-date form. And the more the dialectical tradition paled into insignificance within the German workers' movement, the less it was possible to come to grips seriously with Lassallean tendencies. If the Hegelian factor in Marx and Engels could degenerate to what was at best a matter of antiquarian or literary-historical importance, then of course it became absolutely impossible to assign Lassalle to his rightful place in the evolution of the dialectical method.

And that is absolutely necessary if we are to get to grips with this issue. Mehring is correct in saying that Lassalle is not a pupil of Marx, but we have to enlarge on this and say that Lassalle's method is essentially that of a *pre-Marxist* thinker; his place in the history of ideas is *between* Hegel and Marx. Which means that all the problems of pre-Marxist Hegelianism (which can always, in spite of all other differences, be traced back to Fichte) in the work of Cieszkowski, Bruno Bauer, Moses Hess, etc., must be thoroughly investigated in respect of their relationship to Lassalle, who was by far the most significant thinker in this group of precursors. Such questions, however, are primarily historical questions, since the tendencies involved are primarily historical questions, and have been rendered obsolete once and for all by the emergence and development of materialist dialectics. Not until this historical aspect of the question has been dealt with – and this will become much easier when publication of all the volumes of Gustav Mayer's, with all the valuable material they contain, is complete – will the other aspect of the Lassalle problem become absolutely clear: namely, its relevance to our present-day practice. For it is beginning to look as if revisionism, which of course always follows in the wake of bourgeois science, is likewise bent on following the current tendency in German philosophy to move away from Kant and towards Hegel; as if the neo-Hegelian era is about to succeed the neo-Kantian era in Marxism. However, any such development must of necessity come up against Lassalle; and this is certainly an important factor in the perceptible growth of interest already being shown nowadays in Lassalle's work.

But that does not explain everything. The real reason for the likelihood of a Lassalle renaissance lies deeper: in the political and social situation of

Germany. In part, war and revolution have pushed the problem of the state once again into the forefront of discussion. The Marxist theory of the state is, as Lenin's *State and Revolution* demonstrates quite clearly, the theory of proletarian revolution; it has become increasingly obvious that the only effective and intrinsically homogeneous theory which can possibly be put forward as a counter-force, by the revisionists as much as by the progressive bourgeoisie, is in fact Lassalle's theory of the state. The attempts to turn Marx into a pacifist or a worshipper of the state, or to 'refute' him in the usual way, were bound to fail. Lassalle is the only intellectual authority with any prospect at all of accomplishing anything in a confrontation with Marx. Not only because of his intellectual authority, but because – as we have attempted to point out – it is precisely his Fichteanized Hegelianism which makes him into *the* theoretician of the bourgeois revolution. The Marx/Lassalle controversy that is now getting under way is, in the last analysis, the dispute as to whether the present period is that of the bourgeois or that of the proletarian revolution. The Lassalle renaissance in that respect signifies the theoretical attempt to arrest development at the bourgeois revolution. And this historical perspective seems all the more seductive in view of the fact that the apparent refutation of the revolutionary theory of German unity, Bismarck's establishment of the Reich, collapsed pitifully in the World War. It is as if history had deliberately confronted Germany yet again with the old problem of 1812, 1848, and so on: the *revolutionary achievement* of unity. But this is precisely where every tendency (apart from those bent simply on undoing history, with whom we are not concerned here) must fall back on Lassalle, revolutionary natural right, Fichte and Hegel, as long as it refuses to go along with Marx and his orthodox pupils, Luxemburg and Lenin, in regarding this as the task of the proletarian revolution; that is, as long as it does not realize that a bourgeois revolution, if it is to be accomplished *today,* must pass over into the proletarian revolution. It is highly probable that Lassalle will gradually become the leading theoretician of left-wing revisionism. And a theoretical confrontation between Marx and Lassalle – which, as we can see, is of tremendous importance today – can only be of any real value if it gets right down to the fundamental differences. The foregoing notes do not of course claim for a moment to offer even the merest suggestion of a solution in this matter. The intention is simply to indicate in the light of this extremely valuable new material – which makes a scientific discussion of the whole question truly possible for the first time – the most important problems involved.

Moses Hess
and the Problems
of Idealist Dialectics

Moses Hess and the Problems of Idealist Dialectics[1]

There have been many attempts[2] to revise the scathing and peremptory judgment passed on Moses Hess by Marx and Engels in the *Communist Manifesto*. Quite apart from efforts by people like Koigen or Hammacher[3] to tar the early Marx and Engels with the same brush of 'true socialism', even Franz Mehring considers the verdict of the *Communist Manifesto* too harsh. Not in the theoretical sense, of course. He believes, rather, that the 'true socialists', and especially Hess, should not be considered merely in the light of the *Communist Manifesto*: 'It can be said in analogous fashion that the essence of the German socialism of that period was determined by the critique made of it in the *Communist Manifesto,* rather than that the elements of the critique made by the authors of the *Manifesto* were developed out of the real conditions of life in which both they and the German socialists of their time found themselves'.[4] Mehring points by way of contrast to the honest revolutionary character of these men (again primarily Hess) and to the fact that precisely this tendency boasts far fewer deserters to the enemy camp than any other. 'Of all the different schools of bourgeois socialists of that time and even today, the true socialists have far and away the clearest conscience in this respect.'[5] However,

1. First published in *Archiv für die Geschichte des Sozialismus und der Arbeiterbewegung*, vol. XII, 1926 (Editor's note). All notes in this essay are the author's except where otherwise indicated.

2. Theodor Zlocisti, *Moses Hess, Der Vorkämpfer des Sozialismus und des Zionismus 1812–1875. Eine Biographie*, 2nd completely revised edition, Berlin, Welt-Verlag, 1921. See also Moses Hess, *Sozialistische Aufsätze*, ed. Theodor Zlocisti, Berlin, Welt-Verlag, 1921.

3. Cf. David Koigen, *Zur Vorgeschichte des modernen philosophischen Sozialismus in Deutschland. Zur Geschichte der Philosophie und Sozialphilosophie des Junghegelianismus* ('The antecedents of modern philosophical socialism in Germany. The history of the philosophy and social philosophy of the Young Hegelians'), Berner Studien zur Philosophie und ihrer Geschichte, Bern, 1901, and Ernst Hammacher, *Das philosophisch-ökonomische System des Marxismus. Unter Berücksichtigung seiner Fortbildung und des Sozialismus überhaupt, dargestellt und kritisch beleuchtet* ('The philosophical and economic system of Marxism. A critical account of its development and of socialism in general'), Leipzig, 1909 (Editor's note).

4. *Nachlass*, II, p. 348.

5. Cf. Mehring, *Karl Marx*, Leipzig, 1919, p. 120; see also *Nachlass*, II, p. 349.

the problem of historically classifying and interpreting 'true socialism', particularly that of Hess, is hardly even posed by such statements, let alone resolved. And it is to this problem that we have to address ourselves here. For Mehring's second point – that the 'true socialists' adhered faithfully to the ideals of the then revolutionary democracy, to the bourgeois revolution, in spite of their completely wrong theoretical attitude to the revolutionary role of the bourgeoise – can by no means be settled by this kind of biographical evidence. The problem is essentially that of the relationship of the bourgeois revolution to the proletarian revolution. It crops up in accentuated form in the response of Marx and Engels to Lassalle's agitation, in their rejection of his 'Tory-Chartism'.[6] It branches out into what could, in non-dialectical terms, be conceived of as an antithesis: on the one hand the tactical attitude of the Mensheviks towards the bourgeois and proletarian revolution in 1905 and 1917; on the other, the theoretical attitude of those who proclaimed the 'purely' proletarian revolution (e.g. the Communist Workers' Party (KAP), and the left-wing economism of the extreme Luxemburg school of thought). But it is only with Lenin's theory of revolution,[7] which even today is frequently misunderstood, that a real theoretical solution is found to the problem. The fact that Hess simply abandoned his theory in the decisive moments of action is therefore not only a sign of his honest revolutionary character, but rather an indication that there were still few clear-cut differences between the various elements of the revolutionary movement in Germany at that time. This meant in practice that there was no real choice : those who were not prepared to fight on the left wing of bourgeois democracy – which of course meant constantly coming into conflict with the bourgeoisie as it veered increasingly rightwards – were bound of necessity to make common cause with the forces of reaction. The criticism levelled by the *Communist Manifesto* at the theories of Hess and his companions was therefore absolutely correct. If followed through logically, their theory could not but lead them into the reactionaries' camp. The criticism was unjust in two respects only: first, it underestimated, if anything, the rootlessness, the essentially ideological nature of 'true socialism'; secondly, it failed to take into account that Hess's theory in this respect was so utopian and the terms of his critique of the bourgeoisie so clearly a mere transla-

6. Cf. e.g. Engels to Marx, 13 February 1865 (Editor's note).

7. Cf. my book *Lenin. Studie über den Zusammenhang seiner Gedanken*, Berlin–Vienna, Malik-Verlag, 1924 (English translation, *Lenin. A Study on the Unity of his Thought*, London, 1970).

tion of English and French experiences into the vocabulary of a purely idealist dialectic, that, as soon as it came into contact with the revolutionary reality, it simply melted and – for what it was worth as a theory – disappeared without trace. This 'biographical refutation' of the *Communist Manifesto*'s criticism of Hess's theory serves, as we can see, only to confirm that the criticism was theoretically correct. And where the problem crops up again in a real sense – in the case of Lassalle – the criticism proved its worth in practical terms as well.

Having said this, let us return to Mehring's first point. If we want to understand 'true socialism' as a product of pre-1848 conditions in Germany, we must proceed from the premiss that it was a movement of intellectuals. In taking over the ready-made experiences of the English and French working-class movements, it was no different from later revolutionary movements made up of intellectuals. There, too, in progressive intellectual circles, the ideological awareness that the old society was in the process of disintegrating existed before the disintegration had found appropriate expression in the shape of real social movements (e.g. Narodniks in Russia; eastern intellectual movements). It is perfectly understandable that intellectuals should latch on to the ready-made experiences of the more advanced forms of social development. Such experiences, after all, are always – not only in times of revolution – part of that social environment in which intellectuals live, elements of their material and intellectual development. The situation of the 'true socialists' is special only in that they began their work in a society which was still at the stage of extremely primitive social differentiation and, in class terms, relatively under-developed, whereas the ideological basis of their work was – particularly in the field of social knowledge – very highly developed. What are the components of this highly advanced ideology? On the one hand, there is the social critique of the great English and French utopians, the breeding-ground of which was the tremendous political and social transformation of society brought about by the bourgeois revolution, and the feverishly rapid development of capitalism, which in turn led to the emergence of the proletariat and the first proletarian uprisings. On the other hand, 'true socialism' is linked to the highest form of ideology ever attained by the bourgeoisie, namely classical German philosophy and the Hegelian dialectic – indeed, it played an active part in the disintegration of Hegelianism.

The other supreme intellectual achievement of the bourgeoisie, classical English economics, is virtually non-existent as a component element of 'true socialism', however. This cannot be explained simply by reference to the economic backwardness of Germany. Indeed – even if we ignore Marx and Engels entirely – the critique of bourgeois society, the 'socialism' of Rodbertus, is very much concerned with the problems of classical economics and especially Sismondi's critique of it. And Hess himself, to whom we shall now devote the whole of our attention, became theoretically convinced after his personal association with Marx and Engels that their method, their theory and their mode of agitation were correct; he subsequently tried to the best of his ability to incorporate this newly mastered territory into his system and to make it intellectually his own. Yet it is precisely his economic works[8] which show most clearly the full extent of his inability, however hard he tried, even simply to understand the real significance of the inversion performed by Marx and Engels on Hegelianism, let alone apply and develop it independently.

What was it in Hess that prevented him from from doing so? It was in fact Hegelian philosophy itself. This may at first seem a trivial, tautological remark. But it acquires greater significance as soon as we have progressed beyond the banal level at which the question is generally dealt with, and managed to grasp correctly – as it is imperative we do – the importance of the Hegelian dialectic in both historical and methodological terms for the development of Marxism. Not that that should be seen as an attempt to 'rehabilitate' Hess. Far from it. It is precisely by posing the problem in this way that we can demonstrate that the severe criticism of him in the *Communist Manifesto* is valid in all essential respects; further, that Hess is of no significance at all as regards the present-day theory of the revolutionary working-class movement; and, indeed, that even his purely historical role in the genesis of historical materialism has been frequently exaggerated by his admirers – among them his latest biographer, Zlocisti. If we nonetheless avail ourselves of the opportunity afforded by the republication of his major writings to undertake an analysis of them, we do so in order that they should serve as a contrast which will help us to elucidate briefly the true progress of the dialectic from Hegel to Marx. Seen in this light, Hess himself appears as a thoroughly unsuccessful forerunner to Marx and a tragic figure inasmuch as he was not only an absolutely honest revolutionary in personal terms, but of all the idealist dialecticians the one who – occasionally – came closest to the Marxist

8. Principally the essay 'Über das Geldwesen' ('The nature of money') in *Püttmann's Rheinische Jahrbücher zur gesellschaftlichen Reform*, I (1845), in Zlocisti's edition see pp. 158ff.

version of the dialectic. (In certain respects – e.g. in the integration of Feuerbach into the dialectical method – he came closer even than Lassalle who was incomparably more gifted as a theoretician and politician. Lassalle, however, also shared many of Hess's limitations.) The schizophrenic nature of Hess's thought is aggravated by the fact that his attempts to overcome Hegel by Hegelian methods always leave him trailing behind Hegel. His dissolution of the Hegelian method turns into dissolution in the very literal sense of the word. The elements which were present in Hegel himself and which Hegel had surmounted dialectically re-emerge naked and unsurmounted. Such was also the case with Bruno Bauer and David Friedrich Strauss, as Marx pointed out: with the one it was the Fichtean, with the other the Spinozan aspect of Hegel's system which received exclusive emphasis.[9]

The twist which Hess gave to the Hegelian system is likewise more Fichtean in nature, although Hess himself consistently claimed to be a Spinozan and although his 'Fichteanism' differs radically from that of Bruno Bauer. It does not set out to resubjectivize Hegelian objectivity, as Bruno Bauer's *Philosophy of Self-Consciousness* aims to do, but rather it is an attempt to overcome the contemplative character of Hegelian philosophy and make the dialectic practical. This tendency towards the practical was bound of necessity to lead back to Fichte. And, moreover, not for epistemological reasons, not because, for instance, in Fichte thinking itself becomes an 'active deed', for that is – even if not terminologically – the essence of every dialectic. If the dialectic is to go beyond the lifeless product, if it is to revert to the process of its production and advance to that of its dissolution, its very thought-processes must have an active character about them. In this respect the difference between Fichte and Hegel is little more than terminological. In fact, if we go to the very core of the matter we will find that Hegel's logic, in spite of its more contemplative terminology, is 'more practical' than Fichte's. The terminological difference conceals a substantial difference, namely the methodological connection in Fichte's work between logic and ethics, but we cannot discuss that at this point. Although that aspect of Fichtean philosophy was consciously assigned a more prominent place in Hess's work, the problem of the history of philosophy is objectively more significant for our present analysis of the dissolution of Hegelianism and the gravitation towards Fichte.

Zlocisti also alludes to the thinker who first posed this question clearly

9. *Nachlass*, II, p. 247.

and precisely: August von Cieszkowski.[10] In all essential respects Cieszkowski remains a Hegelian. His object is only to complete Hegelian philosophy, not to dissolve it. His chief reservation about it, about its philosophy of history, is that it does not pose the question of knowledge of the future.[11] However, it must not be forgotten that the question which Cieszkowski poses himself here has already been answered by Fichte. Fichte's *Characteristics of the Present Age* divides history into five epochs, of which the present, as the epoch of 'absolute sinfulness' is the third. The last two epochs, the structure of which is described in detail, belong to the future.[12] It would be wrong to speak of direct influence from this source, the more so since Cieszkowski and after him Hess both regard the matter as a question, as a problem, whereas Fichte, always the naïve dogmatist, turned up straightaway with an answer.

The very fact that Cieszkowski and Hess pose the question in a more critical, more dialectical, less formal fashion shows that, for all their gravitation towards Fichte, they are in fact striving to progress beyond Fichte and that methodologically such gravitation does not mean simply reverting to Fichte's standpoint. The future as the object of dialectical thinking, the attempt to grasp the future *concretely* by means of dialectics and to make it into a criterion by which to judge past and present – all this is a marked advance on Fichtean philosophy of history. In Fichte's work the future is still little more than a somewhat more concrete expression for Kant's infinite progress, for the fact that the demands of absolute (supra-historical) reason have not as yet been fulfilled. Cieszkowski and Hess, on the other hand, attempt to grasp the historical process dialectically in its concrete uniqueness, with the result that for them the future

10. *Prolegomena zur Historiosophie*, Berlin, Veit & Co., 1838. Cf. Hess's comments on it in the anonymously published work *Die europäische Triarchie*, Leipzig, Otto Wigand, 1841. The roughly contemporary attempts of the group associated with the *Hallische Jahrbücher* to historicize Hegel do not concern us directly here. Further information on this point can be found in Gustav Mayer's essay *Die Anfänge des politischen Radikalismus im vormärzlichen Preussen* ('The beginnings of political radicalism in Prussia before 1848'), *Zeitschrift für Politik*, VI (1913), pp. 10–11.

11. Cf. Cieszkowski, op. cit., pp. 8–9. In Hess's *European Triarchy* the issue is already seen in terms of the dissolution of Hegelian philosophy and indeed of philosophy in general. His preface begins with the statement: 'German philosophy has carried out its mission, it has shown us the way to truth in its entirety. Our task now is to build bridges which will lead us back from heaven to earth. – Whatever remains in isolation, becomes untrue, even truth itself cannot escape this fate if it persists in its lofty seclusion. Just as reality is bad if not permeated by truth, so too truth is bad if it is not made real.'

12. *Werke*, Ausgabe Medicus (Meiner), vol. IV, pp. 11–12.

becomes just as concrete an epoch as were the epochs of the past. Hence, for them knowledge of the future was bound to become a methodological problem of the dialectic, whereas for Fichte the periodizing of history followed directly and unproblematically from his – ethical – conception of the absolute. Hence, too, even when they seem to agree fundamentally on certain questions, above all the interpretation of history according to the notion of natural law, they are in fact doing two completely different things: Fichte is taking what in the eighteenth century was the revolutionary concept of natural law to its philosophical conclusion, whereas Cieszkowski and Hess are attempting to establish a new, concrete, historically derived natural law. (The methodological kernel of the 'system of acquired rights'[13] is in many respects the fulfilment of this endeavour.)

The future in this latter case is revealed methodologically as the concrete, *intentional object* of the philosophy of history. This brings both thinkers, Hess more clearly than Cieszkowski, into a certain methodological affinity with the philosophy of history of Fourier, whom, incidentally, Cieszkowski quotes several times. Even so the problematic remains essentially on Fichtean ground, as we hope to demonstrate. For no matter how modified, no matter how historicized, an analysis operating in terms of the concept of natural law cannot but remain burdened with the antagonism – irresolvable on this ground – between supra-historical principles on one side and history itself on the other. Moreover, any attempt to sublate this antagonism by conceptual dialectics must of necessity be unavailing. Thus the methodological affinity with Fichte proves after all to be very pronounced. For the knowledge of the future, even if it is only a matter of the knowledge of its essence and not of the 'infinite multitude of existent contingencies',[14] is only possible if the fundamental logical-metaphysical categories of the system are extended over past, present and future. True knowledge of the whole system (the inner contemplation of logic) must, in other words, include knowledge of the future. This, however, involves the logical necessity of heightening the purely aprioristic, purely speculative and hence purely contemplative nature of knowledge even beyond the level of Hegel's system.

Cieszkowski accuses Hegel of 'proceeding in *a posteriori* fashion', which he attempts to counter by advancing to '*a priori* deduction'. Parallel to this, his intention is to 'make the whole system of categories develop

13. Reference to Lassalle's *System of acquired rights. A reconciliation of positive law with the philosophy of law* in *Werke*, vols. IX–XII (Editor's note).

14. Cf. Cieszkowski, op. cit., p. 10.

dialectically within history'; he demands 'a systematic *quest* for the logical within world history' in contrast to Hegel, of whom it can only be said that he 'merely *finds* it speculatively';[15] and he moves the future so close to the present that for him 'everything future, irrespective of how reasonable and consistent it proves to be, not only has no effect at all against the already existing, but must already *be* in existence before it itself *becomes* existence'.[16]

And yet the effect of all this is in fact to idealize and ideologize the dialectic even more than Hegel does. True, in stopping at the present, at what he calls the self-attainment of the spirit, Hegel's system is reactionary both in substance and in its intentions and consequences. Looked at from the methodological standpoint, however, refusal to go any further reveals Hegel's magnificent realism, his rejection of all utopias, his concern to conceive philosophy *as the conceptual expression of history itself* and not as philosophy *about* history. Hegel has often – and to some extent justifiably – been attacked for this tendency, this 'reconciliation' with reality. But it must be remembered that it derives methodologically from this urge to develop the categories out of the historical process itself, and that only in consequence of his reactionary *hypostatizing* of the present did it change from a dynamic principle impelling reality forwards into a static one designed to fix the stage presently attained as an absolute. In Cieszkowski and in Hess's *European Triarchy*, the problem of knowledge of the future has the function of overcoming such hypostatization. However, in searching for the answer purely by means of a conceptual dialectics, what they have done is to detach Hegelian dialectics from the real historical process, far more than Hegel does himself, and to make it purely conceptual, purely idealistic – without the possibility of eliminating the reactionary components of the 'reconciliation' from the method.[17]

This is no mere chance. For in all cases where the object-forms of historical reality are discovered in conceptually aprioristic fashion, either reality has to be conceived of as being ultimately and at heart irrational, accessible to these categories only in a 'methodological' sense (see Schelling's later works), or reason and reality, category and history, aprioristic form and empirical material, have somehow to be brought together and 'reconciled' with each other. But that involves applying to

15. ibid., pp. 50–51.   16. ibid., p. 36.

17. E.g. *The European Triarchy*, pp. 9, 37–8. It is well known that Lassalle too makes use of the category of 'reconciliation' (see his *Science and the Workers*, *Werke*, vol. II, p. 258). The methodological necessity for it has the same roots as in the case of Hess.

reality a thought-determinant that has not been developed out of historical reality itself. The consequences of such a process of joining together, of 'reconciliation', are inevitable. Either that reality has to be distorted by constructs, or it becomes necessary to adapt the thought-determinants to the superficial, merely empirical phenomena of historical reality, thereby raising such phenomena to the level of categories, of absolutes. All forms of abstract utopianism are therefore bound – by virtue of their very abstractness and utopianism – to make greater concessions to superficial empirical reality than does a truly dialectical realism. They are bound to hypostatize transient forms of the present, bound to nail development down to such moments of the present, bound to turn reactionary.[18]

The question of 'reconciliation' reveals in fact the most problematical aspect of Hegelian philosophy: in defiance of his programme, idea and reality do not coincide, and hence the duality of theory and practice, the 'unreconciled' confrontation of freedom and necessity, remains unsolved. To put it in terms of the history of the problem: the Kantianism in Hegel remains not quite superseded. Cieszkowski claims that the problem of history – in his terminology, knowledge of the future – finds Hegel 'taking up a critical position analogous to that of Kant in regard to the unattainability of the absolute as such, but with the difference that with Kant it was the necessary result of his standpoint and system, whereas with Hegel it was introduced from without and thus disrupts the rest of his system.'[19]

This partially correct observation demonstrates the presumptuousness of talking in terms of really overcoming the limits of the Hegelian position. On the one hand, that Hegel stops at the present is related, as I have already indicated, to the most profound motives of his thinking – to be precise, to his (in the correct sense) historico-dialectical thinking. For instance, in the preface to his *Philosophy of Right* he writes: 'The task of philosophy is to comprehend *what is*, for *what is* is reason. As for the individual each is a *child of his time* anyway; philosophy, too, is *its time translated into thought*. It is just as stupid to imagine that any philosophy can transcend its contemporary world as that an individual can jump over his time, jump across the Straits of Rhodes.' That is incomparably nearer

18. Proudhon or Fourier provide further instances of this. As for Cieszkowski, it is significant that his future, his era of activity coincides with the era of 'the adequate formation of the life of the state' (op. cit., p. 122). The analogy with Lassalle is striking: 'The developed idea of the state is above all the idea of the estate of the workers.'

19. Cieszkowski, op. cit., p. 9.

to a materialistic-historical conception than a construct *à la* Fichte-Cieszkowski-Hess-Lassalle, where history is divided into successive epochs, the order of which is derived from the logical arrangement of a perfect system.

On the other hand, of course, Cieszkowski is correct in drawing attention to the Kantian thing-in-itself problem – more correct, even, than he himself realizes. But it is precisely in his correctness that it becomes clear where the 'supersession' of Hegel actually leads back to a position less advanced than Hegel's. For, even with Kant himself the problem of the thing-in-itself is very closely connected with the problem of history, with the problem of becoming.[20] It is not by chance that the transcendental dialectics of the *Critique of Pure Reason* lead into the forecourt of dialectics: to the insoluble antinomies. In doing so it demonstrates that to grasp reality contemplatively (and to adopt the intuiting attitude is to dissolve all becoming into being)[21] can lead at best to the discovery of the contradictory foundations of existence, but not to their resolution. Even when the *Critique of Practical Reason* transfers the resolution of these *same* antinomies, the solution of the thing-in-itself problem, into the realm of practice, it cannot – in the final analysis – advance to a proper formulation of the question because the practice of individual action (the only one which Kant knows) cannot be anything more than pseudo-practice. It is a form of practice which is unable to shake the foundations of reality and for which, therefore, the object-forms of (contemplatively grasped) reality remain unaltered. Its new attitude to reality leaves reality untouched and cannot be more than something formal and subjective: the Ought. Now Hegel senses very acutely the emptiness, the transcendent and abstract nature of this Ought. But since he is likewise unable to indicate concretely the real subject of revolutionizing practice, he cannot go beyond a mere rejection of the Ought – which leaves the problematical nature of the concept in Kant's system unsolved. Hegel, too, cannot con-

20. For a discussion of this issue see my book *History and Class Consciousness*, particularly the chapter entitled 'Reification and the Consciousness of the Proletariat'. On the similarity, here very close, between Kant and the materialism of the eighteenth century, see Plekhanov, *Beiträge zur Geschichte des Materialismus* (Contributions to the history of materialism), Berlin, 1957, pp. 20ff., where becoming, origin, appears as the unknowable.

21. This is very clear in Feuerbach, who attacks the 'monarchist tendency of time' in Hegel, in the name of the 'liberalism of space'. See Ludwig Feuerbach, *Zur Kritik der Hegelschen Philosophie* (A critique of Hegel's Philosophy), *Werke*, Ausgabe Jodl, vol. II, pp. 160–1.

ceive of a transformation of given being, of the present, except in the form of an 'Ought'. The continuation of the passage quoted above reads: 'If his theory actually goes beyond that, if he builds himself a world *as it ought to be,* then of course it exists, but only in his mind – a soft element prone to every possible kind of fantasy.' That in itself represents an enormous advance on Kant in that it grasps the present concretely as present, that is, as the product of a historical process and no longer as an essentially immutable being.

In contrast to Fichte with his revolutionary Utopia, Hegel developed very early on in his work the tendency to 'understand what is', a tendency which originally pointed energetically in the direction of the future. His concern to comprehend the present as at once become and becoming is expressed, for example, in an epigram written during his first Jena period:

Strive, attempt more than today and yesterday; you will be, not better than time, but time as good as it can be.[22]

Here was the germ of a true historical dialectics (the dialectics of history translated into thought). For it is precisely in the present that all forms of objectivity (*Gegenständlichkeit*) can be revealed quite concretely as processes, since it is the present which shows most clearly the unity of result and starting-point of the process. Given that, the rejection of all 'Oughts' and futuristic utopian thinking, the concentration of philosophy on knowledge of the present (grasped dialectically) emerges precisely as the only possible epistemological method of knowing what is really knowable about the future, the tendencies within the present which impel it really and concretely towards the future.

However, implicit within this self-same tendency of Hegel, his realism, his rejection of all forms of Utopia and all merely formal 'Oughts', was the limitation which not only prevented him from going any further, but even forced him into an increasingly reactionary position. As a result, his 'present' lost its immanent tendency to point to the future and ossified more and more until it became a hard and fast result. It ceased to be dialectical. The fundamental problem confronting the philosophy of right at that time was posed by the fact of the revolution. Constitutional changes were recognized as being necessary; but since the attempt to solve the problem was undertaken in constitutional terms – that is, in formal terms: immanently juristically, and in terms of social content: within the

22. *Dokumente zu Hegels Entwicklung*, ed. J. Hoffmeister, Stuttgart, 1936, p. 388 (Editor's note).

framework of bourgeois society[23] – it was bound to lead increasingly in that direction, especially if the revolutionary, 'eternal' law of reason was abandoned. Whereas Fichte's philosophy of right seeks guarantees which would establish this law of reason in the face of empirical reality and the actual wielders of power, Hegel attempts to find the indications of further development within contemporary development itself. The more realistically he conceives this present and the closer he moves to the Prussian Junker state, however, the less he is able to recognize developmental tendencies concretely and the more he is obliged to accept this state absolutely, thereby – from the point of view of the philosophy of history – bringing the historical process to a halt in the present.

Thus the result of Hegelian philosophy is to put an end to the process as process. Historically and logically, every form of abstract petrification and thing-ness has been dissolved into a concrete becoming, a process, only for the product of the process, the present, to petrify once again into a mere product, a thing. Dialectics turns into yet another metaphysics – a change which penetrates deeply into the structure of Hegelian logic, where (even in terms of pure logic) it dissolves dialectics into an appearance and transforms it into a kind of aesthetics. Hegel relegates to the level of sham movement the crowning achievement of his dialectics, the dialectics of being and becoming, while at the same time raising it, as he thinks, to the level of a pure movement in itself. He writes: 'The movement of the concept is to be regarded, as it were, merely as a game.'[24] The 'reconciliation' in which this construct of the Hegelian system finds concrete and historical expression is therefore manifestly and essentially dualistic. Looked at in relation to earlier philosophy it is the resolution of Kant's antinomies; turned forward, however, it represents their reproduction on a higher level. It is not possible to preserve the this-sidedness of philosophy unless the real, dialectical tendencies, the direction of the real dialectical process can also be shown as effective, as real, as *process* in the present; unless, that is, the present points in real and dialectical fashion beyond itself and into the future. This Hegel fails to do. Hence, in terms of the motives which led him to posit it, Hegel's 'reconciliation' is an expression – albeit a resigned one – of his self-criticism and his realism *vis-à-vis* history. In its methodological, systematic and objective conse-

23. We may consider Condorcet and Sièyes in this light. The line of development of revolutionary bourgeois philosophies of right culminates in Lassalle's *System of Acquired Rights*.

24. *Encyclopaedia*, Para. 161, Addition.

quences, however, it represents the fixing of the present as an absolute and the elimination of dialectics – in other words, it is a reactionary principle.

It is therefore only too understandable that the philosophically radical Young Hegelians should take up this problem. However, they attempt to transcend the logical limitations of Hegel's system, which are only a consequence – albeit a necessary one – of his attitude towards the real historical process, in and by logic itself. (That this logic is supposed to be a logic of history alters nothing substantial in the situation.) As a result, the future – knowledge of which is possible only as the object of a revolutionizing practice and which only becomes something concrete and real for us at all through practice – becomes for them the object of mere contemplation. Past, present and future appear, it is true, on the same level of comprehensibility. The level, however, is to an even greater extent that of 'pure' cognition, the purely logico-systematic development of the dialectical triad. Such 'knowledge' of the future means that the dialectical connection between past and present established by Hegel has disappeared.

The full significance of this regression to Fichte – and beyond him to Kant – emerges clearly in the theory of freedom which Hess formulates in his *European Triarchy*. This theory is significant for our discussion in that it is, after all, precisely in the positive relationship to the future that freedom should manifest itself. According to Hess, since Hegel 'draws only the past as such into the realm of speculation, necessity is therefore predominant'. 'What happened *before* us,' says Hess, 'even if it happened for itself with freedom, nonetheless happened for us of necessity because it did not happen through us. Only what is achieved *by us,* although in itself it happens of necessity, happens *for us* with freedom – insofar, that is, as our innermost being, consciousness, is the determining element in it.'[25] Anybody familiar with the Kantian theory of freedom will immediately realize that in this passage the contradictory antithesis of freedom and necessity, the merely subjective nature of freedom, the transference of freedom and necessity into two completely separate spheres[26] – that all this, although formulated in Hegelian terms, is wholly Kantian in spirit, and that Hess has fallen back way behind the stage of a dialectical union of freedom and necessity already reached by Hegel.

Because of this basic attitude, even the attempt to historicize the dialectical categories beyond the level of historicization in Hegel is bound to fail.

25. *The European Triarchy*, p. 14.
26. *Critique of Practical Reason*, (Phil. Bibliothek 38), Leipzig, 1915, pp. 121–3.

It turns into a wholly arbitrary assignment of types of categories to certain historical epochs: neither the necessity of their connection with these epochs, nor the development of the historical epochs out of each other emerges from the exercise. This, of course, is not to deny that the Young Hegelians are sincere in their attempts to transcend Hegel. The most radical of them are fully aware that changes within society become illusory if the authority of a *single* – essentially supra-historical – system of logic is spread across history. And yet they are unable to be radical in drawing the necessary conclusions from this understanding – which would involve applying Hegel's dictum on philosophy in general (that it 'translates its time into thought') concretely to logic itself. Cieszkowski's phrasing is truly Hegelian![27] 'Just as everything in the world is subject to history, so history in turn is subject to God', whereas Hess's treatment of the same problem acquires a Spinozan accent.[28] The *methodological aspect* of the question, however, remains unaffected.

To go into a detailed analysis of Cieszkowski's and Hess's historical constructs would take us too far. For whether Cieszkowski applies the category of mechanism derived from Hegel's logic to antiquity, that of chemism to the Middle Ages and that of organism to the modern age as a special category; or whether Hess defines the three periods of world history as being from the Flood to the migration of nations and from there to the French Revolution, after which the modern age begins, as attempts to transcend Hegel and really historicize dialectics, they both amount to the same thing. In each case we are presented – as in Fichte's history of philosophy – with aprioristically construed, logical characteristics of historical epochs, with differentiations *within the concept*. These are then applied – not without a good deal of violence – to historical reality. At which point, of course, all the contradictions underlying the exercise come to light in all their crudeness.[29] With Hegel himself, the inconsistency in the relationship between historical and logical succession of the categories was – at least in part – an instinctive corrective to the decline into formal apriorism and its vacuous constructs. The radical Young Hegelians, however, think this idealistic and formalistic aspect of Hegel's system through to its conclusion; in so doing, they loosen the relationship between the

---

27. op. cit., p. 69.

28. E.g. *The European Triarchy*, pp. 148–9, where Spinoza is made to supersede Hegel.

29. Via Grün this Fichteanized Hegelianism also influenced Proudhon. Marx scathingly uncovers its contradictions in *The Poverty of Philosophy*, op. cit., pp. 127ff.

dialectics of real history and conceptual dialectics which, although he had not worked it out consistently, was already present in Hegel's work.[30]

The more constructed the philosophy of history becomes and the looser its connection with historical reality, the more it is bound to become basically contemplative in character. As this occurs, so the 'deed' which Hess henceforth makes the focus of his thinking is less able to be real practice, revolutionizing and transforming reality; so, too, philosophy is bound to succumb to the methodological dualism of Kant, the separation of 'pure' and 'practical reason'. We have already established Hess's tendency to regress via Fichte to Kant in our discussion of his treatment of the question of freedom in *The European Triarchy*. His abstract separation of theory and practice, however, becomes more strikingly obvious the more he exerts himself trying to use his philosophical 'supersession' of Hegel as the philosophical basis of socialism. Here the duality of theory and practice assumes the form of a duality between the historical movement, whose 'mission' it is to bring socialism about in a real sense, and the philosophical theory of this movement, which is supposed to give it clarity and direction and explain its real goals to it.

It must be emphasized that this duality existed within the contemporary working-class movement itself at that time. And not only in socially undeveloped Germany: even in France and England the theory of social revolution and the revolutionary practice of the proletariat had still not yet come together. No socialist theoretician before Marx and Engels had been able to perceive in the social being of the proletariat itself the process whose real dialectics has only to be made conscious in order to become the theory of revolutionary practice.[31] At this point, the central problem in the emergence of socialist theory in the 1840s, the theoretical blind-alley into which Hess's supersession of Hegel led him, becomes blatantly obvious. Although he imagined he was going beyond Hegel by including the future in the triadic progression of his logic, what he was able to say about it amounted to no more than a few at best abstract and utopian

30. In his polemics with Rosenkranz, Lassalle, in contrast with Cieszkowski, treats mechanism, chemism and organism as general logical categories applicable to any epoch. This does indeed enable him to overcome Cieszkowski's abstract scheme, but at the cost of referring the relation between logic and history back to the level of Hegel's logic (rather than to an essentially more historical phenomenology or to the particular disciplines). Cf. Lassalle in his essay *Die Hegelsche und die Rosenkranzsche Logik*, *Werke*, vol. VI, pp. 5off.

31. Marx describes this dualism, its causes and its cure in *The Poverty of Philosophy*, op. cit., pp. 140–1.

generalities. The price he had to pay was high: his theory raised to the level of a category and perpetuated the duality of theory and practice in the shape of the duality of socialism and proletariat (the ideological consequence of the undeveloped state of the working-class movement of the time); philosophy was forced to 'reconcile' itself to this reality. In his first attempt to provide a philosophical basis for socialism he talks of the old duality in religion and politics. For him the break-up of that duality means the beginning of 'revolution *and* criticism'.[32] What he fails to realize is that this is simply to reproduce the old duality in a new guise. On the contrary, he even attempts to preserve the purity, scientific status and objectivity of this philosophy (which, it should be remembered, is supposed to lead to 'action'). In his otherwise commendable critique of Lorenz von Stein he attacks Stein for 'repeating ad nauseam the connection between communism and the proletariat'. 'This,' he goes on,[33] 'is the only vital aspect which Stein is capable of getting out of communism. But when it is a question of justifying the claims of the proletariat, he glosses over the problem with a few philosophical flourishes. The insubstantiality of his reasoning reveals his inability to achieve understanding on this point. The only way he could have come to such an understanding, of course, would have been through the insight into the connection of communism to socialism and science. As I have said, he lacks this insight altogether.'

Hess could not possibly have been totally unaware of the problematic nature of his method – as is evidenced by the constant changes he made to his system and his frequent attempts to draw on Marx. That he nevertheless clung to it is of course explicable in terms of his class position. Hess philosophizes from the standpoint of the revolutionary *intelligentsia* sympathetic to the coming social revolution. The sufferings of the proletariat form the starting-point of his philosophizing, the proletariat is the

32. *Die Philosophie der Tat* (The Philosophy of Action') in Herwegh's *Twenty-one Sheets from Switzerland, 1843*, see Zlocisti, p. 47.

33. *Sozialismus und Kommunismus*, ibid., p. 72. His view does not alter even *after* reading Marx's and Engels's essays in the *Deutsch-Französische Jahrbücher*. Cf. the way he derives the origins of socialism 'from without', i.e. from the nature of the proletariat, and 'from within', i.e. from the theoretical necessity of science arising from Marx's *Critique of Hegel's Philosophy of Right*, which he actually cites in his essay *Über die sozialistische Bewegung in Deutschland* ('The Socialist Movement in Germany'), in Grün's *Neue Anekdoten*, 1845, see ibid., p. 106; see further the polemic against the idea of socialism as the problem of the Have-nots (*Magenfrage*), ibid., p. 129, and the introduction to the *Gesellschaftsspiegel*, quoted by Struve in *Die neue Zeit*, XV/II, 1896–7, pp. 269, etc.

object of his concern and his struggle, and later on he even acknowledges
the proletariat's struggle for emancipation as an important element in the
imminent liberation of humanity from the yoke of capitalism. Besides –
or rather, over and above this, however, hovers theory, knowledge,
philosophy, which impartially and selflessly takes over the intellectual
leadership of the good cause.[34] The fond belief that he inhabits a sphere
above all class antagonisms and all egoistical interests of his fellow-men is
typical of the intellectual who does not participate – directly – in the process of production and whose existential basis, both material and intellectual, seems to be the 'whole' of society, regardless of class differences.
(The less developed the class antagonisms in any society, the easier it
is for this illusion to take hold – and the more difficult it is to see through
it as an illusion.) Hence, when he strives honestly to recognize and proclaim the truth, he claims that he can see no social basis for the construction of his 'truth'. In the Germany of the 1840s it was all the easier for
such an illusion of 'neutral' classlessness to emerge, in that the still primitive class-differentiations virtually ruled out the possibility of an 'intelligentsia' as an independent stratum with independent interests such as
existed, for example, at the time of the growth and blossoming of social
revolutionism in Russia. Even there, of course, there arose the illusion
and the ideology of classlessness. But there is one important difference:
the ideology of the social revolutionaries was already permeated with the
out-and-out hypocritical ideology – the state as being 'above and beyond
classes', and so on – put out by a bourgeoisie that had come to the end of
its development. At the time of the 'true socialists', however, the real
ideologues of the bourgeoisie were still openly and clearly proclaiming
bourgeois class interests. (One only has to think of the significant French
historians of the time, for instance.)

If theory is thus assigned a place above the struggle of the different
groups, estates and classes, the necessary consequence is a moralistic
and moralizing verdict on the present, and specifically on those tendencies
opposed to the social revolution. For if communism is not the class-truth
of the proletariat; if it does not emerge from the proletariat's class-situa-
tion as its conceptual expression; if rather, it is the 'objective truth' of the
historical process – then the motives for resisting the 'truth' can only be
ignorance or moral inferiority. The first mentioned played an important

34. Much of this is echoed by Lassalle, e.g. in the famous speech *Die Wissenschaft
und die Arbeiter* ('Science and the Workers'), which Lassalle describes as the 'two opposite poles of society' (*Werke*, vol. II, p. 248).

role in the thinking of the Utopians. Hess and company criticized bourgeois society, the capitalist system of production, by subsuming its economic principles under the – ethical – category of 'egoism' and condemning it morally as such.[35]

There is no denying that 'egoism' did in fact play a big part in the growth of bourgeois ideology; in this sense, then, it was not wholly inappropriate to relate the critique of the bourgeois class to this question. But it must be remembered that for the first great champions of this ideology (Hobbes, Mandeville, Bayle, *et al.*) the struggle to establish the new morality was a very real one. Not only was there a close connection between the war on feudal morality (and that of the Puritans when the bourgeois class was just emerging) and the elaboration of the theoretical cornerstone of the whole bourgeois ideology, classical economics, but this ideology also provided very important weapons for the bourgeoisie's actual class struggle. By Hess's time the frankness with which the morality of egoism was first proclaimed had already begun to evaporate. This was partly because the growing contradictions of capitalist production forced the bourgeoisie to resort to hypocrisy in the moral sense as well, preventing it increasingly from 'expressing what is' in clear and bold tones; and partly because the development of classical economics had robbed this moral theory of much of its practical significance for the class-consciousness of the bourgeoisie. Smith and Ricardo concretized in economic terms what someone like Mandeville had not been able to express except in much more ideological form. Already in Smith's economics the 'egoism of conduct' had found quite unmythological expression, and it was only the 'extra-economic' aspects of life – that is, what seemed to them to be 'extra-economic' – which were still connected with the ethics of the great growth-period of bourgeois ideology (cf. Smith's relation to Shaftesbury).

That Hess was unable to advance beyond a moral condemnation of 'egoism' – even though he represents it as a necessary product of bourgeois society and draws constant parallels with that society's (somewhat superficially conceived) economic foundations – proved fatal to his theoretical development. True, he regarded it as a necessary product of bourgeois society, but only as a petrified one: he saw it metaphysically and not dialectically..Hence he could only take up a moralizing attitude towards it. And since Hess's socialism, his logico-dialectically 'known

35. Cf. 'Über die Not in unserer Gesellschaft und deren Abhilfe' ('Poverty in our society and how to alleviate it') in *Püttmanns Bürgerbuch*, 1845, in Zlocisti, p. 138; and also 'Über das Geldwesen' in Zlocisti, p. 164, etc.

future', did not sprout from the real soil of the concrete class struggles of the present either, but was logically sublimated from the antagonisms thereby produced – with the result that those antagonisms, once transformed into pure thoughts, were bound to harden idealistically into autonomous essences – the future simply stood there opposite the 'problems' of the present as a ready-made 'solution'. There is therefore no real mediation between present and future: Hess failed to recognize in the elements of the present, in the tendencies which have brought it into being and make it problematic, the real forces which impel it to transcend itself.

His attitude is made very clear in his criticism of Lorenz von Stein.[36] He writes: 'The gross mistake which Stein makes, and to which he is driven primarily as a result of his wrong understanding of the French mind, is to see in the striving for equality only the purely superficial, material trend towards pleasure. On the one hand he can find excuses even for the so-called materialism of today, seeing in it only the first attempts of the abstract personality to give itself a concrete content. On the other, he detects in communism only the striving of the proletariat to secure for itself the same pleasures as those enjoyed by the owners. One of the chief virtues of communism, however, is that it does away with the antagonism between pleasure and work. Only where ownership is divided is pleasure distinct from work. The state of community is the practical fulfilment of the philosophical ethic which recognizes free activity as the true and sole pleasure, the so-called highest good. As against this, the state of divided ownership is the practical fulfilment of egoism and immorality, which on the one hand negates free activity and degrades it to slave-labour, while on the other it replaces man's highest good by bestial pleasure, the goal worthy of that equally bestial labour. Stein is caught up in these abstract notions of work and pleasure, whereas communism has long since advanced beyond them. It has already become – in the minds of its foremost representatives, of course – what it is destined one day to become in reality: practical ethics.'

This is how the present is abstractly and moralistically condemned. In his *Philosophy of Action* Hess says:[37] 'We know full well that there are tame and lame philosophers who, because they lack the wrathful courage of action, poke around by the light of their Diogenes lantern in the dung-heap of lies that passes for religion and politics, in the hope of fishing out something or other which they might yet find a use for. But it is not worth

36. Zlocisti, pp. 70–71.   37. ibid., p. 43.

the trouble of raking out the miserable rags buried in the debris of the past. . . .' And in keeping with this attitude towards the present, the only possible bridge to the future is therefore the new morality, translated into effective action. 'You have been told,' Hess goes on,[38] 'that man cannot serve two masters at once, God and Mammon. We, however, tell you that man does not have to serve either as long as he thinks and feels *as man*. *Love* one another, unite in *spirit*, and you will possess in your hearts that blissful consciousness which you have vainly sought for so long above yourselves, in God. *Organize* yourselves, unite in *reality*, and you will possess in your actions and works all the wealth which you have sought for so long *outside* yourselves, in money.'

That passage reveals the decisive influence of Feuerbach on the 'true socialists', particularly on Hess. He gave them a new, positive morality with which to confront the 'morality of egoism'. What Marx and Engels received from Feuerbach was at most the final encouragement they needed to eradicate the remaining traces of Hegelian idealism from their thinking and to transform the dialectic in a definitively and completely materialist way. Hess and company, however, took up (Hess far less wholeheartedly than Grün or Kriege) precisely that aspect of Feuerbach which remained essentially idealistic[39] and which Marx and Engels even at that early stage regarded indifferently or critically. The difference is brought out very clearly and characteristically in Engels's letter of 19 September 1844[40] to Marx at the time of Marx's collaboration with Hess, who had just written his pamphlet, *The Last Philosophers,* as an attack on Stirner and Bauer. Referring to Stirner, Engels writes: 'But we must also take up those elements of the principle which are true. And it is certainly true that we must first make a cause our own, selfish cause before we can do anything for it – that in this sense, therefore, even disregarding possible material hopes, we are communists for selfish reasons; that it is for selfish reasons that we want to be *human beings* not mere individuals.'

38. 'Poverty in our society and how to alleviate it', p. 149.

39. Idealistic in the sense in which for instance Plekhanov describes the view of history held by the eighteenth-century materialists as idealistic.

40. *Briefwechsel*, vol. I, p. 7. Incidentally, it is worth remarking that the necessary connection between the 'idea' and 'egoistic interest' had already been noticed by Hegel, albeit in somewhat mythologized form, and was dropped only by his successors; cf. the role of the 'passions' in his philosophy of history or his treatment of the 'useful' in the *Phenomenology*. The healthy side of Stirner which Engels acknowledges in this letter – while emphasizing Stirner's similarity to Bentham – is the likewise mythologizing attachment to the (bourgeois) theory of bourgeois society.

201 of Idealist Dialectics

Even Hess, of course, is not uncritical of Feuerbach, and his criticism is sometimes very incisive: as, for instance, when he applies to Feuerbach Marx's critique of conditions in Germany. He writes:[41] 'The Feuerbachian "philosophy of the future" is nothing but a *philosophy of the present*, but of a present which still appears to Germans as future, as ideal. What in England, France, North America and elsewhere is already present reality – the modern state with its counterpart and complement, bourgeois society – still finds only philosophical and theoretical expression in *Principles of the Philosophy of the Future*.' At the same time Hess realizes that the flaw in Feuerbach's thinking is that it ignores the *social* nature of man: consequently: 'man' as he is in Feuerbachian anthropology cannot be real, concrete man. In his essay, *On the Socialist Movement in Germany*, Hess argues:[42] 'Why did Feuerbach not attain these important practical consequences of his system? – the essence of God, says Feuerbach, is the transcendent essence of man, and the true theory of divine essence is the theory of human essence: *theology is anthropology*. That is true, but it is not the whole truth. Man's essence, it needs to be added, is the social nature and the cooperation of the various individuals for one and the same purpose, for wholly identical interests. And the true theory of man, true humanism, is the theory of human socialization. That is: *anthropology is socialism*.' And immediately following this Hess, while conceding that Feuerbach advances beyond the individual human being, accuses him of locating 'the human-species-act' essentially, if not exclusively, in 'thought'. Hess correctly assesses as inconsistencies Feuerbach's attempts to overcome the purely contemplative nature of his philosophy and his acknowledgement that the 'species-act' expresses itself in other areas. 'We cannot understand why Feuerbach admits it,' he writes, 'since nowhere does he arrive at *philosophical* consequences other than those which follow from the correct version of the act of thinking.'

In spite of this valid criticism – at some points fairly close to that of Marx and Engels, into which an equally incisive critique of the Young Hegelians is woven – Hess nonetheless succumbs to the very weakest, most idealistic aspect of Feuerbach's work: his ethic of love. We have already indicated the social factors which defined Hess's position in this respect as that of an intellectual who merely enters into an 'alliance' with the revolutionary proletariat but is never capable of thinking from the standpoint of the proletariat in its actual class situation. Philosophically

---

41. *The Last Philosophers* (1845), in Zlocisti, p. 192.
42. In Grün's *Neue Anekdoten* (1845), in Zlocisti, pp. 115–16.

this finds expression in Hess's uncritical adoption of Feuerbach's basically wrong attitude to the Hegelian dialectic and in particular his theory of the relationship between immediacy and mediation. 'Feuerbach,' he says,[43] 'proceeds from the correct principle that man as he alienates his essence or develops himself is the creator of all collisions, contradictions and antagonisms: hence, that there can be no question at all of a speculative *mediation* since there is in truth nothing to mediate, no identity of *opposites*, but only and everywhere man's identity with himself to be re-established. Antagonisms and contradictions exist only in the imagination of speculative mystics.' By identifying alienated man as the essence of Christianity Feuerbach 'has identified the root of all theoretical mistakes and contradictions – although he does not carry on systematically to demonstrate how *all* antagonisms and contradictions arise from self-alienating man'. It becomes very clear here how ill-equipped Hess is, despite his critique of Feuerbach's failure to include a social dimension, to perceive the fundamental mistake in Feuerbach's whole formulation of the question. By that, of course, we mean the way in which he abstracts from the historical process, and his consequently uncritical attitude to the socio-historical character of the religious phenomena which he sets out to criticize and dissolve anthropologically. In his seventh thesis on Feuerbach,[44] Marx formulates this objection with the utmost precision: 'Feuerbach therefore fails to see that "religious sentiment" is itself a *social product* and that the abstract individual whom he is analysing belongs to a certain form of society.' Hence, according to Marx, the standpoint of the old materialism – to which in this sense even Feuerbach belongs – is merely bourgeois society (ninth and tenth theses). This is the kind of criticism which Hess strives to achieve in his identification of Feuerbachian 'philosophy of the future' with advanced bourgeois society in England, etc., but at every decisive juncture where his critique of Feuerbach needs to be concretized he veers off to work the weakest aspects of Feuerbach into his own philosophy.

The false methodological terrain on to which Hess allowed himself to be lured is Feuerbach's rejection of the Hegelian concept of mediation, the attempt to restore immediate knowledge to its rightful position. True, Feuerbach protests that what he means by immediate knowledge is not to be confused with earlier versions – e.g. that of Jacobi.[45] But even if we

43. ibid., p. 114.
44. *The German Ideology*, London & Moscow, 1965, p. 661 (Editor's note).
45. *Zur Kritik der Hegelschen Philosophie*, op. cit., p. 168.

could grant that he was absolutely correct in this respect, one of the most important achievements of Hegelian philosophy, one of the points in which it contained the *possibility* of being developed further into materialist dialectics, would nevertheless have been lost in doing so. That possibility is, namely, the *methodological possibility* of acknowledging and recognizing the social reality of the present in its reality and yet still reacting to it critically – not moralistically-critically, but in the sense of practical-critical activity. In Hegel, admittedly, no more than the possibility existed. But it proved to be decisive for the development of socialist theory that, methodologically, Marx took over *directly* from Hegel at this point, purging Hegel's method of its idealistic inconsistencies and inaccuracies, 'setting it on its feet' and, no matter how much he owes to Feuerbach's encouragement, rejecting the Feuerbachian 'improvement' on Hegel. The 'true socialists' on the other hand, Hess included, followed Feuerbach uncritically. Precisely because 'true socialism' from its very beginning idealistically watered down Hegel and transformed his objective dialectics of the historical process itself into a mere conceptual dialectics, Feuerbach's opposition to Hegel must have seemed to them like a way out at last from the blind alley in which they had become stuck. (If Lassalle in spite of his idealistic dialectics maintained his superiority over the 'true socialists' in many respects, it was largely owing to his *more orthodox* Hegelianism.) The great influence which Feuerbach had on the radical young Hegelians rests, then, on the fact that in this question he stood on the same methodological ground as they did – albeit often with inverted *value*-symbols for the elements which go to make up the method. In terms of the problem to be discussed now, that can be put as follows: both treated mediation as something purely conceptual. With the Bauer brothers and their philosophy of self-consciousness, it was turned into a thought-fetish as the real motive force of world history;[46] while Feuerbach denied its claim to any real objectivity.

46. Hess consistently rejects the philosophy of self-consciousness, but often comes closer to it than he himself realizes. Thus in establishing the methodological foundations of the *Philosophy of Action*, he writes: 'Change, the different aspects of life, cannot be understood as a change in the law of activity, as objectively different life, but only as a difference of self-consciousness. Reflection, which turns everything upside down, asserts the opposite: "Objective life has different aspects, the ego is always the same" ' (ibid., p. 39). Hess's Kantian and Fichtean idealism is revealed by the fact that he can see the dilemma here, but does not consider, even as a methodological possibility, that these two factors could enter into a process of dialectical interaction, mutually modifying each other.

Feuerbach argues in the *Principles of the Philosophy of the Future*:[47] 'Only that is *true* and *divine* which *needs no proof, immediately speaks for itself and carries conviction,* and entails immediately the affirmation that it is – the positive as such, the indubitable as such, the crystal clear. . . . Everything is mediated, says Hegelian philosophy. But nothing is *true* unless it is no longer mediated, but immediate. . . . The *self-mediating* truth is *the truth still afflicted with its opposite.* We start with that opposite, but it is later transcended. But if it is something to be transcended, something to be negated, why should I start there, why not straightaway with its negation? . . . Why should what is certain and proven *through itself* not be higher than what is certain through the nullity of its opposite? Who, then, can elevate mediation to necessity, to the law of truth? Only he who is still caught up in that which is to be negated, who is *still fighting and struggling with himself and has not yet completely squared matters with himself. . . .*'

From this follows, as it were, as an epistemological foundation of the

47. Feuerbach, *Principles of the Philosophy of the Future, Werke,* ed. Jodl, vol. II, p. 301. I have quoted only the passage relating to the problem of immediacy and mediation. Feuerbach's equation of immediacy and sensuousness explains his great impact on Hess, but is of no interest here since we are concerned with the distinction between dialectical and undialectical thought, not between idealism and materialism. The question only becomes crucial with Marx since the problem of materialism forms the demarcation line between himself and Hegel, just as here the problem of dialectics divides him from Feuerbach. The relations between the latter and Marx (and for that matter between Marx and Hegel) have not been clarified either theoretically or historically. In my view Mehring has overestimated Feuerbach's influence. He can appeal to a number of individual comments by Marx, but these are far from sufficient to prove that the *objective* influence was really as great as the *impression* Feuerbach made on him. Thus Hammacher, for instance, cites a number of passages from *The Holy Family* in support of his contention that for a time at least Marx, like the 'true socialists', subscribed to Feuerbach's ethics of love. But on closer inspection, these very passages seem to prove the opposite. It seems to me that at the time when the young Marx was attempting to fight his way out of the conceptual jungle of Young Hegelianism and back to reality, Feuerbach's materialism – despite profound disagreements – must have been congenial to him for the same sort of reasons as made Hegel at the period of his great reckoning with Kant and Fichte take to the naturalist philosophers of law (above all, Hobbes) whom he treated much more sympathetically than ever before and much more gently than Kant or Fichte. Marx very soon saw through Feuerbach quite clearly. And in later years the sections of *The Holy Family* where he praised Feuerbach struck him as 'very humorous' although he did not repudiate the work in its entirety (see his letter to Engels of 24 April 1867). (For Mehring's views on the influence of Feuerbach on Marx, see *Karl Marx: The Story of his Life,* London, 1951, pp. 52ff. On Hammacher, see Emil Hammacher, *Das philosophisch-ökonomische System des Marxismus,* p. 78 – ed.)

only true immediate knowledge, the unity of being and essence. At the same time, Feuerbach as an honest thinker finds himself obliged to admit that 'in human life', 'but then only in *abnormal, unfortunate cases*', being is separated from essence. Then 'it happens that one does not also have one's essence where one has one's being, but precisely because of this separation one is also not truly, not with heart and soul there where one is bodily. You are only where your heart is. But all beings – *with the exception of unnatural cases* – are willingly where and what they are. That is, their essence is not separated from their being, nor their being from their essence.'[48] Mediation is then no longer the conceptual expression of the dialectical structure of being itself, which consists of opposites dissolving one another and producing new antagonisms. Nor is it any longer the logical form in which we reproduce conceptually the dialectical process of being and thereby conceive the results of the process (which, viewed in isolation, are necessarily given as petrified products and hence can be grasped immediately only in metaphysical terms) really as results – that is, not in a static metaphysical fashion but within the context of the process as a whole, as in Hegel. Instead, it is a formalistic means of *communicating* immediately evident thought-contents. Feuerbach expresses this very clearly in his *Critique of Hegelian Philosophy*:[49] 'Thinking is an *immediate* activity insofar as it is *self-activity*. . . . Demonstration is nothing other than showing that what I say is *true*; it means nothing other than taking back the alienation of the thought to the *primary source* of the thought. . . . Now, it is only in the communicative activity of the thought

48. *Principles of the Philosophy of the Future*, op. cit., p. 286 (my italics). The identity of being and essence, together with the very characteristic reservation, is the logical formulation of the same utopianism that we found in Hess's identity of work and enjoyment. The similarity is by no means fortuitous. On the contrary, it arises inevitably when a thinker attempts to resolve a socially given antinomy in purely conceptual terms. Interestingly enough (though we cannot probe the matter further here) it turns out that both utopians and apologists have to face *the same logical consequences*. Thus vulgar economists are forced to posit an identity between consumption and production (an identity which, as we shall demonstrate, will be taken over by Grün and Hess); thus too Hegel is reduced to a similarly utopian solution to such a fundamental ideological fact of bourgeois society as the separation of legality and morality, and so on. *The fact that on this point* Kant and Fichte uphold a realistic position *vis-à-vis* Hegel – which admittedly amounts to no more than the insistence that it is a fundamental fact of the contemporary world – became of great importance for the later contribution of Fichte to the break-up of Hegelianism. A detailed discussion of the relations between Fichte and Hegel would take us too far from our theme.

49. op. cit., pp. 169–71.

for others that the demonstration has its *raison d'être*. If I want to prove something, I prove it for others. . . . Every demonstration is therefore, not a mediation of the thought in and for the thought itself,[50] but a mediation by means of language, [between my mind], *insofar as it is mine*, and the mind of the *other insofar as it is his*.' 'Hegelian philosophy,' says Feuerbach,[51] *'lacks immediate unity, immediate certainty, immediate truth.'*

Such arguments do not in any sense overcome Hegel's idealism definitively, as Feuerbach hoped they would. All they do is rather to raise moralizing utopianism to what is philosophically certainly its highest conceptual stage and to create an epistemological justification of ethical utopianism. An immediately certain unity, an immediately obvious truth, can only be attained in two ways. In the first place, the basic societal forms of the present are given to us as immediate realities – in fact, the more subtle and complex (in Hegel's terms, the more mediated) the forms, the more immediately evident they are. In the case of the economically social foundations, such immediacy can be seen through as mere appearance from the standpoint of the proletariat. (We shall return later to the remarkable contribution made by Marx and Engels on this question.) Of course, the fact that we can see through these forms does not in any way alter the immediately obvious certainty that they are the forms of existence of our present, but it can on the other hand give our *practical behaviour* towards them a new quality, which in turn reacts upon our immediate behaviour. In the case of the more complex, severally mediated formations, by contrast, this dialectical dissolution of immediacy into a process of mediation has far weaker repercussions in the immediate, practical sense. The process therefore seems to be a mere conceptual one, a merely theoretical or logical operation. For example: we may well perceive clearly that our existence as isolated individuals is a consequence of capitalist development; but as long as our insight is merely theoretical, the individualistic structure of our feelings, etc. will survive in unshakeably immediate form. In the same way (although it must be stressed that the following example is intended to serve *only* as a *psychological illustration*), total understanding of the correctness of Copernican astronomy in no way affects the immediate impression that the sun comes up and goes

50. The turn taken by the argument here shows the extent to which Feuerbach understands and interprets Hegel in a Young Hegelian and Fichtean sense.

51. *Vorläufige Thesen zur Reform der Philosophie* ('Preliminary Theses on the Reform of Philosophy'), *Werke*, ed. Jodl, vol. II, p. 227.

down, and so on. Only the practical tendency towards transforming the real, social foundations of this immediacy itself is able to bring about a transformation in behaviour in this context – and that does not in all cases have visible effects straightaway.

This structural state of affairs strongly influenced the thinking of both Hegel and Feuerbach. For all his serious attempts to get to grips with the problem and solve it (we shall speak of this later), Hegel was seduced into treating it as a purely theoretical and logical question. For him, therefore, the categories of mediation turned into autonomous and real 'essences', detaching themselves from the real historical process, from the basis of their real comprehensibility, and thus petrifying into a new immediacy. Feuerbach's polemics, on the other hand, took up only this unsuccessful aspect of Hegel's attempt, overlooking not only what Hegel had already achieved in terms of correctly posing and resolving the problem, but even the actual problem itself. He therefore treated the whole question of mediation as a purely logical one, which can be resolved partly by pure logic,[52] partly through recourse to immediate intuition and sensuousness. In so doing, however, he falls into a completely uncritical position. As Marx points out in *The German Ideology*,[53] he overlooks the fact that 'this world of the senses is not a thing given direct from all eternity, remaining ever the same, but the product of generations, each of which stands on the shoulders of the previous one'.

This is the one form of immediately given reality; closely connected with it is the second, the immediate acceptability of ethical Utopia. Its premiss, in a nutshell, is that the objective forms of man's concrete environment are immediately given to him and that the degree of their immediacy,

52. The furthest he will go is to ascribe to it a (negatively assessed) mythological ability to bring about real changes in man. For example, 'Hegelian philosophy has alienated *man from himself'(Preliminary Theses*, ibid., p. 227).

53. The fact that this vital work has not yet been published represents a major obstacle to the proper understanding of this period. It is to be hoped that an edition – including a German version – will shortly be made available through the agency of the Marx-Engels Institute in Moscow. My quotation comes from the excerpt printed by Gustav Mayer in *Friedrich Engels*, vol. I, Berlin, 1920, p. 247. (The precise wording of this quotation is as follows: 'He does not see how the sensuous world around him is not a thing given direct from all eternity, remaining ever the same, but the product of industry and of the state of society; and indeed, in the sense that it is an historical product, the result of the activity of a whole succession of generations, each standing on the shoulders of the preceding one, developing its industry and its intercourse, modifying its social system according to the changed needs' [*The German Ideology*, Moscow, 1968, p. 57] – ed.)

far from providing a measure of their supra-historical essence, is the consequence of, on the one hand, the objective strength of those economic forces which produce them and, on the other, the class-specific prejudices and vested interests of man in the survival of his social environment. Hence, however, the concrete scope of his spontaneous emotional reactions to this social environment is likewise given. That is, he reacts to those given attitudes of his just as immediately as to the environment itself. And it is precisely in the separateness of 'objectivity' and 'subjectivity' that it becomes most clearly manifest that they are derived from one and the same social root and that the immediate nature of each is a function of the most thoroughgoing reciprocal action of the one on the other. In the case of a simple affirmative attitude towards reality, this connection hardly calls for detailed analysis. But if it is a question of Utopia, of the imperative ethical mode of behaviour, then their merely immediate nature seems at first sight less obvious.

But two points must not be forgotten: first, that we are dealing here only with the appearance of practice – with a practice, that is, which either leaves the structure of objective reality fundamentally untouched, hence confirming the contemplative attitude towards it and not transcending it (Kant's Ought), or is incapable of posing the transition from given reality to 'transformed' reality as a concrete problem (utopianism). 'Transformed' reality is thereby treated as a *state* – in other words, contemplatively – and contrasted as such to immediately given objective reality, without the way which leads from the one to the other being in any way elucidated. And secondly: in neither case is the attempt made to demonstrate concretely the *genesis* of the ethico-utopian mode of behaviour. It is taken for granted in just the same way as contemplatively grasped objective reality (or its so-called 'ultimate principle') was taken for granted. In his *Critique of Practical Reason* Kant proceeds from the 'fact' of conscience in just the same way as in his *Critique of Pure Reason* he proceeds from the 'fact' of synthetic *a priori* judgments. For Smith the economist the objective laws of free competition, etc. are an immediately accepted fact, in just the same way as 'feelings of sympathy' are for Smith the moralist.

Feuerbach appears to represent an advance in just this respect. His dissolution of theology into anthropology, his dissolution of the 'alienated' essence of man, appears to represent a true genesis. But it is in fact only appearance. And this is chiefly because he replaces one abstract concept (God) by the equally abstract one of 'species', thereby rendering illusory the derivation of concepts from reality. (This is not to deny the advance which his theory nonetheless represents. That, however, is irrelevant to the present discussion.) Marx comments in his Feuerbach theses: 'Feuerbach dissolves the religious essence into the human essence. But the human essence is no abstraction inherent in each single individual. In its reality it is the ensemble of the social relations. . . . The human essence, therefore, can be grasped by him only as "species", as an internal, dumb generality which *naturally* unites the many individuals.'[54] However, if this genesis, this demonstration of the *real* roots of the concepts, is only the appearance of a genesis, the two basic principles of his world-view, 'alienated' man and the dissolution of this 'alienation', solidify into rigidly opposed essences. He does not dissolve the one into the other, but rejects the one and affirms (morally) the other. He opposes one ready-made reality to another ready-made reality, instead of showing how the one must arise – in the dialectical process – out of the other. His 'love' allows the 'alienated' reality of man to survive unaltered, just as Kant's Ought was incapable of changing anything in the structure of his world of being.

In this case 'practice' consists in 'evaluation'. With the purely contemplative position of Feuerbach, this necessary consequence of his methodological limitations manifests itself less blatantly in his own work than in that of his successors, the 'true socialists'. In applying the Feuerbachian formula of 'alienation' to society and opposing Feuerbach's notion of God with that of money as socially alienated essence ('Money is the product of mutually estranged men, *it is alienated man*'),[55] Hess is led to condemn this world of 'alienation' in moral terms and to oppose it with a utopian world of transcended 'alienation'. *True* property replaces *false* property. 'Existing property is not reprehensible because it is personal, individual, integrated into the individual; on the contrary, it is reprehensible only and precisely because it is not personal, not integrated into the individual,

54. Sixth Thesis on Feuerbach, ibid., pp. 660–1 (Editor's note).

55. *The Nature of Money*, in Zlocisti, p. 167. Cf. the similar statement in *The Philosophy of Action*, ibid., pp. 58ff. Cf. the seemingly related passage in *The Jewish Question*, 'Money is the alienated essence of his labour and life' (*Writings of the Young Marx on Philosophy and Society*, trans. and ed. by L. D. Easton and K. H. Guddat, New York, 1967, p. 246). Although this last statement suffers from the abstract immediacy of the category of 'labour', it already exhibits a strong tendency towards concretization and true dialectics. By contrast, the thought of the young Lassalle moves entirely along these lines (cf. Lassalle's letters to Arnold Mendelssohn, Alexander Oppenheim and Albert Lehfeldt, middle of September 1845, see his posthumous writings, ed. G. Mayer, vol. I, p. 216).

but detached and remote from him, confronting the individual from without as a remote, wholly alienated and general means of life and intercourse, as external wealth, as money.'[56] At several points in his studies, Hess compares Feuerbach with Proudhon. This is not the place to discuss the tenability of this parallel in terms of genetic history (it is a necessary consequence of Hess's method that he operates consistently with such parallels – e.g. Babeuf/Fichte, Saint-Simon/Schelling, Fourier/Hegel – very much on the lines of Heine).[57] But it is noticeable that his application of Feuerbachian principles to society is itself Proudhonian in one respect: in the way it contrasts the 'good' and the 'bad' aspects of a social phenomenon and defines progress, the resolution of the given antimony, as the preservation of the 'good' aspect and the eradication of the 'bad' one. That Feuerbach is not done any injustice when such petty-bourgeois, ethical utopianism is treated as the application of his method, is shown by, among other things, Engels's critique of his ethics. Engels contrasts Feuerbach's treatment of the conflict between good and evil with the dialectical treatment of the same problem in Hegel.[58]

It is by no means coincidental that both Marx, in his refutation of the Proudhonian notion of 'good' and 'bad' times, and Engels, in his critique of Feuerbach's ethics, should refer back to Hegel. For Feuerbach, Proudhon and Hess in this question all fall back far behind Hegel. Their attitude towards the basic phenomenon of bourgeois society is far less critical, far more immediate that that of Hegel himself. True, even he treats 'alienation' as a general philosophical problem. But in the most significant exposition of his theory of consciousness, the *Phenomenology of Mind*, he poses the problem to himself as a problem of the structure of society, as a problem of the consciousness of man arising out of this structure about himself as social being. This is not the place to describe, even in outline, Hegel's position in respect of these problems. But if we are to understand the methodological situation obtaining during the period when communist theory was emerging in Germany, we must at least point out briefly that the whole problem of 'alienation', of man's 'estrangement' from himself as a historically and philosophically necessary stage

---

56. 'Poverty in our society', etc., in Zlocisti, p. 153; similar statements can be found in *The Nature of Money*, ibid., pp. 179ff. The proximity to Proudhon is perfectly plain here.

57. Cf. Heine's *History of Religion and Philosophy in Germany*, 1833 (Editor's note).

58. See Engels, *Feuerbach and the End of Classical German Philosophy*, in Selected Works, vol. II, pp. 345–6 (Editor's note).

towards his final coming-to-himself, is the chief concern of the decisive chapters of the *Phenomenology of Mind*. It is generally known that 'alienation' is a Hegelian term. Feuerbach's polemic against Hegel, however, on the one hand made the question appear to be a problem of idealistic logic in general, while on the other it shifted the debate essentially on to the problem of Hegelian philosophy of nature, the problem of nature as the 'other-ness', the being-'external'-to-itself of the idea.[59] In spite of the thorough knowledge which some of them had of Hegel, Hess and company shared Feuerbach's basic position and chose to follow him in this respect, applying *his* theory of 'alienation' back to society. In so doing they overlooked the fact that Hegel posed the whole question in a basically socio-historical way. For what is so very remarkable, fascinating and – at the same time – confusing about the *Phenomenology of Mind* is that it is the first work in the history of philosophy to treat the so-called final problems of philosophy, the questions of subject and object, ego and world, consciousness and being, as historical problems. And moreover, not in the sense of applying an aprioristic (i.e. 'timeless') formulation of the question, typology, etc., to history as empirical material (as is the case with Kant and Fichte); but rather in such a way that these problems, as *philosophical* problems, in their 'apriority', in their purely philosophical distinctiveness, are at the same time treated as forms of the historical development of human consciousness. Of course Hegel was far from consistent in the matter. It is usually held that the *Phenomenology of Mind* is confusing precisely because, in it, historical and supra-historical concept-formations are jumbled up together, contradicting and cancelling one another out. As in other areas, here too we can see at once the strengths and limitations of Hegel. When he treats the 'phenomenology' as a prelude to philosophy proper; when the stages of consciousness occurring within its pages are conceived as aprioristic stages which the 'mind' has to pass through in order to raise itself from the level of ordinary consciousness to that of the identical subject-object – i.e. the level of philosophical consciousness – there are two consequences. On the one

59. Hegel, *Encyclopedia*, para. 247. The question cannot be treated here, beyond remarking that Engels in particular never wholly abandoned Hegel's philosophy of nature. In a letter to F. A. Lange on 29 March 1865 (*Neue Zeit*, XXVIII/I, p. 186) as well as in another to Marx on 21 September 1874, he describes the second part of the *Logic*, the theory of essence, as its true centre. And in my view it is indeed the case that the theory of essence does contain the really seminal part of the Hegelian dialectic, that part which decisively influenced not only Engel's view of nature, but also the historical dialectics of Marx and Engels, their analysis of the structure of capitalist society.

hand, this whole development is reduced to a merely subjective process (even if not in the terms of empirical psychology), and on the other the material of history is degraded to the level of mere illustrative material.

But Hegel does not keep to this idealistic programme. The assignation of stages of consciousness to historical epochs is – as an example we shall shortly adduce will make clear – incomparably more profound: in spite of the purely conceptual terminology, the aprioristic treatment appears as a mere reflection, a merely conceptual expression of the historical material underlying it, the historical epoch intended to serve as an illustration for that aprioristic stage. But it is not only in details that the *Phenomenology* outgrows the place in the system which Hegel himself allotted it. He is unable to allot even the whole of it to a position in keeping with his system. The phenomenology which Hegel in his *Encyclopedia* places between anthropology and psychology as the second stage of the subjective mind has, precisely in the crucial problems, very little in common with the *Phenomenology of Mind*. The latter contains, rather, the *whole* of Hegel's philosophy. It is one of his attempts to summarize his world-view in a unified fashion. Seen in this perspective, the 'subjectivity' of the *Phenomenology* (just like the 'reconciliation' referred to earlier) reveals a double physiognomy. On the one hand, the real-ness of the 'forms of consciousness' which fill the pages of the *Phenomenology* is diminished from the outset; on the other, however, it is in this very diminution that Hegel's remarkable (albeit unconscious) historico-social self-criticism reveals itself. The phenomena he discusses, the emergence of bourgeois capitalist society with its political climax in the 'reign of terror' of the French Revolution, *were* after all mere forms of consciousness for the Germany of that time – and not concrete historical reality. This situation allowed for two possible responses: either the conceptual substance of these phenomena was turned into an ethical postulate of natural law and opposed to German reality (this is what the young Fichte did) – in which case, however, the very fundamental philosophical problem of the age, the notion of reality as being 'created' by 'us', by man, remained unsolved. Or the answer had to be sought in the Hegelian manner.

The salient point in Hegel's treatment of this question is that he establishes the *this-sidedness* of social reality. The chapter on the 'Truth of Enlightenment',[60] which leads on to the discussion of the French Revolution, closes with the words: 'Both worlds are reconciled and heaven is

60. Hegel, *The Phenomenology of Mind*, trans. J. B. Baillie, London, 1964, pp. 590–98.

transplanted to the earth below.' For Hegel, moreover, this tendency is not by any means restricted to the ideological plane. The decisive category that actually brings about this this-sidedness is, rather, an economic one (albeit in mythological form): the useful. And this category of the useful already exhibits very clearly the dialectical double nature of the commodity, the unity of use-value and exchange-value, the appearance of thing-ness along with internal relatedness in itself. 'It is,' says Hegel, 'something that subsists *in itself* or a thing; this being in itself is at the same time only a pure moment; it is in consequence absolutely *for something else,* but is equally for an other merely as it is in itself; these opposite moments have returned into the indivisible unity of being-for-self.'[61] Through the useful, this stage of consciousness achieves what the earlier stages lacked: reality. 'What is wanting is reached in the fact of utility so far as pure insight secures positive objectivity there; pure insight is thereby a concrete actual consciousness satisfied within itself. This objectivity now constitutes its world, and is become the final and true outcome of the entire previous world, ideal as well as real.'[62] This world, the world of bourgeois society translated into thought, is the Hegelian world of 'alienation' and 'estrangement'. Consciousness is confronted by an objective, legitimate world, which in spite of – or rather, precisely in and through – its strangeness and autonomy is its own product. In his introductory remarks to this section Hegel says: 'But that spirit, whose self is absolutely discrete, finds its content over against itself in the form of a reality that is just as impenetrable as itself, and the world here gets the characteristic of being something external, negative to self-consciousness. Yet this world is a spiritual reality, it is essentially the fusion of individuality with being. Thus its existence is the *work* of self-consciousness, but likewise an actuality immediately present and alien to it, which has a peculiar being of its own, and in which it does not know itself. ... It acquires its existence by self-consciousness *of its own accord* relinquishing itself and giving up its essentiality. ...'[63]

The terminological affinity between such statements and those of the radical Young Hegelians is so obvious that it does not need to be analysed in detail. And likewise it follows from what has previously been said that we are not dealing with a merely terminological affinity, but, rather, that this is where the Young Hegelians took over from Hegel. What we must remember, of course, is that they took over only the subjective, idealistic aspects of such statements, only the limitations of his thinking. But in

61. ibid., p. 595.   62. ibid., p. 597.   63. ibid., p. 509.

doing so they overlooked precisely what was crucial: namely, that Hegel comprehended the objective forms of bourgeois society in their doubleness, in their contradictoriness: as moments of a process in which man (Hegel's mythological term is 'mind') in alienation comes to himself, to the point where the contradictions of his existence are driven to their extremes and produce the objective possibility of the upheaval and sublation of the contradictions themselves.[64] Alienation, abstraction from oneself, is therefore an appearance, it is true, which reveals itself as appearance in the self-attainment of 'mind'. But *as* appearance it is at the same time an objective reality. In his later system, where he attempts to grasp the same problem logically, Hegel says: 'Being has not vanished: but, firstly, Essence, as simple self-relation, is Being, and secondly as regards its one-sided characteristic of *immediacy*, Being is *deposed* to a mere negative, to a *seeming or reflected light* (Schein) – essence accordingly is Being thus *reflecting light into itself* (scheinen in sich selbst).[65]

It is impossible at this juncture to analyse, even in outline, the various forms in which Hegel wrestles with this problem (apart from the theory of essence, both in the *Encyclopedia* and in the *Logic*, it is chiefly his account of bourgeois society in the *Philosophy of Right* which would have to be discussed). The main methodological issue at stake here has in any case been clarified by these few allusions. First, it is clear that for Hegel 'alienation', the 'abstract' forms of life – indeed, abstraction and estrangement themselves – are neither pure thought-constructs nor a 'reprehensible' reality, but the immediately given forms of existence of the present as forms of the transition towards their self-overcoming in the historical process. (The *Philosophy of Right* ends with the transition to world-history.) Hence, they cannot be overcome either epistemologically or in ethical-utopian fashion; only by self-sublation in the identical subject-object of history can they attain their resolution. Secondly and consequently, 'alienation' appears as immediacy and immediacy as 'alienation' not yet overcome. Thus Hegel refutes in advance Feuerbach's critique of his philosophy. Which means, thirdly, that immediacy has been relativized both historically and methodologically: at every stage of development, the result of the previous process appears as an immediate datum.

64. On this point see ibid., p. 596.
65. Hegel, *Encyclopedia*, para. 112. (The inherent difficulty of this passage is aggravated by Hegel's pun on the word 'Schein', which can have both a negative and a positive force: (1) *mere* appearance, as opposed to being or essence; (2) that which is manifest shines, is reflected light – ed.)

Its immediacy is appearance: the categories of mediation through which it has passed in the process in order to become this – new – immediacy remain unknown. Fourthly, however, this appearance itself is a – necessary and objective – form of being, and can be correctly grasped only when this its double character is grasped in its dialectical interactions – when, that is, those categories of mediation have been pinpointed which have made it into the necessary appearance of essence, the necessary phenomenal form of being. In other words, it must be comprehended not only as a product, but also at the same time as a moment of the process. Thus, finally, the historical and the philosophical approaches join forces as it becomes clear that each on its own is bound to remain stuck fast in immediacy, and it is shown, on the one hand, that true philosophical 'deduction' of concepts or categories can consist only in 'creating' them, in demonstrating their historical genesis, and, on the other, that history consists precisely in the constant transformation of those forms which earlier modes of thinking, undialectical and always stuck fast in the immediacy of their present as they were, regarded as suprahistorical.

Of course, even Hegelian philosophy issues into the immediacy of its present. The dialectical process in which everything constantly dissolves for it, finally petrifies to yield a metaphysical, non-dialectical object. It thereby abolishes itself as a process. And yet – Hegel's road to failure nonetheless provides the methodological basis for a new, critical (practical-critical, historico-critical) approach to the present as a moment of the historical process. It is an approach in which the duality of theory and practice is transcended: on the one hand, the present is grasped as concrete and immediate, but comprehended as a result of the historical process – i.e. genetically – by pinpointing all the mediations which underlie its immediacy; on the other, however, this same process of mediation demonstrates that the present is a mere moment of the process which transcends it. For it is precisely this critical approach to the immediacy of the present which relates it to human activity: it is in the moments of the present which are pushing onwards beyond themselves that the guidelines and real scope of practical-critical activity, revolutionary practice, are given.

But only for those whose approach takes the same direction as these onward-driving tendencies, which transform the present not only into a *retro*gressive, but also into a *pro*gressive process. Such an approach was unattainable for Hegel himself. He was able to achieve the supreme conceptual account of bourgeois society, grasping its construction as a process, historically, dialectically.[66] And it was precisely Hegel's real understanding of the antagonistic structure of bourgeois society – something also achieved by Ricardo – which drove him to transcend it conceptually. But he did so purely logically, purely methodologically. Since he lived in a less highly-developed capitalist society than did Ricardo, where remains of past epochs mingled much more obtrusively with the forms of existence of his social environment, and since, therefore, he saw bourgeois society much more as developing than as developed, he was able to approach the forms of existence created by it with fewer prejudices. His method was devised in order to achieve knowledge of the present; hence it contains within itself all the contradictions of the present in the form of methodological problems. It is driven by these contradictions beyond the present, beyond bourgeois society. But for the same reason it cannot concretize itself into a true critique of bourgeois society. Hegel either stops his critique at the present (reconciliation), or he directs the impulsive dialectical movement to a formal standstill in the purely contemplative regions of mediated social forms (absolute spirit). This deviation from the dialectical tendencies of the dialectic does not manifest itself merely at those points where it is obliged to become concrete and obvious, but it reacts on the design and structure of the whole method, making Hegel's entire dialectics problematical. Thus, further progress, the attempt to transcend bourgeois society, cannot be achieved by simply continuing Hegelian dialectics – this was where Lassalle failed methodologically. Nor is progress possible by making the limitations of Hegelian thought into the basis of a system (Bruno Bauer). On the other hand, to engage in a one-sided polemic against these limitations and simply throw away all that has been achieved within them, as Feuerbach did, is equally pointless. But the attempt least likely to succeed is the one made by Hess: namely, to amalgamate the two rigid opposites. That none of the radical Young Hegelians possessed anything remotely like Hegel's knowledge of economics, let alone managed to cope with the economic developments of the intervening years, is symptomatic of their lack of understanding of

66. It is in general too little appreciated that Hegel's understanding of economics always stood at the highest theoretical level available to him historically. Unfortunately, the relations between his thought and economic developments have been largely neglected. Extensive material for badly needed investigation into this question can be found in F. Rosenzweig, *Hegel und der Staat*, Munich and Berlin, 1920, vol. I, pp. 131–2, vol. II, pp. 120ff, which provides references to earlier literature, e.g. Rosenkranz's observations on Hegel's early commentary on Steuart.

what was crucial in his historical dialectics and their inability to realize which aspects of his problematics were fruitful and susceptible of development.

We have just described as symptomatic the lack of real economic knowledge and the inadequate acquaintance with continuing developments in economic theory manifested by Hess and the other radical Young Hegelians. It needs to be added that, although these deficiencies were of course a symptom and a consequence of the wrong way in which they *posed the question*, the fact that they posed the question wrongly stems itself from their position as members of the revolutionary intelligentsia. In other words, Hegel, the ideological champion of bourgeois development itself, is superior to them simply by virtue of his initial position.[67] For in striving to transcend bourgeois development ideologically, they repudiate *on principle* the typical class science of the bourgeoisie, economics, in just the same unconditional manner as they repudiate the class science of the absolutist Junkers, theology.[68] Instead, they seek liberation by means of Feuerbach's undialectical and unhistorical genesis: by unmasking the 'alienated', inhuman nature of these disciplines, to which the correct reaction can only be 'understanding' and the conscious discovery of 'man'.[69] For Hegel, on the other hand, knowledge of economic phenomena constituted an integral element of his systematic orientation. But Hegel's position was itself fraught with insurmountable limitations. In the first place, as the thinker who made knowledge of bourgeois society culminate in the state and drove philosophy beyond that realm and into the 'pure' regions of the absolute spirit, he also found that economics 'is a credit to thought' only 'because it finds laws for a mass of accidents'.[70] As a result the economic elements become, in part merely unconsciously, systematic components of this thinking, and he is unable to retain and put to use the historico-social understanding he has already achieved. Secondly, however, his bourgeois attitude prevents him from exposing the limitations of economics even methodologically. Alongside a number of extremely acute

67. Hegel's various studies of bourgeois society show that he increasingly pressed forward in this direction. Thus Rosenzweig rightly points out (op. cit., vol. II, p. 120) that the definition of 'Estate' (*Stand*) becomes more and more 'economic' as time goes on. In the *Philosophy of Right* the ethics appropriate to an Estate has become no more than the product, rather than the precondition of an Estate, as it had been in his youth.

68. Hess establishes a parallel between the two in *The Nature of Money*, in Zlocisti, p. 167.

69. ibid., p. 163.

70. *The Philosophy of Right*, Para. 189, Addition.

observations,[71] some of them of much wider relevance than the economics
he was working on, we find Hegel describing Say as a representative of
economic science on a par with Smith and Ricardo, obviously not even
noticing the difference in standard.[72]

This is the starting-point for the critique by Marx and Engels. The
epoch-making essays in the *Deutsch-Französische Jahrbücher* introduce
an entirely new *method of criticism* into thought: criticism as the demonstration of the underlying social causes of a problem and of the social prerequisites of its solution. Only with this approach to the problem did it
become possible to carry dialectics over the point of inertia in the Hegelian
version. And in spite of all the apparent affinity with their contemporaries,
Marx and Engels are working even at this early stage on completely different lines from those pursued by the radical Young Hegelians and the
socialist supporters of Feuerbach, who, instead of following the Hegelian
path to the end and leading thought about society and history out of the
blind-alley into which Hegelian philosophy had stumbled, settled down
and made themselves at home in this blind-alley, uttering praise or criticism as they did so. It is not possible at this point even to sketch the out-
lines of the change brought about in the dialectical method by Marx and
Engels. The contrast was intended merely to demonstrate the methodological necessity which condemned the efforts of even such an honest
thinker as Hess to abject failure from the very outset. It is often claimed
that the Young Hegelians tried to resolve philosophically the philosophical contradictions of Hegel's system and that they failed in their task.
That is correct. But we must amplify this by showing how deeply the
reasons for their failure are rooted in the nature of philosophy itself and to
what extent the change wrought by Marx and Engels in fact created a
theory of a completely new kind (albeit profoundly connected with the
Hegelian dialectic): *the critique of political economy*.

The critique of political economy is based methodologically on the
Hegelian theory of the dissolution of immediacy by pointing out the
historical categories of mediation, by concrete, historical genesis. Marx
and Engels are able to execute these changes because they look at bourgeois
society from the standpoint of the proletariat, whence proceeds the dialectical unity of the immediate reality of capitalist categories and, at the same

71. 'It hence becomes apparent that despite an excess of wealth civil society is not
rich enough, i.e. its own resources are insufficient to check excessive poverty and the
creation of a penurious rabble' (ibid., para. 245).

72. ibid., para. 189.

time, the resolution of the rigidity, their fetishistic character.[73] The obtuseness of bourgeois economics lies in the fact that it accepts all the phenomena of its underlying existence in the forms in which they are immediately encountered, and hence in its theory – at least in the work of the great representatives of classical economics – reflects, unconsciously, those contradictions which are really operating behind this immediacy. By contrast, the shallow vulgar economists and the committed apologists for capitalist society attempt – theoretically – to transcend these contradictions. The idealism of the – more or less conscious – proletarian critics of bourgeois economics is based on their inability to see through this dialectical double nature. The 'true socialists' in Germany were not the only ones to succumb to such idealism (although it manifested itself most blatantly in their work because of their Hegelian, superficially dialectical reasoning); others to do so were Proudhon, Bray[74] and the English socialist critics of Ricardo. Writing about Hodgskin, whom he also characterizes as an idealist,[75] Marx points out: 'Thus, in other words, Hodgskin asserts: The effects of a specific social form of labour are attributed to the thing, to the products of that labour; the relation itself is clothed by fantasy in the form of a *thing*. We have seen that this is a specific characteristic of labour based on the production of commodities, on exchange value, and that this quid pro quo can be seen in the commodity, in money (though Hodgskin fails to realize this) and, at a higher level, in capital. In capital the effects which things have as objective moments in the process of labour, are attributed to them, as if they owned them, as if they had become autonomous, personified beings *vis-à-vis* labour. They would cease to have these effects once they ceased to confront labour in *this alienated form*. The *capitalist* as capitalist is no more than the personification of capital, he stands opposed to labour as its creation, but endowed with a will and personality of his own. Hodgskin regards this as a purely subjective delusion behind which the deception and the interests of the exploiting classes lie concealed. He does not see how this manner of seeing the situation springs from the real facts of the matter, how the latter is not

73. I have discussed this issue in detail in my essay 'Reification and the Consciousness of the Proletariat', in *History and Class Consciousness*, pp. 83ff.

74. John Francis Bray, 1809–95, a compositor by profession, was an Anglo-American utopian socialist, the co-founder and treasurer of the Leeds Working Men's Association; his main work, *Labour's Wrongs and Labour's Remedy, or the Age of Might and the Age of Right*, in which the influence of Robert Owen is apparent, was published in 1839 (Editor's note).

75. *Theories of Surplus Value* in *Werke*, vol. 26, part 3, p. 263.

the expression of the former, but vice versa.'[76] Marx underlines the – relative, historical – justification[77] of this subjectivist standpoint of Hodgskin's *vis-à-vis* the fetishism of the economy, but makes it explicitly clear that this inability to recognize the reality-factor in their fetishistic formations of capitalist production and in their theoretical reflections is based on the fact that Hodgskin takes the problems posed by the economy (and the reality which underlies them) as he finds them (for example, the distinction between fixed and circulating capital).[78] This, however, leads in turn to his overlooking the process-like nature of even the 'simple' phenomena of capitalist society (e.g. in the question of compound interest, where he fails to notice that 'simple profit' is in fact as much compounded as compound interest proper – that, in other words, it is not a question of a 'thing' in the midst of the process, but rather of 'thingness' as being simply a manifestation of the process).[79]

'True socialism' is just as obtuse in this decisive question as bourgeois economics. For example, when Marx, referring to James Mill, stresses that 'he makes the unity of opposites into the immediate identity of those opposites',[80] he is merely continuing his earlier polemic against the economics of 'true socialism', in which he poured scorn on Grün for his inept, vulgarly economistic notion of the 'unity of production and consumption'.[81] 'We can see how, for all his extravagant carryings-on, nothing emerges but an apologia for the existing conditions.' And the harsh criticism in the *Communist Manifesto* is only the logical elaboration of this critique: in the case of the bourgeois economists, the economic structure of bourgeois society is simply accepted theoretically in its immediacy; as for the attitude of the 'true socialists' towards the revolutionary movements of the bourgeoisie, the concretely revolutionary kernel of the process of social development is misunderstood in abstract, utopian

76. ibid., p. 290.

77. ibid., pp. 263–4. In general the whole *tone* of this polemic differs from his attacks on the Young Hegelians. This is not simply due to the fact that it was written *after* he had achieved self-understanding and not *before*, but much more to the circumstance that the pamphleteer Hodgskin among others had really advanced a stage beyond Ricardo and hence was an *objective* precursor of Marx, whereas Hess and Co. cannot be regarded as links between Hegel and Marx.

78. ibid., p. 263.   79. ibid., p. 300.   80. ibid., p. 84.

81. Cf. his critique of Grün's *History of Socialism* in *Die Neue Zeit*, XVIII/I (1890–1900), pp. 138–9 (see *The German Ideology*, ibid., pp. 58off. – ed.). This view can be found in Hess. e.g. in his essay, 'Poverty in our society', etc. in Zlocisti, p. 153. On the alleged dialectics of these categories see the *Introduction to a Critique of Political Economy*, pp. xx–xxxiv.

fashion – without in any way escaping from the realm of the immediate. These two points of view – seemingly opposed and actually contradictory – are nonetheless closely related methodologically. They are necessary consequences of the idealistically basic notion of 'true socialism': the separation of theory and practice and hence of the theoretical and historical examination of social phenomena. Hegel's enormous intellectual achievement consisted in making theory and history dialectically relative to each other, conceiving them in terms of a process of dialectical interpenetration. But even this attempt finally failed. Hegel was never able to advance to a real unity of theory and practice; instead he merely either saturated the logical arrangement of the categories with a wealth of historical material or rationalized history into a succession of sublimated and abstracted forms, alterations of structure, epochs, etc., which he raised to categories. Marx was the first to see through this false dilemma: he did not deduce the order of sequence of the categories from either their logical arrangement or from their historical succession, but he recognized that 'their order of sequence is rather determined by the relation which they bear to one another in modern bourgeois society'.[82] In doing so, he not only provided dialectics with the real foundation that Hegel had sought in vain, setting it, as Engels put it, 'right side up', but at the same time he rescued the critique of political economy – which he had made the basis of dialectics – from the fetishistic petrifaction and abstract pettiness into which economics was bound to decline even in the hands of its greatest bourgeois representatives. The critique of political economy no longer stands as 'one' science alongside the others, nor is it merely ranked above the others as a 'basic science'; but rather it comprises the entire world-history of the 'forms of existence' (the categories) of human society.[83]

With materialistic dialectics thus established, 'true socialism' lost its whole *raison d'être*, even from a subjective point of view.[84] And after serious inner struggles, Hess, who was an honest thinker and revolutionary, admitted as much – unconditionally, in fact, in a letter written in 1846

82. *Critique of Political Economy*, p. XLIV. The deduction of consciousness from *social* existence (rather than the other way round), a deduction which the 'true socialists' could never discover, but which they did not seek with any seriousness, follows necessarily from the dialectical conception of the categories as 'forms of being, determinations of existence' (ibid., p. XLIII).

83. This is perfectly clear from the scheme set out by Marx in the Introduction, ibid., pp. XLV–XLVI.

84. Marx acknowledges that this is true of Hess's early period. Cf. the critique of Grun, *The German Ideology*, p. 552.

and quoted by Mehring.[85] But he was unable to make the new standpoint truly his own. His essay published in 1847 in the *Deutsche Brüsseler Zeitung* comes very close to Marx terminologically and indeed, attempts to apply the Marxist mode of thinking. But the title itself – *The Consequences of the Proletarian Revolution* – makes it clear that, even at the time when he most closely approached Marx, he still remained the old idealist and ethical Utopian. And in the work which he published immediately after the 1848 revolution – *Jugement Dernier du Vieux Monde Social* – he turns back once more to his old point of view. Talking about Marx and Engels he writes: 'They understand perfectly the art of dissecting our society, analysing its economy and revealing its sickness. But they are too materialistic to possess that electrifying élan which inspires the people. After giving up idealistic philosophy, they threw themselves into the arms of materialistic economics. They have exchanged the nebulous standpoint of German philosophy for the narrow and petty standpoint of English economics.'[86]

But a real return to the old standpoint was of course no longer possible. The economic approach remained henceforth decisive in the development of Hess's theory; but since his thinking continued to be basically idealistic, it functioned methodologically as a foreign body. Thus the pamphlet quoted above contains a number of moves in the direction of historical materialism, but always Hess stops half-way (sometimes even three-quarters of the way) and reverts to his old moralistic idealism, reinforcing it with all kinds of wildly mythological, cosmic or racial theories. For example, he writes: 'Labour has always been organized for progress, the progress of labour has always increased and perfected the forces of production, and the great revolutions have always erupted for the purpose of raising the mode of production to the level of the forces of production and organizing labour for progress.' Attacking Saint-Simon, he even formulates the economic mode of the coming socialist society in the following terms: 'From each according to his abilities, to each according to his needs.' And yet the whole presentation of the problem remains obstinately ideological: the old rigid confrontation of necessity and freedom, immediately accepted world and equally immediately accepted ethical demand (which goes hand in hand with moral judgment of being),

85. Cf. Moses Hess to Karl Marx 28 July 1846, in Moses Hess, *Correspondence*, ed. E. Silberner and W. Blumenberg, The Hague, 1959, p. 165 (Editor's note).

86. F. Melly, Geneva, 1851. Extracts have appeared in Bernstein's *Dokumente des Sozialismus*, vol. I, p. 540.

is unchanged – or, at most, assigned in a seemingly less rigid way to past and present. Thus, after admitting the objective necessity for the past of class antagonisms, he goes on to say: 'Today, of course, enlightened people are not wrong to attribute the continued existence of this antagonism to the malevolence of a handful of privileged persons.'[87] The sudden and complete change which is supposed to occur in a revolutionary situation could hardly be formulated more ideologically.

Since Hess was unable either to maintain his old standpoint or to understand and apply the new one properly, his writings after he was 'converted' by Marx show him floundering helplessly to and fro between totally empty and abstract thought-constructs, fantastic conceptions of a philosophy of nature, justification of Zionism in terms of racial theories and the history of philosophy, etc., etc.[88] As an honest revolutionary he participated in the Lassallean workers' movement and remained in the ranks of the struggling proletariat until his death. As a theoretician, however, he was destroyed by his contact with materialist dialectics. Hess's strange fate, the almost total separation of theory from practice, the anonymous persistence of the wrong theoretical formulations even after he himself had – unconciously, at least – abandoned them, the possibility for a typically philosophically orientated revolutionary to act at decisive moments with complete disregard for his theories – all this can be explained only in terms of the under-development of the class antagonisms in Germany at that time. Whenever such thoughts have cropped up since then, they have always led with a certain inevitability from the camp of the proletariat into that of the bourgeoisie. Hess's case – both his utter failure in the objective realm of theory despite all his talents and his sometimes correct approach to individual problems, and his personal loyalty to the cause of revolution – is one of the most illuminating paradigms of the intellectual situation in Germany at the time the theory of proletarian revolution was beginning to emerge. Both in his faults and in his virtues, Hess is the most typical representative of this transitional period; and it is as such – not, as some would have it, as the theoretical link between Hegel and Marx – that he will keep his place in the history of the working-class movement.

87. op. cit., pp. 547, 549 and 545.
88. For Hess's development see Zlocisti's industrious, but unprincipled, confused biography, heavily biased in Hess's favour.

Blum Theses
1928-1929

Blum Theses (Extracts)*

Foreword by the editors of *Párttörténeti Közlemények* ('The Journal of Party History'), vol. II, no. 3, 1956, published by the Institute for Party History under the auspices of the Central Committee of the Hungarian Workers' Party (PUW).

Comrades working on the period 1929–1930 have discovered in the course of their researches in the archives of the Institute for Party History, in the PUW central committee headquarters, a document of great significance in the history of the Hungarian Communist Party. The document is the so-called 'Blum Theses', and its author is Comrade Georg Lukács.

The draft of the theses was written late in 1928 as a preliminary outline of the political report to be made to the second Congress of the Hungarian Communist Party (HCP). It interprets both the situation of the party and the general situation in Hungary. In the light of the programme agreed on by the Sixth Congress of the Communist International, it alludes to the necessity of a change in the party's strategic objectives and to the notion of a democratic dictatorship of workers and peasants. However, despite setting out what were basically correct objectives, the draft did not draw from them the necessary consequences in respect of alliance policy, agrarian policy, and the tactics of the party in general.

This draft of the theses was discussed in the party in 1929.

Following the dispute in the party and the open letter of the executive committee of the Communist International,[1] the Central Committee and subsequently the Second Congress of the HCP (February–March, 1930) rejected the theses as a false and opportunistic document precisely with respect to its reference to strategic objectives.

The draft of the theses is sub-divided into five chapters:

I *The situation of the HCP during the first Congress and its development to the first Plenary Assembly of 1928.*

II *The fundamental changes during the Bethlen regime and the classes.*

---

* For the Open Letter of the ECCI and the dispute about the Blum Theses see the Introduction (pp. XIX–XX). All notes to this essay have been added by the editor except where otherwise indicated.

III *The situation of the working class.*
IV *The activity of the HCP since the Plenum.*
 V *The main problems of the present situation.*

Chapters I and IV of the draft and sections A and D of Chapter V are reproduced below.

Theses concerning the political and economic situation in Hungary and the tasks of the Hungarian Communist Party[1]

I. THE SITUATION OF THE HCP DURING THE FIRST CONGRESS AND ITS DEVELOPMENT UP TO THE FIRST PLENARY ASSEMBLY OF 1928.

1. The HCP held its first congress[2] in a period when the development of left-orientated mass movements was very marked. The best left-orientated elements of the working-class were beginning to join together to form an opposition. The HCP succeeded at the very beginning of the movement in establishing contact with the most self-conscious section of this opposition and bringing it under its influence. In the spring of 1925, when the new bourgeois coalition was elected at the communal elections, the movement led to the split in the Social Democratic Party.

2. The political course of the Hungarian Socialist Workers' Party (MSZMP)[3] was from the beginning correctly centred on the fundamental problems of the class struggle: it was directed towards the overthrow of the counter-revolutionary system which was at that time consolidating itself, and towards the mobilization of the dissatisfied masses. This is why the programme put forward by the MSZMP rejected from the outset any form of coalition policy and why the party proposed that the working class should conclude a workers' and peasants' alliance instead of an agreement with the bourgeoisie. It was in this spirit that it emphasized the land question – i.e. the notion that the land should belong to the peasantry as of right – as forcibly as was legally permissible. In as much as all the theoretical and practical problems relating to democracy in Hungary at that time were submitted to a detailed analysis, the congress in the main resolved the strategic questions of the mass movement.

1. See pp. 227–8 above.
2. The first congress of the reconstituted illegal HCP took place in Vienna from 18 to 21 August 1925.
3. This party was founded on 14 April 1925, following a decision of the HCP in Vienna on 1 November 1924. Officially led by a directory, its actual leader was István Vági (1883–1940). It formed the legal counterpart in Hungary to the illegal HCP in Vienna and the links between the two parties were very close, despite the inability of the police to prove that they existed.

3. Shortly after the congress, the entire leadership of the HCP was arrested,[4] and it was not possible to disseminate the lessons of the congress among the party members. A completely new leadership had to be formed. This process of consolidation took place quickly. By the spring of 1926 the party was once more capable of action. However, the process of consolidation was not completed. True, an illegal organization had got under way and the party had dealt with those liquidationists who clung to the illusions of legality (Weisshaus[5] and his comrades) without any serious repercussions, but still it could not manage to establish the leadership on a firm, party-orientated communist basis. True, the party succeeded in mobilizing a relatively large number of people among the mass movement that began in 1926 (2,000 signatures at the elections), and it also succeeded in getting across to the masses the central slogan of its transitional programme – a republic governed by workers and peasants. But the process of re-organizing, of consolidating in organizational terms the influence they had already achieved, lagged far behind the extent of its political influence. By Christmas 1926 the plenum of the central committee had recognized the hidden dangers in this situation, and therefore made the expansion of the illegal HCP the focal point of its work, thereby emphasizing that the MSZMP represented only one sphere of activity incumbent on the HCP. Once again, political persecution made it impossible to carry out this resolution: in February 1927 the entire leadership of the HCP was arrested.[6]

4. These arrests, which forced the MSZMP almost completely underground and deprived it of its contact with the masses, were followed by a period full of crises and a heavy defeat. It was not simply that the building of the party was progressing at best laboriously, nor was it simply that the formation of cadres was creating great difficulties; beyond that, a whole range of liquidationist tendencies of all shades was coming to the fore again. The liquidationists put forward what seemed to be fundamentally distinct

4. Mátyás Rákosi was sent to Hungary immediately after the first congress, but was arrested, together with another fifty members, at the very start of his illegal activities.

5. Aladár Weisshaus (1887–1963) played a decisive role in the illegal HCP, particularly in the years 1923–5, and was the leading force behind the foundation of the MSZMP. In the last years of the decade he pursued an increasingly right-wing radical course and was finally expelled from the HCP.

6. Among those arrested was Zoltán Szántó, who had been commander of the First Red Battalion in the Commune. He and a further 52 members were put on trial in May 1927.

and even contradictory points of view: on the one hand, complete with-drawal into illegality; on the other, however, a complete acceptance of the legal possibilities and rejection of illegality. Had their activity been suc-cessful, it could have led only to the liquidation of the HCP. In this context the liquidationism of the renegades also manifested itself: it pursued a policy of merely ideological work and waged a stubborn, demagogic campaign – even going as far as outright denunciation – against practical work in cells. After a number of serious disputes the HCP succeeded in excluding all the liquidationist tendencies from the party, eliminating the influence of the renegades within the party, and to a large extent isolating them even among the party sympathizers.

The fact that the MSZMP was three-quarters illegal forced the party to adopt new tactics. It was necessary, first, to advance beyond the line put forward by the Christmas plenum; secondly, to build up regular party work in all mass organizations – and to create the basis for such work in the illegal organization of cells; and thirdly, to disseminate the technique and the spirit of conspiracy throughout the party. After considerable objective and subjective obstacles had been surmounted, this work finally began. With the impending collapse of the Bethlen coalition,[7] which the party had seen coming in good time and correctly interpreted, the party's influence grew steadily, as did the dedication (*Parteilichkeit*) of the leader-ship and of the organization. And yet there continued to be a gulf between the political influence of the party and the transformation of that influence into organizational terms. These problems generated a mutually strength-ening process which could not be halted, either by the differences over the Julius question that came to light before the external commission, or by the numerous arrests to which the party was still subjected. But it is a clear indication of the organizational consolidation of the party that the number of arrests made both in Hungary and abroad (Béla Kun)[8] was relatively small and did not for a moment hinder the progress of party work. In the summer of 1928 the enlarged plenum of the central committee drew the necessary lessons from this period and laid down guidelines for the further activity of the party. The party participated in the Sixth World

7. Count István Bethlen (1874–1946) was made Prime Minister by Horthy in April 1921. After elections in May 1922 he ruled throughout the twenties by means of a coalition of the United Christian National Party and the Party of small farmers and farm labourers. From 1927–8 his power was gradually eroded by the problems of internal politics and he finally resigned in 1931. His successor was Count Gyula Károlyi.
8. Béla Kun was arrested on 26 April 1928 in Vienna and tried in June of that year.

Congress of the Communist International with a delegation consisting of comrades from home and abroad.

IV. THE ACTIVITY OF THE HCP SINCE THE PLENUM

1. The political perspective and the line advanced in the theses of the plenum proved to be correct. The general political situation as well as the development of the workers' movement were moving in the direction they had forecast. The plenum theses gave the party the possibility of responding on the whole correctly to the tendencies they had drawn attention to. And yet, in what was at the time the most important issue for the workers' movement – the formation of a left-orientated workers' front – the party had achieved only minimal successes.

2. The rapid development of these tendencies in the autumn forced the party to adopt a decisive attitude as regards the MÉMOSZ[9] and the Hungarian fitters. The change of direction which had thus become necessary in its trade-union tactics – in other words, in an area of vital importance in the present situation – was completed by the party quickly and in all essentials correctly.

3. The most important successes of the party in the period up to the present:

a) The formation of a dedicated (*parteilich*) leadership. As a result of the intensification of the party work undertaken by the upper and lower echelons, the political preparedness of the party has grown considerably, although it would even now still be unable to organize all party members immediately and lead them into struggle on behalf of a campaign which it recognized as correct.

b) This growing dedication has also brought with it an improvement in conspiratorial methods, and hence both a reduction in the number of arrests and a lessening of the effect of those arrests already made. The political consequence of this state of affairs has been the eradication of liquidationism within the party, by which we mean those forms of liquidationism which were widespread during the 1927–28 crisis. This in turn has brought the party an increase in influence and success in its struggle to destroy liquidationism outside the party. From which it follows that the party is slowly but surely combating the fears of left-orientated workers

9. MÉMOSZ – National Union of Hungarian Building Workers.

in respect of the illegal communist party. (It is often the case today that left-wing workers approach the party either to join it or because they feel that even though they wish to remain party-less, they cannot work effectively without close links with the party.) These fears are the chief obstacle to the formation of a unified left-wing workers' party because they prevent the best section of the left-wing elements among the workers from playing a dedicated part, i.e. under party discipline, in an organized and planned fashion, in all the various industrial, professional and political movements.

c) The strike in Salgótarján[10] signifies a decisive step in the party's development. This was the first large-scale strike to break out and be conducted under communist leadership, in accordance with the instructions of the HCP and in spite of the opposition of the bureaucracy. No matter how many mistakes and vacillations marked the leadership of the strike (especially *vis-à-vis* the strike-breaking bureaucracy), the movement must nevertheless be classed as a success, the more so since the extension of the strike from Salgótarján to the rest of the country was the result of the action taken by a delegation which – at the suggestion of the communists – travelled round the mines.

The positive influence of the strike was revealed in the strong opposition which the miners, particularly those from Tarján and Tata, put up at the national conference when the Pilisvörösvár strike was called off.

d) The party's influence on the fitters who have been made redundant is growing steadily; this is especially evident in the increasingly militant and class-conscious tone of our leaflets. The party work that has grown up among the fitters and turners is preparing the ground for the creation of a metalworkers' union orientated towards militant class struggle.

e) Formation of a class-militant MÉMOSZ opposition – this was a particularly noteworthy success because, in the process, the inevitable pseudo-opposition put up by the centralists (Palotás)[11] had to be combated just as the bureaucracy had to be prevented from taking any rapid measures to isolate the leaders of the movement from the opposition masses.

f) The growing impact of the communists on the working masses at

10. Strikes took place in the mines in Salgótarján, Pécs, Tata and Pilisvörösvár in November and December 1928 (original editorial note).

11. Imre Palotás (b. 1894), a building worker and an active communist since 1921; as one of the leaders of the illegal communists within the union movement, he was arrested several times. In 1923 he was expelled from the MÉMOSZ along with seventeen others, because he had stood out against the bureaucracy which planned to wage open war on the communists.

large and an extension of the party's political influence in general, even though it has not succeeded either on the trade-union or the political level in drawing together and uniting the left-orientated working masses in a homogeneous, ideological (let alone organizational) entity under its own leadership.

4. The causes of the deficiencies in the party's work among the masses.

a) Organizational: the weakness of the cells, their lack of influence in the factories, faulty constitution of factions (MÉMOSZ), unplanned and incoherent work of the factions (social-democratic opposition, cultural organizations).

b) Lack of functionaries, low standard and general political inexperience of those we have, and especially their inexperience in combining legal and illegal work, which is one of the main reasons for the inability of the cells to achieve the relevant influence in the factories.

c) The correct analyses and slogans of the party often reached the party members – and through them the masses – only after considerable delays or in an insufficiently effective form.

d) Irresolution among the power-echelon leadership, especially during the metalworkers' campaign.[12]

e) The inadequate and irregular contacts with the young workers' movement. Although marked improvements have been made in this respect since the plenum, the relationship as it manifests itself during the campaigns is still unsatisfactory and too tenuous.

f) The complete absence of women's work, which is responsible for the lack of influence on the textile workers' strike.

5. These organizational factors, however, by no means wholly explain the situation. The gulf which still exists between the party's political influence on the one hand, and the exploitation and consolidation of that influence in organizational terms – and hence the party's ability to act – on the other, also has political causes. The following are the most important:

a) The party still does not show its face as often as it should, even when it is responsible for initiating and leading an action. No one doubts the difficulties and dangers involved; but the illegal experience of other

12. This refers to a movement for higher wages among the metal workers, which the HCP supported and which reached its climax in August 1929.

countries shows that the problem is not insoluble. People must be trained for conspiracy, and more is needed than just conspiratorial politics. When the cells have grouped around themselves those people who sympathize with them, and when they are capable of mobilizing such people for their actions – then the appearance of the party in public no longer entails the risk of arrest. But in stepping up these actions, the party cannot afford to make any concessions to this fear of showing oneself in public, a fear which the lower-level organizations have inherited in an exaggerated form from a stage of development which has long since been passed. Only by remaining firm can the party ensure that its actions meet with a really serious response from the masses and exert any influence on those groups of workers who are politically more remote.

b) In its agitational and propaganda work, the party has not always proved capable of incorporating the central strategic slogans of the plenum theses into the immediate, day-to-day issues, and thereby turning such struggles – whether spontaneous or party-inspired – into the conscious section of a nascent left-wing workers' front.

c) The party was incapable of getting across a number of its strategic slogans ('Fight against War', 'Fight for "democratic demands"') to the masses adequately.

d) In the application of the plenum theses and the elaboration of the party line, rightist deviations manifested themselves both in the central leadership (Julius, Robert)[13] and among party members; they often prevented the party from responding quickly or resolutely enough to events. Such rightist deviations often crop up simply in the shape of pessimistic moods, the cause of which is the feeling common to party members working under conditions of stress that their efforts and organizational power are unrelated to the tasks confronting them. We cannot afford to shut our eyes to this state of affairs, for all forms of rightist deviationism are basically expressions of the feeling that there is some such discrepancy between the forces available and the tasks to be fulfilled. This kind of ideology of weakness, which involves turning aside from the

13. Julius – Gyula Alpári (1882–1944), the leader of the 'Luxemburgist' opposition in Hungarian social democracy before 1914 and one of the most prominent leaders of the Hungarian youth movement after 1907; in the twenties he was the editor-in-chief of the *Internationale Presse-Korrespondenz*. Robert – Béla Szántó (1888–1951), people's commissar for the Red Army under the Soviet Republic and active in the Red Trade-Union International during the twenties; after 1945 he became Hungarian ambassador to Poland. The Institute for Party History was unable to discover any material relating to the rightist deviation to which Lukács refers.

concrete tasks of militant struggle, is at the root of most rightist deviations We must of course use our discrimination in dealing with the problem – and that means adopting different approaches to these rightist deviations, depending on whether they manifest themselves at a higher or at a lower level, whether they are part of a system or merely isolated points of view. In general these deviations crop up in different quarters and in an unorganized fashion, and they do not constitute a faction. Objectively, however, they are connected in that they represent a misconstruction of the contemporary situation in Hungary and thereby retard the efforts of the party to solve its immediate and decisive questions and arrive at a clear theoretical position.

6. The following are the most important rightist deviations:

a) The standpoint of Comrade Julius and his assessment of the Bethlen regime and the social democrats, as shown in the speech he gave to the international secretariat of the Communist International (reprinted in the appendix to the theses). In that speech Comrade Julius makes it clear that he is totally out of sympathy with the policies which the HCP has been pursuing in recent years. His attitude constitutes a coherent rightist-orientated system. He denies that the Bethlen regime is fascist in character, denies that the Social Democratic Party is moving towards Bethlen-type fascism, assessing it instead as a party of opposition fighting for democratic reforms. If this were true, the HCP would clearly have to revise its entire politics.

In reality, the practical consequence of Comrade Julius's analysis would be to deprive the party of all activities except that of supporting the Social Democratic Party in opposition in its struggle for democratic reforms and giving it – at most – a push to the left. The only task left to the HCP as an independent organization would be that of making purely theoretical propaganda for the dictatorship of the proletariat. Apart from the complete wrongness of his analysis, Comrade Julius's platform would serve only to cast the party back into the kind of situation that immediately follows the overthrow of a dictatorship – in other words, reduce it to the level of a pure propaganda group. Although his line has been tailored to suit the anomalous situation in Hungary, it is in keeping with the standpoint of other rightist groups abroad, and is essentially an expression of faintheartedness at the thought of trying to resolve the urgent and difficult tasks which confront the party.

b) Comrade Robert's standpoint (cf. his three articles in the appendix to the thesis) bears even more clearly the stamp of an ideology of weakness. He sees the approach of fascistoid tendencies and the constant decrease in the membership of the trade unions, but he understands nothing of the concrete reasons for this development, which is why he mechanically equates the lack of numbers in the trade unions with lack of life in the workers' movement in general. The fact that the masses are unorganized is for him simply an indication that the movement is disintegrating; in the same way he sees spontaneous movements as a sign that those taking part are waiting for the Messiah. This short-sighted view completely ignores the radicalization of the masses and the complex forms and circumstances in which radicalization comes about; the consequence is an evasion of the concrete and fundamental tasks facing the party today. Robert covers up his evasiveness with a show of pseudo-radicalism. He claims that there is a contradiction between the political and the organizational theses of the plenum, between party line and party perspective. He fails to notice the necessary dialectical antagonism which any spontaneous movement is bound to cause between the party's perspective and its line: that is, that the aim of the party's work is to turn the spontaneous movement in a different direction from the one which it would take if left to its own – spontaneous – devices.

Beyond that Comrade Robert is not prepared to admit that a move to the left which develops spontaneously can be of significance for all kinds of different areas (culture, social-democratic opposition, etc.). He attempts to confine the party exclusively to work in factory cells, his argument being that only in that way, 'on the line of strongest resistance', can the masses be reached. But if we avoid the struggle against centrism; if we equate the retrogressive development of the trade unions with the disintegration of the workers' movement as a whole; if, in consequence, we represent the trend towards fascism as inevitable because the working class does not even recognize it, let alone defend itself against it; if, in other words, we do not recognize that the working class is already moving to the left and is at this moment fighting, even if only spontaneously, against the moves to introduce fascism – what, then, are the practical possibilities for work in factory cells? To set up factory cells in isolation from the work of the factions and without any political content would be a retrograde step, taking the party way back beyond the stage it has reached in recent years. Such factory cells would then only exist formally, without any possibility of taking real action or of becoming politicized. The task of the HCP, especially now, is to continue their work – helped, of course, by the central position occupied by the factory cells – on *all* the fronts of the working-class movement, everywhere where the masses are to be found, with the ultimate aim of building up a left-wing working-class movement under its leadership. In this respect, too, Comrade Robert's point of view is basically an ideology of weakness. He bridges the gulf which exists between the party's political influence and its organizational strength by simply cancelling out the political influence.

c) Under-estimation of centrism, and the vacillating and irresolute attitude towards the centrists. This kind of attitude was widespread even among the party workers active in Hungary. (It also forms part of Comrade Robert's system.) It crops up in various forms, some of which even seem to be mutually contradictory. On the one hand, there is the view that social democracy is even now no longer able to exert any influence on the masses, that it is only political persecution which holds us back from a victorious struggle against social-democracy, that nobody supports Jenö Kis, and so on. On the other, there is the fear that communists, at present working in illegal opposition, would too clearly give the game away about the communist character of the militant opposition if they were to take up the ideological struggle against centrism in a precise and direct fashion. Both of these points of view represents a deviation to the right – or at least a tendency which, if it becomes conscious, could develop into one – because they evade the immediate concrete tasks of the party. Centrism is one of the means which social democracy uses to keep left-inclined but not yet conscious masses away from the Communist Party, or at least away from its influence. Therefore, if the communists intend to get the left-orientated working class under its leadership, they must take up the struggle against centrist ideology right down the line. It is not enough to prove in concrete individual cases that the centrists serve the interests of Peyer and company;[14] the aim must be to show the working class that the entire ideology of centrism is the main obstacle to the class struggle and to knock it out of the workers' heads. To be ignorant of or to under-estimate centrism, which is our most dangerous enemy, can lead to a serious deviation to the right – in Hungary just as much as in the international movement generally.

14. Károly Peyer (1881–1956), a prominent trade-union leader and social democrat; sympathized with the Fascists; in 1919 he was Minister of the Interior under Peidl, in 1920 Minister for Public Welfare under Huszár, in 1927 he was General Secretary of the Trade-Union Council; from 1925–44 he was member of the National Assembly and in 1947 he emigrated from Hungary.

d) It is likewise rightist-inclined attitudes, and not ineptitude or in-experience, which are concealed behind the terror of combining legal and illegal work, behind the insistence on remaining hidden in illegality, behind the fear of showing oneself – or indeed, of the party's showing itself – in public. The party has now outgrown the period of propaganda and has set itself the task, contained in the plenum theses, of conducting a campaign independently, without the mediation of front-organizations. This means that there has been a change of direction in the party's entire tactics, with profound repercussions on the position of every single party member. Some members are still unable to draw all the tactical and organizational consequences from this change and therefore do not under-stand that, the wider the circle of real and effective sympathizers the communist base organizations can gather round themselves, the greater their security will be. Such people are terrified by the idea of the party showing its face during its actions; they are afraid that the organizations concerned will be discovered. Two kinds of fear of coming to grips with the concrete tasks of the party thus fuse into a single rightist position; on the one hand, these particular members do not know how to surround the cell or the faction with this kind of wide circle of sympathizers, and on the other – because of the resultant feeling of their own weakness – they are afraid to appear in public themselves. This position is reprehensible, because the party can never have any influence on the broad masses it has not yet reached, nor can it ever become the leader of the entire left-orientated working class, if these masses know only the principles of the communists, but never get to see any concrete actions on the part of the party.

e) There is another position which springs from weakness and which has equally damaging consequences. It manifests itself in the attempt of individual members and organizations to evade the concrete tasks by sub-stituting all kinds of complicated manoeuvres and digressions for the mass work which has to be done by the party's organizations. It includes setting up extra-party organizations and far-fetched 'parallel' campaigns. The frenzy and aimlessness involved in such activities not only diminishes the party's standing in the eyes of the masses, but it also disorientates the party members themselves.

The party must wage an ideological struggle against all rightist tenden-cies and positions. But in doing so it must differentiate clearly between those tendencies which are very largely the result of subjective weakness and inexperience, and those conscious rightist deviations which form part of a coherent theoretical system. The way to counter the former is through continuous enlightenment. Regular work must be undertaken in an attempt to eradicate the organizational weaknesses which are most often at the root of such attitudes. But at the same time it has to be made quite plain to the comrades concerned that the organizational weaknesses cannot be eradicated unless the attitudes themselves are in turn combated and over-come. As for those rightist deviations which are part of a coherent system, however, the party must take up the ideological struggle clearly and re-solutely against them. Such deviations must be eliminated root and branch from the party – precisely because they concern the crucially important strategic questions facing the party, and because they obscure from the party members those objective economic and political conditions which determine the party's strategy. They thus make it impossible for party members to understand the party's political principles and apply them correctly.

V. THE MAIN PROBLEMS OF THE PRESENT SITUATION

1. The consequences of re-grouping within Hungarian political life and of the foreign-policy setback suffered by the Bethlen regime manifest themselves in three main developments which are closely connected with one another and constitute different moments of the same process. The party's response to them must therefore be such that this unity is made visible and intelligible to the masses in the day-to-day struggle. The main problems are: a) a complete liquidation of democratic reforms and bourgeois democracy – while preserving democratic forms; b) a systema-tic extension of fascistoid developments, in all likelihood on 'western' and not Italian lines, so as not to clash with democratic principles; c) preparation of a war against the Soviet Union; war as the forger of the national united front.

2. The question of the party's attitude towards democratic reforms is thereby posed more precisely than ever before. The party's earlier line both on the question of the republic and in respect of its attitude towards the electoral block then emerging, was correct. Also correct was the blunt rejection of the form of rightist opposition presented as an alternative to the party (Julius). Thus far the HCP has correctly exposed the fact that the parties of so-called democratic reform do not fight seriously enough even for bourgeois-democratic reforms. However, the present situation

holds open the possibility that the broad masses are becoming awake to this kind of betrayal of bourgeois reforms, this disguising of the increasingly fascist state machinery in democratic apparel – all of which is happening with the consensus of every one of the bourgeois parties, including the social democrats. The facts reveal more and more clearly that the HCP is the only party in Hungary today which is fighting seriously for bourgeois democracy. This struggle of the party must be widened into a mass struggle, it must be taken beyond the confines of the proletariat. The central slogan of this struggle, which is directed towards bringing down the entire Bethlen régime, is: a democratic dictatorship of the proletariat and peasantry.

A. *Democratic dictatorship*

3. The programme passed by the Sixth World Congress[15] very correctly numbers Hungary among those states in which the question of a democratic dictatorship to mark the transition towards the revolution of the proletariat plays a decisive role. The party must therefore use every available means to explain what is involved, in the first instance to the party members, and then to the broadest masses of the workers. In clarifying the issue, the following factors must be borne in mind:

a) A struggle must be waged among the workers against the nihilism which has arisen out of disappointment in the Social Democratic Party's politics in relation to bourgeois democracy. The Marxist view – that bourgeois democracy is the best battlefield for the proletariat – must be made popular among the party members. It has got to be understood that serious revolutionary efforts are needed in order to create such a battlefield. The lessons of the 1917 revolution in Russia and the 1918/19 revolution in Hungary in this respect must be taken to heart and made popular. (Lenin said in the spring of 1917: 'Russia constitutes the most progressive democracy in the world.')

b) It is necessary from the outset to combat that school of thought which maintains that a democratic dictatorship is a transitional form of government between the Bethlen regime and the dictatorship of the proletariat. That argument runs something like this: first, the Bethlen regime exists, then we will establish a democratic dictatorship, and when we have fully developed and realized that, then and only then will the era of the

15. The programme of the Communist International adopted by its Sixth Congress on 1 September 1928 can be found in Degras, op. cit., vol. III, pp. 471–526.

dictatorship of the proletariat dawn. A democratic dictatorship can take various different forms. Early in 1917, Lenin pointed out to Kamenev, who wanted to pin the party down to the 1905 form of democratic dictatorship, that democratic dictatorship had already been achieved in quite definite form by the beginning of the 1917 revolution: one of these forms was a counter-government made up of workers' and soldiers' soviets. Democratic dictatorship, then, as a complete realization of bourgeois democracy, is a battlefield in the strict sense of the word, a field on which the all-deciding battle is fought between bourgeoisie and proletariat. At the same time, of course, it is also the most important means of the battle, a chance to address the broadest masses directly, to spur them on and lead them to spontaneous revolutionary action, as well as a chance to loosen the organizational and ideological forms which, under 'normal circumstances', help the bourgeoisie to keep the broad masses of the working people disorganized. A democratic dictatorship provides the possibility of creating those organizational forms which can help the broad masses of the workers to assert their interests in the face of the bourgeoisie. At the present stage of development a democratic dictatorship is irreconcilable in principle with the economic and social power of the bourgeoisie, even though the explicit class content of its concrete objectives and immediate demands, far from going beyond the bounds of bourgeois society, is in fact the perfect realization of bourgeois democracy. (In 1793 the realization of a complete democracy did not conflict in principle with the power of capitalism – in fact, it promoted it.) Hence it was inevitable, in both Kerensky's and Károlyi's revolution,[16] that the bourgeoisie should attempt to dismantle abruptly 'the most highly developed democracy' which followed the outbreak of the revolution and re-establish 'normal democracy' – which secures the power of capitalism – as quickly as possible. The object of such efforts is always to bring about the situation where the re-established state apparatus, the social organizations, the economic superiority of the bourgeoisie and so on, once more cancel out the spontaneity of the masses; and where the masses are once more thrown into disarray by the bourgeoisie and its agents, chiefly the

16. Kerensky's revolution – the period between July and October 1917. Kerensky became Prime Minister in July 1917, after the effective elimination of the soviets. Károlyi's revolution – the bourgeois democratic revolution in Hungary, which resulted in the proclamation of a republic on 16 November 1918 by the National Council led by Count Michael Károlyi. Károlyi formed a government in January 1919 which survived until the Soviet dictatorship in March of that year.

social democrats. A democratic dictatorship, then, although in terms of its immediate concrete content it does not go beyond bourgeois society, is a dialectical form of transition towards the revolution of the proletariat – or towards the counter-revolution. To stop at democratic dictatorship, conceived as a fixed, 'constitutionally determined' period of development, would necessarily signify the victory of the counter-revolution. Democratic dictatorship can therefore be understood only as the concrete transition by means of which the bourgeois revolution turns into the revolution of the proletariat. 'There is no Chinese wall between bourgeois revolution and the revolution of the proletariat' (Lenin).[17]

c) Hence, the contradictory functions of bourgeois democracy must be made intelligible to the party members in very precise terms. It is imperative to make a clear distinction between a democracy where the bourgeois is the politically dominant class and one where – although it maintains its economic exploitation – it has ceded at least part of its power to the broad masses of the workers. The function of democracy in the former case is to scatter, mislead and disorganize the working masses; in the latter, to undermine and disorganize the bourgeoisie's maintenance of political and economic power, and to organize the working masses for independent action. To ascertain the value or valuelessness of a democracy, therefore, the communists must pose this question: which class's power is disorganized by that democracy? Does that democracy have a consolidating or a destructive effect from the standpoint of the bourgeoisie? (Social democracy's 'fight' for democratic reforms has always proceeded under the banner of consolidation, with a view to preventing a revolution.) All the slogans of democratic dictatorship, then, must be judged from one particular standpoint, that of mobilizing the masses and disorganizing the bourgeoisie. Take, for example, proletarian control of production, which becomes an immediate issue under such circumstances. There must be no illusions on this score, no believing that proletarian control of production can of itself have any kind of 'consolidating' effect. Unmasking the sabotage perpetrated by the bourgeoisie, and if need be just stopping it: such measures do not have any particular value except as instruments in the struggle for power and the mobilization of the masses.

4. If we intend to make use of the notion of democratic dictatorship as a concrete strategic slogan nowadays, we must be clear what post-war

17. See V. I. Lenin, *The Proletarian Revolution and the Renegade Kautsky*, 1918, in *Collected Works*, vol. 28.

imperialism in its present third phase (a term used by the Sixth World Congress) actually means and what guises democracy assumes in order to consolidate the power of the bourgeoisie. This issue is obscured in the minds of the broad masses of European workers by the fact that, in most European countries, democracy came about as the result of bourgeois revolution, with the oppressed and exploited classes fighting for centuries or at least decades together with the bourgeoisie for the overthrow of feudal absolutism and the establishment of a bourgeois democracy. Hence, it is difficult for the masses to recognize the completely new situation to which imperialism has given rise, although the democracy which prevails in the USA provides us with an almost perfect example. There the bourgeoisie as the dominant class (which did not have to destroy feudal power with the help of proletarian and semi-proletarian masses) has succeeded in creating the very forms of democracy in which every possibility for the free development, accumulation and expansion of capital is given, while at the same time the external forms of democracy are preserved – but in such a way that the working masses cannot exert any influence whatever on the actual political leadership. America represents, not only economically but also politically, an ideal for today's ruling bourgeoisie. The political development of the great 'western democracies' has been tending more and more in recent years towards the creation, in all kinds of variations, of some such democracy. Apart from the previously mentioned revolutionary traditions, which are very much alive in France but also active in Germany, the illusions cherished by the working masses are encouraged by the politics of social democracy. Social democracy, which concentrated all its resources during the period immediately after the Russian revolution on campaigning against the dictatorship of the proletariat, is now doing its best to help set up democracies on American lines in all European states. It is a policy which has very serious economic causes – from the point of view of the working-class bureaucracy. For post-war imperialism can no longer afford to tolerate trade-union struggles of the pre-war type, no matter in what form. It cannot do so for two main reasons: first and foremost, because of the preparations for a new world war; but also on account of the intense competition for the world market. In other words, it is obliged to turn the trade unions into fascist organizations. This can be done in a number of different ways. Mussolini has created one type, which, with the help of a counter-revolution staged by the petty bourgeoisie and the better-off peasantry, smashed the old trade unions and set up new ones in their place. As a solution this method involves certain dangers, both for the bourgeoisie and the working-class bureaucracy. It costs the bourgeoisie a great deal of effort to transform the petty-bourgeois counter-revolution into the consolidation of the big bourgeoisie; some of the working-class bureaucracy lose their positions in the working-class movement (Italian emigration); and last but not least, those who conform with the fascist system find themselves in dangerous confrontation with the working-class masses. From the point of view of both the grand bourgeoisie and the working-class bureaucracy, a better, less troublesome and less dangerous solution would seem to be the method which has already been put into effect in Germany by means of state arbitration, which has already come partly into force in England, by means of trade-union legislation, and which finds its perfect culmination in 'Mondism'.[18] It is clear that the class content of the two systems is the same as far as the proletariat is concerned. Only the methods are different. This difference in method means, of course, that in every fascist state it is different strata which exercise power – that is, they share power in different degrees. Given this situation, it is understandable that the entire international social-democratic movement should nowadays pose the question as: democracy or fascism? By posing this question it hides from the workers the real class goals of the kind of democracy which is possible under present-day imperialism, and lends its support to the suppression of class struggles, the institutional prevention of wage struggles, the fascization of the trade unions, and the integration of social democracy and the trade-union bureaucracy into the fascist state apparatus. (Among the consequences of this entire system are preparations for war; this can be seen most clearly in the parliamentary bill proposing general mobilization proposed by Paul-Boncours,[19] which of course is also inspired by American models.) Hence, just as during the first period of the proletarian revolution it was a task of the first order to expose the erroneous formulation of the question of dictatorship and to define the real question – i.e. dictatorship of the bourgeoisie or of the proletariat – so now it is a primary task to expose the misleading alternative, 'democracy or fascism'. It must be shown that the democratic development now getting under way both

18. Lukács refers here to the legislation on state arbitration in Germany of 30 October 1923, and the Trade Disputes and Trade-Unions Acts of 1927 in England. 'Mondism' derives its name from the English industrialist and politician Sir Alfred Mond (Lord Melchett) and refers to a movement which aimed at bringing about an end to conflict between employers and unions by establishing a working community.

19. Joseph Paul-Boncours (b. 1873), French socialist, member of the Assembly from 1919 and French representative at the League of Nations until 1928.

here and in the 'western democracies' is a genre of fascisization which – in contrast to the Italian type – is based on the cooperation of the big bourgeoisie and the working-class bureaucracy. We must therefore counter the slogan 'democracy or fascism', with a different one, 'class against class'; and counter a fight for democratic demands that secure possibilities of movement for the working sectors with – the fight for democratic dictatorship.

In the imperialistic post-war period, the role of the state also undergoes fundamental changes as a result of the transformation in the system of production. A close relationship develops between the state and capitalist production: on the one hand, as a steadily growing influence of the state on the possibilities of capitalist production, capital investment and capital accumulation, etc.; on the other, as a steadily growing influence of large-scale capital (bank capital and heavy industry, which is controlled by it) on the state. This kind of merger between large-scale capital and the state was already evident even in pre-war developments. Development during and since the war has merely accelerated the tendency. The constantly growing intensity of the class struggle, however, forces the state increasingly to create institutional safeguards for itself. The disorganization of the masses, their lack of influence in the life of the state, and the prohibition by legal means of the working class's class struggle – these are not new, but they now appear in a new context. For: a) the political importance and the political level of the masses is at present higher than it was in earlier stages of development. Against that, however: b) the mass media (press, etc.) which large-scale capital has at its disposal are also much more highly developed; and c) we are confronted with an entirely new moment, namely the fact that such tendencies towards a union of large-scale capital and the state are being supported by the official leadership of the working classes. Here, too, the United States serves as the model. However, there are fundamental political and economic differences between the USA and Europe: a) the upper stratum of the working class in America (as in the European imperialist states before the war) can be materially satisfied by accumulation, export of capital and the great scope and rapid increase of extra profits – whereas the basis in Europe for such a development is very narrow; b) America lacks the class-militant traditions of the European working-class; c) in numerous European states, the bourgeoisie either did not become a politically dominant class until the post-war period (Germany), or it acquired a far greater share in the political leadership of the country than ever before (Hungary). Hence the attempt to combine the kind of political democracy where the masses actually have no political influence with the institutional or arbitrary suppression of the class struggle in Europe has not achieved anything; nor will it reach the American ideal. Not that that prevents the bourgeoisie and the working-class bureaucracy from wanting to get closer to the American model. But the pre-conditions are bound to be shakier in Europe than in America, and therefore no European bourgeoisie is going to completely abandon the possibility of the 'classical' (Italian) type of fascism: it will always keep even that option open in case of an intensification of the class struggle and a separation of the masses from the bourgeoisie. Hence, today's imperialistic capitalistic state is equally concerned to render the masses completely ineffective politically and to combine and organize them within the state (or within 'society', under state supervision). The democratic form of fascisization is the most appropriate, but by no means the only form which this double objective can take.

5. Hungary's development therefore differs from both the Italian and the English model by reason of different historical and social conditions. The defeat of the revolution in Hungary brought petty-bourgeois and peasant-farmer strata to power. But they did not succeed in smashing or dis-organizing the trade-union movement; they had even less success, unlike Mussolini, in winning support from within the working class. (The causes of this resistance are to be found largely in the way in which the revolution was put down and in the democratic illusions of the working class as regards social democracy.) An amalgamation of big landowners and capital-ists took over from the counter-revolution of the petty-bourgeoisie and middle peasantry and incorporated its organs into the state apparatus. They had been operating with contradictory methods in this area for a long time, and to some extent they still do today (both a pact with the social democrats and their support). In recent years the Bethlen regime has pushed through a rapid reconstruction of the state apparatus and of the social organizations. And this will soon make it possible to take over the methods of 'western democracy'. (Whether Bethlen or someone else actually conducts the takeover, is completely incidental.) The most im-portant measures involved are: a) the question of parliamentary rules of procedure, and the necessity of public nominations in those constituencies where elections are secret. This would enable the regime to extend secret elections to the provinces as well, and even to the villages – all without running any risks. b) A new press law which can easily use the amount of

caution money levied and the principle of increased personal responsibility to obstruct any form of opposition press by legal methods, or to destroy at any time those publications which already exist – again, by entirely legal means. c) The abolition of autonomy in the towns and elsewhere. d) An upper house, to ensure the unlimited hegemony of large-scale capital, alongside any kind of parliament. e) A revision of the right of combination and assembly, to give legal backing to the present state of affairs, i.e. the complete abolition of the right of combinations and assembly for workers and peasants. f) Fascisization of the country. g) Fascist cultural policy. And last and most important: h) The abolition of the right to strike through the introduction of state arbitration. Once this edifice is complete and sufficiently stable, there will no longer be anything to prevent the Bethlen regime or its liberal successor from going over to universal and secret suffrage and dismantling all the emergency laws and decrees – from switching over, that is, to the standpoint of complete western democracy. A legitimate king would crown such a democracy perfectly. The democracy itself would provide the social basis for the Hungarian counter-revolution, enabling it to serve England and go to war against the Soviet Union. As far as this kind of democratic liquidation of the sum total of bourgeois democracy and bourgeois-democratic reforms is concerned, complete unity reigns from Bethlen down to Jenö Kis. The resistance of petty-bourgeois fascists against this block does not count for very much. The most enthusiastic supporter and proclaimer of such a system of democracy is the Social Democratic Party. Thus with the intensification of capitalist production and the counter-revolution, and with the revolution now a long way off, the Hungarian counter-revolution enters the period of 'western development'. The HCP is the only party which represents the true struggle for democratic reforms in opposition to the Bethlen regime.

6. During this struggle, the high-point of which is necessarily the fight to achieve democratic dictatorship, the party must retain its earlier slogan of the 'republic'.[20] As long as the tranquil and unruffled power of large-scale landed property and large-scale capital expresses itself in advocating the coronation of the legitimate king, the struggle for the republic will also continue to represent, in the eyes of the masses, the struggle for all

20. The idea of the 'republic' was the central slogan of the MSZMP. It had played a role in the transitional programme, formulated after the Fifth Congress of the International and adopted at the First Congress of the HCP.

basic liberties, for the right to combine, assemble, and even to strike. In propagating this slogan, no communist should allow himself to be misled by the so-called republican propaganda of social democracy. On the contrary: it must be pointed out that the slogan of the republic means nothing more to the social democrats than a screen for legitimism; its main role is as a watch-dog *vis-à-vis* the fascists of Albrecht's petty-bourgeois party. Naturally, the party must not, either now or in the future, employ the republican slogan in isolation. The republican slogan can only be used in the sense of a struggle for total democracy, for the republic headed by a government of workers and peasants, a struggle against the democratic liquidation of democracy, a fulfilment of the slogan, 'Class against class', a mobilization for the struggle which has to be conducted to secure democratic dictatorship. (However, this attitude towards the republic is valid only as long as the union of large-scale landed property and large-scale capital advocates a legitimate monarchy. If it were to give up this aspiration for reasons of foreign policy and install a bourgeois republic on German or Austrian lines, then the HCP would have to revise its tactical slogans, without in any way changing its strategic line.)

7. This struggle for the workers must be conducted in the closest co-operation with the demands of the workers, understood in the strictest sense. It must be pointed out that a drop in the living standard of the workers and the liquidation of the right to strike are central to the whole system of democratic fascism. The struggle for democratic dictatorship must therefore always be dinned into the workers in connection with the fight against fascisization and state arbitration. In the course of this struggle, of course, the practical significance of all democratic liberties (the right of combination and assembly, freedom of the press, etc.) for the day-to-day class struggle of the workers must be pointed out; the fight for the workers' freedom of movement in the factories must be taken up (shop-steward system, factory committee); and the measures taken by the regime against any kind of movement on the part of the workers (deportations, the role of the police, the miners' and farm labourers' strikes) must be exposed. In short: the struggle for bourgeois liberties must be connected with the everyday needs of the workers. It is precisely with regard to these everyday questions that it becomes imperative to expose the treachery of the social democrats, the way in which social democracy organically accommodates itself to democratic fascism. But however strongly the struggle has to be waged against all the forms of

nihilism that manifest themselves in the bourgeois liberties, it is just as imperative to emphasize constantly the relative value of democracy from the point of view of the workers – in bourgeois society, and hence, too, in the democratic dictatorship. 'There can be no equality between oppressor and oppressed, between bourgeoisie and proletarian' (Lenin).[21] Even the most perfect realization of bourgeois democracy does not in any sense do away with the exploitation of the working class.

8. The peculiarity of Hungarian development is that the feudal form of distribution of landed property remains unchanged alongside relatively highly-developed and still developing capitalism. In fact, it has, if anything, got worse rather than better as a result of the reform of landed property. There are individual members of the ruling classes, those who have risen above the provincialism of the gentry, who are clear that the present state of affairs as regards the distribution of landed property bears within it the seeds of a peasant revolution, and who, in order to avoid this, talk about the possibility of a new land reform. But it is objectively impossible to make even the slightest changes in the distribution of landed property through reforms, since landed property and large-scale capital are growing closer and closer together. The middle-ranking peasantry and to an even greater degree the lower peasant strata do not have any parties. And the urban petit-bourgeois parties and the social democrats follow large-scale capital in this respect without demur. Here too, then, the HCP remains the only party which inscribes the consistent implementation of the demands of the bourgeois revolution on its banner: expropriation of the large landed-property owners without compensation, revolutionary occupation of the land, free land for the peasants! The alliance of workers and peasants, the democratic dictatorship, will remain simply an empty phrase unless there is a consistent propaganda effort and a resolute struggle aimed at putting it into practice. The HCP must do its utmost to win ever wider sections of the land-labourers and the poor peasants over to this programme. Accordingly it must also draw in those sectors of the working class which have not yet lost their connections with the land. It must attempt to get a firm footing among the lower strata in the villages by building up contacts with the land labourers in a regular and organized fashion. In order to regain the trust of the peasantry, which was disillusioned by the counter-revolution, the party must be ruthlessly self-

21. Cf. the chapter entitled 'Can there be equality between the exploited and the exploiter?' in Lenin's *The Proletarian Revolution and the Renegade Kautsky*, op. cit.

critical about the failures in agrarian policy made by the dictatorship of the proletariat. It must be stated, without beating about the bush, that the party has given up the position it held during the dictatorship. Within the party itself, it must be made clear to each and every member that this is a decisive strategic issue for the party, an inevitable pre-condition of the seizure of power and the liberation of the proletariat. There must be no concessions to the view that this is 'a long way from socialism' or that maintaining production and providing for the working class are interests which call for very different policies, etc. All party members must understand that what is at issue is a question which is fundamental to the transition from the bourgeois revolution to the revolution of the proletariat; they must understand that the power of large-scale landed property and large-scale capital cannot be destroyed except by this kind of revolution, and that the remnants of feudalism cannot be wiped out except through the elimination of capitalism.

D. *Slogans and immediate tasks of the party*

30. In accordance with the interpretations and tasks outlined above, the activity of the HCP is centred on the following slogans:

a) Fight for the overthrow of the Bethlen regime. Fight against all forms of pseudo-opposition to the Bethlen regime, and against bourgeois and social-democratic pseudo-opposition. No pact with the bourgeoisie. Class against class – long live the alliance of workers and peasants.

Fight against the implementation of fascism in a democratic framework. Fight against the slogan 'democracy or fascism', which misleads the workers. Fight against social democracy as a mainstay of fascism. Fight for universal freedom which assures freedom of movement for the working class (the right of combination and assembly, freedom of the press, right to strike). Fight on the basis of conglomeration of these basic liberties for a republic headed by a government of workers and peasants.

Fight for the democratic dictatorship of the workers and peasants. Fight for the dictatorship of the proletariat.

Fight for the revolutionary occupation of the land by the poor peasants; fight for confiscation without compensation of all landed property in excess of 100 acres. Free land for the peasants.

Fight for the class-militant unity of the workers' movement. Fight against the division and disintegration of the workers' movement, and against the politics of the bureaucracy, which serve to break up the organization of the party. Defend the class-militant character of the trade unions within – and, if need be, outside – the old trade unions against the bureaucracy. In defending the class-militant character of the trade unions, we must not allow our hands to be tied by trade-union rules.

Defend the trade unions against fascism – against the Bethlen regime and its ally, the bureaucracy. Liquidate conciliatory criticism. The financial situation of the workers cannot be remedied except by the prosecution of the class-struggle to its end.

Eight-hour working day. Peace-time real wages.[22] Unemployment payments. Fight against rationalization.

The question of the class struggle concerns the entire working class. Bring the unorganized workers into the wage struggles. Bring the unorganized workers into the militant trade unions.

To be 'unpolitical' is to kill the economic struggle as well. 'Non-political' professional prejudice or syndicalism leads the workers to fascism. Politicize the economic struggles. Solidarity of all striking workers. Fight against the strike-breakers. Fight against the state, which supports the strike-breakers, restricts the possibilities of striking and supports the anti-strike laws. Fight against the fascists. Fight for control of the streets.

The factory is the bastion of the class-militant workers. Shop-steward system. Factory committees, factory-level wage movements against the wishes of the bureaucracy. The basis for organizing militant class struggle is the factory. Propaganda to assist in the realization of the idea of an industrial union (factory treasurers).

Long live the VSZI.[23] Spread the ideology of the VSZI. Attempt to affiliate to the VSZI.

c) The Bethlen regime is leading Hungary into war. The enemy is not to be found outside, but in our midst. No regional integrity. Fight the revisionist confidence-trickster. The liberation of the nation cannot be achieved except through the international revolution of the proletariat.

The Social Democratic Party is the militant reserve of the Bethlen regime. The Social Democratic Party is the Centrists' reserve as 'opposition'. Away with Peyer and Jenö Kis, the advocates of Bethlen's war policy.

The Bethlen regime is preparing for war against the Soviet Union. The

22. By 'peace-time real wages' was meant the real wages, obtaining in 1913 (original editorial note).

23. VSZI – Red International Labour Unions (RILU or Profintern) (original editorial note).

Soviet Union must be defended against the attacks of the imperialists. Make the war into a civil war. Worker and peasant soldiers, go over to the Red Army of the Soviet Union.

Down with pacifist illusions. The 'peace' of the League of Nations is – preparation for a war against the Soviet Union. 'Radical' pacifism deceives the workers. They believe that war can be prevented at the last moment. (However, this cannot be achieved whether with a boycott or with a general strike.)

Call off the boycott of the army. Go into the army. Go into the Levente.[24] Go into the munition factories, join the railway, the post office, the telegraph offices. Enter all the organizations necessary for war in order to disorganize them, in order to turn the bourgeoisie's weapons and means of war against the bourgeoisie itself.

Agitate among the soldiers. (Demands must be worked out.)

31. The slogans and tasks of the HCP enumerated above move the party's basic organizations, the factory cells, more than ever into the centre of its political work; they turn the politicization of the cells into a fundamental task. No matter to which 'area of labour' the slogans of the HCP are related, they constitute a unified system and cannot be explained to the workers in isolation. And it is even less feasible to lead the workers into the struggle simply on the basis of individual slogans. The real basis of this unity is: the worker's life and his everyday problems. Only thus is it possible for these slogans to penetrate properly into the workers' bloodstream. The task of the cell, then, is to seize on everything that happens in the factory, all the immediate concrete problems of the factory, and connect them with the total situation – that is, the liberation – of the working class. By adapting their work to this kind of development, by generalizing the concrete, everyday problems of the factory, and by bringing their work into line with national and international standards, the cell must help the workers to overcome the spontaneous and narrow limits involved in that method of struggle, without losing contact with the concrete day-to-day problems.

The factory should be our bastion. The factory is the starting-point of our strategy. The success of all our struggles and the entire mass work of the HCP (through the factions) cannot be assured until they are based fully and firmly in the life of the workers and in the class struggle – that is, in the life of the workers in the factory.

24. The former state youth organization for 14- to 18-year-olds; it provided paramilitary training.

Index

The names of Karl Marx and Friedrich Engels
are not included in this index
as their names occur throughout the book.